Zones of Conflict

D0782911

Zones of Conflict

US Foreign Policy in the Balkans and the Greater Middle East

Vassilis K. Fouskas

Pluto Press

LONDON • STERLING, VIRGINIA

First published 2003 by Pluto Press
345 Archway Road, London N6 5AA
and 22883 Quicksilver Drive,
Sterling, VA 20166–2012, USA

www.plutobooks.com

British Library Cataloguing in Publication Data
A catalogue record for this book is available from the British Library

ISBN 0 7453 2030 9 hardback
ISBN 0 7453 2029 5 paperback

Library of Congress Cataloging in Publication Data
  Zones of conflict : US foreign policy in the Balkans and the greater
Middle East / Vassilis Fouskas.
        p. cm.
Includes bibliographical references and index.
  ISBN 0–7453–2030–9 — ISBN 0–7453–2029–5 (pbk.)
  1. United States—Foreign relations—Middle East. 2. Middle
East—Foreign relations—United States. 3. United States—Foreign
relations—Balkan Peninsula. 4. Balkan Peninsula—Foreign
relations—United States. 5. United States—Foreign
relations—1993–2001. 6. Balkan Peninsula—Foreign relations—1989– I.
Title.
  DS63.2.U5 F68 2003
  327.730496'09'049—dc21

                                                            2002015830

10   9   8   7   6   5   4   3   2   1

Designed and produced for Pluto Press by
Chase Publishing Services, Fortescue, Sidmouth, England
Typeset from disk by Stanford DTP Services, Towcester
Printed and bound in the European Union by
Antony Rowe, Chippenham and Eastbourne, England

To my father Constantine,
who taught me
what democracy and morality mean
through his humble but difficult life

Contents

Maps

Acknowledgements

This book is a by-product of a large history and international relations project entitled *Greece, Europe and the Balkans: Greece's Foreign and Economic Relations in the 20th Century*, for which I received a fellowship from the Leverhulme Trust (2002–03) in order to conduct research in Turkey, Greece and Cyprus.

My profound gratitude goes to Van Coufoudakis, Bulent Gokay, Peter Gowan, Peter Loizos, Stevan K. Pavlowitch and Donald Sassoon, who have read the manuscript, or parts of it, and enlightened me with invaluable critical comments and scholarly insights.

I am also indebted to the editorial team of the *Journal of Southern Europe and the Balkans*. The work that they have carried out since the mid-1990s has been of enormous intellectual value to me.

My colleagues in the European Research Centre at Kingston University (KU) and the teaching team of the MSc in International Conflict have been more than stimulating. I also thank the staff working at the inter-loan library service at KU, who have managed to put up with me on several occasions.

Over the years, I have also benefited enormously from discussions with a number of scholars and policy practitioners, some of whom brushed aside their busy schedules and accorded me interviews. Out of discretion, I will only mention here Michalis Attalides, Tozun Bahcheli, Chris Brewin, Richard Clogg, Theodore Couloumbis, Soteris Georgallis, Pauline Green, Panayiotis Ifestos, Nikos Kotzias, Heinz Kramer, Nicos Makris, William Mallinson, Farid Mirbagheri, Brendan O'Malley, James Pond, Heinz Richter, Christos Stylianides, Mehmet Ugur, Thanos Veremis and Diana Weston Markides.

I am obliged to Katy Patrick of the Open University and to my copy-editors Laura Harrison and Oliver Howard, and to András Bereznay for the maps. I also thank Katryna Turner for editorial help with the Conclusion.

The third chapter is an extended version of 'The Balkans and the enlargement of NATO: A sceptical view', published in *European Security*, V. 10, N. 3, Autumn 2001. I would like to thank the publisher for giving me permission to reproduce this material here.

A version of the sixth chapter has been presented to a conference on 'Cyprus and the EU', held at Intercollege, Nicosia, in April 2002. It took its final form thanks to the research I was able to conduct in Nicosia and Brussels with the support of a travel grant from the Laiki Bank and the London-based refugee organisation Lobby for Cyprus.

List of Abbreviations

ABM	Anti-Ballistic Missile Treaty
AMBO	Albanian–Macedonian–Bulgarian Oil
CAP	Common Agricultural Policy
CDU/CSU	Christlisch Demokratische Union (Germany)/ Christlich-Soziale Union (Germany–Bavaria) – Christian Democratic Union/Christian Social Union
CFSP	Common Foreign and Security Policy (EU)
CSCM	Conference on Security and Co-operation in the Mediterranean
DC	Democrazia Cristiana (Christian Democracy – Italy)
EBRD	European Bank for Reconstruction and Development
EEC	European Economic Community
EMU	European Monetary Union
EOKA	National Organisation of Cypriot Fighters
EPC	European Political Co-operation
ESDI	European Security and Defence Identity
EU	European Union
FCO	Foreign and Commonwealth Office
FIR	Flight Information Region
FYROM	Former Yugoslav Republic of Macedonia
GATT	General Agreement on Trade and Tariffs
IGC	Inter-Governmental Conference (EU institutional practice)
IMF	International Monetary Fund
INOGATE	Inter-state Oil and Gas Transport to Europe
ISAF	International Security Assistance Force
KLA	Kosovo Liberation Army
MHP	Milliyetci Hareket Partisi (Nationalist Action Party – Turkey)
NATO	North Atlantic Treaty Organisation
NSC	National Security Council (US)
OPEC	Organisation of Petroleum Exporting Countries
OSCE	Organisation for Security and Co-operation in Europe
PASOK	Panhellenic Socialist Movement (Greece)
PCI	Partito Comunista Italiano (Italian Communist Party)

PDS   Partito Democratico della Sinistra
            (Party of the Democratic Left – Italy)
PfP   Partnership for Peace
PLO   Palestine Liberation Organisation
PSI   Partito Socialista Italiano (Italian Socialist Party)
SPD   Sozialdemokratische Partei Deutschlands
            (Social Democratic Party – Germany)
TACIS   Technical Assistance to the Commonwealth of
            Independent States
TRACECA Transport Corridor Europe–Caucasus–Asia
UK   United Kingdom
UN   United Nations
US   United States
USSR   Union of Soviet Socialist Republics
WMD   Weapons of Mass Destruction
WTO   World Trade Organisation

1 Introduction

The Realist Chessboard

'Ever since the continents started interacting politically, some five hundred years ago,' Zbigniew Brzezinski notes in the opening lines of *The Grand Chessboard*, 'Eurasia has been the centre of world power'.[1] Russia, Austro-Hungary, France, the Ottoman Empire, Britain and Germany all wanted to dominate this bizarre landscape ranging from the French shores of the Atlantic down to the Persian Gulf, and from the Chinese land mass to Central Asia, the Black Sea, the Turkish Straits and the Suez. Brzezinski observes that all of the powers claiming mastery over Eurasia in the past were part of its landscape, but now 'for the first time ever, a non Eurasian power has emerged, not only as the key arbiter of Eurasian power relations, but also as the world's paramount power'. America is indeed the sole world superpower after the fall of 'really existing socialism' and has taken a firm grip of a great part of the economic and political resources of the vast Eurasian continent.

In the midst of the great debates about the future of NATO and the EU, Brzezinski, like many other Anglo-Saxon analysts, attempts to elaborate a comprehensive strategy for America, so as to make impossible the emergence of any other challenger capable of thwarting America's primacy in Eurasia. Quite rightly, he argues that 'Eurasia is the chessboard on which the struggle for global primacy continues to be played, and that strategy involves geo-strategy – the management of geo-political interests.'[2] In other words, if America lacks the proper strategy to streamline the development of key Eurasian actors according to her national interests, then Eurasia will be lost and America's primacy in world politics will wither away too.

Brzezinski's account is clear, comprehensive and instructive. The overall message of his book can even be perceived by a *tout court* reading of it. He makes everybody understand that globalisation via power projection is not an 'illicit' method by which the US may promote its national interests across the globe. What is more, these interests are best served by making realist geo-political use of the power innate in certain Cold War institutions, such as NATO and the IMF, as well as of the US paramount military might per se.

1

Brzezinski suggests not a contraction of American power after the eclipse of the USSR, but an expansion of it.

The second, more specific, message is a direct consequence of the first: there is no such thing as 'ethical foreign policy', or a power projection based on moral and 'human rights' values. 'In Paris in 1998 to promote the French edition of his book', Diana Johnstone acutely observed, 'he was asked about the apparent "paradox" that his book was steeped in *Realpolitik* whereas, in his days as National Security Adviser to President Jimmy Carter, Brzezinski had been the "defender of human rights".' But the man waved the 'paradox' aside. 'There is no paradox', he replied. 'I elaborated that doctrine in agreement with President Carter, as it was the best way to destabilise the Soviet Union. And it worked.'[3]

We have come to the crux of the matter. The world we live in is still a realist/neo-realist world dominated by states, national interests, geo-politics and power politics. The more 'globalised' and lopsided it becomes under the sway of the dominant power (i.e. the US) the more the possibilities for conflict, terrorist activities and ethnic and religious wars will be in the ascendant.[4] The zones of conflict and conflicting regional micro-interests multiply, and with them the difficulties and contradictions of world-rule policies grow inexorably. The collapse of the USSR opened up new peripheral corridors and regions for US hegemonic engagement, but this US engagement proved to be not entirely problem-free. After all, not everything that happens in the world and which affects US interests is predicted by US strategic and contingency planning. The US engagement policies are, at times, reactive rather than proactive. This is due in part to pressure exercised by domestic political factors, such as public opinion, ethnic lobbies, legislative institutions, state departments and other organised class and corporate interests. This overall set of vicissitudes of US policy for world domination is the overarching theme that runs through the pages of this book, a theme that Brzezinski and the majority of US policy-makers fail to address critically. How do we explore and infuse that theme in the present discussion and what is the key set of arguments developed here?

My first objective is to present the ways in which the US has attempted to hold sway in Western Eurasia since the collapse of the USSR and its satellite states.[5] Some of the vicissitudes of US policy necessarily take the form of contradictions inherent in the very process of formulation and implementation of US policy per se. Others pertain to the differences between peripheral states and regions that the US wants to engage and lead in a direction that serves its own national interest: not always coinciding, however, with the interests of those regional/peripheral powers. This overall nexus of contradictions, inherent in the politics of globalisation and world domination, is the explosive material that leads to conflicts and wars, rather than to peace and security. The EU, which has achieved a remarkable degree of economic prosperity and political security since the Second World War, finds itself in an awkward dilemma. It can either stand up to global challenges engaging itself with or without the US, with or against the US; or, alternatively, adopt a pacifist and democratic position, while making sure that it is able to defend and spread such a position around the globe. The fundamental prerequisite for each option is for Europe to produce a coherent federal polity, thus becoming an independent actor in world politics.

Brzezinski is against this reasoning. He wants the EU to expand eastwards, but not to deepen its political integration as this might challenge America's supremacy, particularly in the Middle East:

> A larger Europe will expand the range of American influence – and through the admission of new Central European members, also increase in the European councils the number of states with a pro-American proclivity – without simultaneously creating a Europe politically so integrated that it could soon challenge the United States on geo-political matters of high importance to America elsewhere, particularly in the Middle East.[6]

We now arrive at the second major objective of this book, which is to examine the potential of the EU to become an independent political actor in world affairs. This potential is limited because the US–EU partnership goes back a long way, as the hegemony of the US over EU political affairs was established during the Cold War and is thus very well embedded. Yet the evidence we possess to date shows that the development of a robust EU is not impossible. In the wake of the disappearance of the Soviet threat, European economic and political interests have gained more freedom of action in the 1990s and received an additional boost with Germany's reunification. The completion of the process of European economic integration and the launch of the euro are further indications fostering this aspect of emancipation of the EU from the US. I pay particular attention to the development of a potentially independent EU foreign policy guided by Germany and France, by looking into relations between Cyprus and the EU. I view the decision taken by the EU in the 1990s to open accession negotiations with Cyprus, a republic *de facto* divided since 1974, as a major step forward, showing the refusal of the EU to completely surrender its foreign policy to the demands of the US and Turkey. I compare and contrast the pivotal roles of Germany and Turkey for the US in Western Eurasia, and I conclude that the former is far more important a player than the latter. A major defect of Brzezinski's strategic assessment is his failure to compare and contrast the postures of both Germany and Turkey in Eurasia's Western belt, that is to say the geo-strategic significance of those countries in the formulation of US policies.

The principal guidelines of US foreign policy, as well as the institutions destined to produce strategies for global domination, were established in the wake of the Second World War and in the Cold War. The US–EU antagonism itself began during the Cold War period. In order, therefore, to decipher the range of difficulties of US policy in the Balkans and the Middle East, it is often necessary to adopt a historical perspective. We shall indeed become aware that some of the major problems facing the US and its allies today have their origins in the Cold War years.

The same applies to the case of Cyprus and the Middle East. The US's substantial engagement with Cypriot affairs is traceable back to the early 1960s, following a British decision to confine Britain's role on the island to the strategic maintenance of its two sovereign bases guaranteed by the Zurich–London constitutional arrangements of 1959–60. However, whereas the US schemes of the 1960s and early 1970s aimed at dividing Cyprus between Greece and Turkey in order to keep both NATO allies satisfied – thus also avoiding turning the dispute into a major Cold War confrontation – the EU has seen the issue in a different way. It has refused to surrender itself to the situation that arose in 1974 and has also rebuffed the Turkish notion of having two independent sovereign states on the island. The EU has expressed its preference to have, ideally, a united and independent Republic of Cyprus in its ranks. Moreover, the EU decided that the (Greek-led) Republic of Cyprus should join the EU regardless of whether a solution to the division of the island is found before accession. This was a major foreign policy initiative that strengthened further the leverage of the EU over Eastern Mediterranean and Middle Eastern affairs. In addition, it further distinguished the EU's policy towards these two Eurasian subregions from that of the US.

The Structure of the Book

This text is selective and, at times, discursive. It would have been impossible to discuss here in detail the foreign policy of the US towards every Balkan or Middle Eastern state: such a task goes beyond the real and ideal capacities of any one individual.

The opening chapter sets the overall scene of the discussion. I explain the nature of US policy in Eurasia in the 1990s by focusing on the 'energy factor'. There is a new type of geo-politics employed by the US and other Eurasian actors in the wake of the collapse of the USSR, that is to say the collapse of the centralised system of corporate economic governance. This new geo-political game is inextricably linked to oil and gas pipeline projects, connecting Asian and European zones. I examine the ways in which the US has tried to control the production and transportation of oil and gas from Central Asia to the Balkans and, from there, to Western markets. I also look at how the Balkans are geo-strategically and geo-politically linked with the Caspian region and the Middle East. The evidence I bring to the fore suggests that the US has not dramatically changed its policies since 1989 or, for that matter, since September 11, 2001. Rather, the US has extended its pre-existing Cold War policy framework towards global domination, precisely because since the Cold War it has encountered far less politically organised resistance. Demystifying the agreement reached between Russia and the US in May 2002, I lay out the parameters of an argument which holds that the Cold War has not really 'ended'. All the major Cold War actors fighting for diverse geo-political and geo-economic interests are still around, the sole difference being that European Germany and Asian China are economically stronger; Russia, although not a spent force, is fundamentally weak and the US is the aggressive and unstoppable politico-military global victor. This chapter also underlines that the 'energy factor' provided NATO and the US with an additional crucial reason to violently orchestrate developments in Yugoslavia via the Bosnian and Kosovo crises, thus halting and putting a check on both Germany's and Russia's influence in the Balkan zone.

But policies, either domestic or foreign, cannot be reduced to economics or the 'energy factor' alone. Foreign policy projection is a multidimensional strategic act, which is deeply political and diplomatic, and which has strong security, defence and preventive aspects. This has driven me to take up the example of Yugoslavia and go on to unravel the contradictions of NATO and US policies, particularly when their actions are justified by the doctrine of 'human rights' abuses. I contend that the Kosovo war was not intended to protect the Kosovo Albanians from Milosevic's brutal grip. Rather, it was a preventive war aiming to guarantee NATO's eastward expansion, US energy interests, as well as to halt German and European influence in the Balkans. Yet, this war inspired Albanian irredentism in the Balkans and threatened the cohesion of the multi-ethnic Republic of Macedonia, thus putting in jeopardy European security. Therefore, occasionally, I compare the EU and NATO eastward enlargements and I highlight the inability of the EU to put forward a comprehensive political agenda to solve the Yugoslav conflict. I also look at the roles of Greece and Turkey in the Balkans and the Near East. I offer a critical overview of NATO's reform and expansion processes of the 1990s, and I argue that its transformation from a defence pact into a political organisation, upholding and selectively implementing liberal-democratic principles, may lead the alliance into serious political deadlock in years to come.

US global leadership in parts of Eurasia during the Cold War was bound up not only with US leadership in Western Europe, but also with the control of developments in the Near Eastern theatre. In the main, the Truman Doctrine and the policy of containment (1947) had created a link between a successful defence of Western Europe and a successful defence of the Near/Middle East, with Greece, Turkey, Iran and Afghanistan constituting the 'front-line' zone of politico-military engagement *vis-à-vis* the Soviet threat. I analyse this link and I place the Cyprus issue in the 1950s and 1960s in context. I argue here that UK/US policies towards Greece, Cyprus and Turkey were mainly unsuccessful, not least because they failed to produce a lasting and permanent solution to the Cyprus issue. In particular, the 'divide and rule' policy of the UK in the 1950s created further animosity between Greece and Turkey, and between the Greek and the Turkish Cypriots. The US had inherited this policy failure from the UK in the 1960s, but its inaction to prevent the Greek junta's coup in Cyprus (July 15, 1974), and the first Turkish invasion five days later, had brought two NATO allies to the brink of war. But I also see a connection between the strategic need of the US to defend Israel after the experience of the Yom Kippur war of October 1973, and the Turkish invasions of Cyprus in July and August 1974. I thus also dwell on the Arab–Israeli conflict, trying to link up the importance of Israel for the US, with the significance of defending Greece, Turkey and Iran from possible Soviet encroachments. This chapter is more systematically structured through a historical perspective.

An analysis of Turkish domestic and foreign policies follows. This is necessary because the US, today as well as during the Cold War, has connected its strategy in the Middle East and Central Asia with Turkey's geo-strategic primacy in South-western Eurasia, particularly since 1979 with the loss of Iran. An analysis of the 'Turkish pivot', will enable us to balance Turkey's weight in NATO and the EU in relation to that of Germany, France, Greece and the Republic of Cyprus. Although these issues constitute the main subject of discussion in the following chapter, my tentative, pre-emptive argument is that the US considers its strategic partnership with Germany and France as more important than that with Turkey. To put it another way, Germany matters for the US more than Turkey in the overall Western Eurasian zone, that is the thick security belt stretching from the Baltic states, southwards to the Caspian Sea and the Persian Gulf. This is tantamount to saying that if the US was forced to choose between a European Germany leading the EU's eastward enlargement on the one hand, and Turkey on the other, then the superpower would opt for Germany. Although never officially said, I tend to believe that Greece's gamble in the 1990s that it would block the EU's eastward enlargement if the Republic of Cyprus was not admitted to the EU, was almost entirely placed within the remit of this strategic assessment.

I then exemplify further the issue of Germany's geo-strategic primacy in Western Eurasia. This chapter looks closely at Cyprus' European perspective and, by focusing on the position of both Greek and Turkish Cypriot sides, tries to diagnose the strategic factors that underpin their respective arguments. I argue here that Greece and the Republic of Cyprus employed the EU/Germany diplomatic card in the background and the legal card up front, as Turkey has lacked legitimate grounds since 1963–4 to defend its claims and politico-military position in Cyprus. Turkey, in contrast, has drawn its arguments from its own regional geo-strategic primacy and military superiority, with almost all other arguments put forward being epiphenomena of this power-politics dimension, in order to buy time. This is far from arguing that Greece 'forced' Germany to go along with its position on Cyprus. Quite the opposite: I attempt to show that Germany and France, in the institutional context of the EU, have had a vested geo-strategic interest in the incorporation of the Republic of

Cyprus to the EU as an independent united state. 'The real criterion for choosing the countries which will be in the "fast track" for membership', Peter Gowan wrote, 'will be neither democratic stability nor economic strength, but the criterion of Western geo-political interests, above all the need to consolidate the incorporation of the states constituting the Eastern flanks of Germany and Austria.'[7] I would add to this the strategic criterion of consolidating the EU interests in the neuralgic zone of the Eastern Mediterranean, the Suez Canal and of the Near Eastern theatre. The US was, and is, vehemently against this perspective. In this context, I argue that Cyprus constitutes a major testing ground for the emancipation of the EU's foreign and security policy from the grip of the US.

The concluding chapter provides an overall assessment of US policy in Eurasia. In addition, it attempts to outline the parameters that can underpin the emergence of a Eurasian, non-hegemonic and social democratic political administration, composed of Eurasian powers only.

Globalisation and European Integration

I refrain from a systematic theoretical and historical discussion of the economic issues inherent in any notion of globalisation and European integration. However, it is appropriate to define in this Introduction the concepts of 'integration' and 'globalisation' so as to avoid confusion and facilitate the reading of the arguments running through the text. In any event, a clarification of the terms will lay the ground for a deeper understanding of the antagonism between the EU and the US, one of the main themes of this book.

I adopt a qualified version of the definitions employed by the neo-realist theories of Robert Keohane and Helen Milner: namely, that the notion of globalisation/internationalisation refers to 'processes generated by underlying shifts in transaction costs that produce observable flows of goods, services and capital'.[8] These processes, however, are not spontaneous events innate in the functioning of global, regional and national markets. As I have shown elsewhere,[9] and as I explain when examining the role of the IMF and GATT–WTO in the Yugoslav crisis, these processes are driven by concrete and highly politicised institutions, which are linked to the US, serving specific US national economic and political interests. Globalisation has been the central pillar of US foreign policy since the collapse of the USSR and its satellite states. But it is neither a new phenomenon in modern economic history, nor one that is free from state interference and state macro-economic strategies.[10] The US/UK globalisation agenda to liberalise the domestic and regional environments of other states and organisations presupposes strong, not weak, states or central institutions. As the case of Britain under the neo-conservative rule of Margaret Thatcher in the 1980s has clearly shown, the neo-liberal state has to be strong not only in terms of being able to shift the economic policy agenda, but also to exercise effective policing over the trade unions. I would also add that, at times, Anglo-Saxon globalisation and free trade strategies deliberately favour arms sales over other forms of trade, thus fuelling regional tensions and conflict across the globe.[11] Therefore, the 'underlying shifts in transaction costs' claimed by Keohane and Milner as being the defining element of 'globalisation', should be viewed alongside the political volition of the US public policy-making apparatuses to facilitate and promote this process with a view to servicing specific US national interests. Globalisation induces national governments to domestic structural adjustments along neo-liberal economic lines, thus fostering the formation and re-formation of a system of economic, military and political alliances dominated by the US. Furthermore, and regardless of whether they are economically successful from a US neo-liberal point of view, globalisation movements are necessarily enshrined into the capitalist economic tendencies of uneven economic development. Globalisation brings about neither economic/welfare prosperity for all, nor an economic homogenisation of the various regions of the world. Quite the opposite: it reproduces the historically uneven development of capitalism in an extended form, precisely as it reproduces an extended subsumption of labour to capital. Moreover, as uneven processes, economic/technological modernisation, and modernity in general, confer benefits to some groups and regions and not to others. At times, and under certain economic and political circumstances, modernisation tends to mobilise ethnic elites and foster nationalism in order to alter or reinforce this structured inequality. As we shall see in detail, this trend was prominent in the case of the break-up of Yugoslavia. Reality is indeed staunchly refusing to surrender to the ideologies of liberal orthodoxy and economic prosperity for all.

'Integration', and European integration in particular, is a process that is different from those of globalisation/internationalisation. Although there is an overlap of economic functions that can be seen from the joint financial and capital ventures between European,

Japanese and American interests, economic integration remains 'the convergence of goods, services and capital in specific markets'.[12] As experienced and best exemplified through the process of European integration per se, it is a relatively new historical supranational phenomenon that tends to solidify specific economic interests generated by the protected regional market and its institutional/ political forces. Also, it is indeed new, in the sense that the only parallel that can *reluctantly* be drawn is with the historical process of economic integration achieved within the borders of national states during and after their foundation in nineteenth- and early-twentieth-century Europe. I say 'reluctantly', because Europe has achieved a considerable degree of economic integration, without having managed, as yet, to create a solid and coherent supranational polity. And nor do we know whether it will ever be able to achieve this. The roots of the antagonism between the EU and the US lie precisely in the completed process of the EU's economic integration (e.g. the euro as the dollar's main competitor in world markets) and the incomplete project of its political integration. Time and again, Europe is driven by a constellation of states, whose influence on the policy-making process of the EU is proportionate to the economic and political weight that each of these states carries. This is best exemplified through the various Inter-Governmental Conferences (IGCs) of the EU. In this context, the EU still remains a 'realist/neo-realist' construction, functioning along both centrifugal and centripetal tendencies. Europe's political integration would entail a wholly independent federal polity, with its own supranational democratic institutions able to elaborate and put forward comprehensively independent and single fiscal, industrial, social, cultural, foreign, security and defence policies. The US policy of globalisation and world domination does not want this to ever take place, and the UK/Denmark pair obstructs this process from within.[13] This conflict of interests, in turn, becomes a conflict between the major players inside and outside the EU, while the smaller and less powerful actors have only to jump on the bandwagon of the power(s) that best serve(s) their own micro-national interests. This is a complex game, which becomes even more obscure in the insti-tutionalised and bureaucratic framework of the EU, but it is still a fragmented game of discord that pertains to a realist/neo-realist definition of international politics.

2 The New Geo-politics of Gas and Oil

Broadly speaking, there are a number of speculative themes and discursive questions that can be addressed in relation to post-Cold War international affairs. Should the collapse of the USSR and its satellite states be seen as an isolated and self-consuming event confined to East-Central Europe, the Balkans and Central Asia? Do NATO and the US really design and perform their policies on the basis of moral and democratic principles? Moreover, despite the restructuring of the West's institutions and power system in the 1990s, and despite the US/NATO–Russia agreement of May 2002, has the Cold War really 'ended'? Has the US really altered its foreign policy framework since the break-up of the USSR, or has it simply extended it, at times aggressively? Have we experienced any dramatic U-turn in the US strategy in the 1990s or, for that matter, since September 11, 2001, or have we been witnessing a reform policy and the organisational growth of it built upon strategic institutions and key policy aims established during the Cold War? This chapter constitutes an attempt to provide an informed discussion of these interrelated themes and questions.

First, I offer a brief summary of some key events in the 1990s, which lead us to conclude that the collapse of the East was bound up with a simultaneous 'collapse' and restructuring of the Western system of power. It appears that the break-up of the USSR was inextricably linked to the restructuring of the power relations system of the West. This was a restructuring which, in certain respects, was bound up with a certain 'collapse' of the Cold War organisational structures and modes of political and strategic thinking. For instance, the evolution of NATO would have been completely different if the disintegration and ultimate break-up of 'really existing socialism' had not taken place.

I go on to analyse a key underlying factor that led the West to advance the institutional and organisational restructuring of its power relations system. I argue that it is impossible to acquire a fully-fledged understanding of NATO, US and EU policies in Western

11

Eurasia, or comprehend the EU–US antagonism itself, if the issue of energy is not brought appropriately into context. 'When powers like the US or the UK go to war', Peter Gowan argues, 'they do so for reasons of national interest, in pursuit of state objectives.'[1] In this qualified context, no moral or ethical principles appear in the equation. I reinforce here the principle that behind some key US actions backed by the rhetoric of 'human rights' lie strategic and geo-political imperatives.

I thus look at two major strategic resources, oil and gas, both of which are coveted and contested by many Eurasian national actors. These two resources have strategic significance for every international and regional power, their security being of paramount importance for the well-being of their economies. The US, by any means available to it, including 'co-operation' with Russia, wants to establish its political hegemony over Eurasia, precisely because of the strategic significance of the region's energy resources. I will examine the 'energy issue' in US geo-political and geo-economic considerations, by way of geo-strategically connecting the entire Western Eurasian and Middle Eastern zones, that is Germany's and Austria's eastern flanks, Central Asia, the Middle East and the Balkans. By doing so, we shall become aware of the ways in which global competition over energy resources has been unfolding since the collapse of the Soviet Union, thus deepening our knowledge of the reasons that prompted the US to employ an expansionist/ aggressive policy in Western Eurasia.

Subsequently, I discuss whether the Cold War has really 'ended', or whether US foreign policy has dramatically changed since the tragic events of September 11, 2001. The apparent renewed economic and political competition between all the key Cold War actors (the EU/Germany/France, the USSR/Russia, the US, China and Japan), drives me to argue that there is an indisputable institutional and strategic continuity between pre- and post-Cold War US policy. To a certain extent, this applies to the foreign policy patterns of the other protagonists, that is Russia, China, Germany and Japan. Apparently, the new realist game that has been unfolding since 1990 has to do with the new type of economic and political competition over security and energy matters that have grown out of traditional conflicting geo-political interests and strategic rivalries. In this context, it is clear that the main differences between the pre- and post-Cold War period are that European Germany and Asian China are stronger, Russia is weaker and the US has become the victor.

The 1990s: Years of Pandemonium

The victory of the US in the Cold War has rightly been attributed to a number of structural economic and political weaknesses of the USSR and, more pertinently, to its economic inability to compete with the Reaganite project of 'star wars'.[2] Yet the very process of the collapse of 'really existing socialism' was not an 'isolated' and quasi-structural event – albeit dramatic and at times violent and protracted – confined to East-Central Europe, Central Asia and the Balkans. In fact, the crisis and the ultimate disintegration of the Warsaw Pact regimes were inextricably linked to a number of concomitant transformations in the Western system of power. *In a way, the collapse of the East heralded an almost simultaneous 'collapse' of the West in terms of new power arrangements and institutional restructuring.*

Undoubtedly, the West, under the hegemonic drive of the US, has contributed to the break-up of the East, particularly by promoting 'shock therapy' neo-liberal economic reforms via the IMF and the World Bank, and by encouraging nationalist secessionist movements to flourish. As we shall see in the following chapter when examining the case of Yugoslavia, this IMF-led strategy has often ignored the realities of transition economies that it was supposed to help. Yet the overall economic projection towards the East has been successful in that it weakened the USSR–Russia, splitting the territorial integrity of the USSR and its satellite states.[3] The strategic and geo-economic vacuum created could be filled by the expansion of both NATO and the EU. It is this very participation of the West in the process of the disintegration of the East that has shaken up Western institutions and states.[4]

The following is an incomplete list, presenting a summary of issues, some of which will be developed in the following chapters. This list exemplifies the way in which the collapse of the East mirrored a parallel and simultaneous restructuring of the Western system of power:

a. The reunification of Germany (1990) rebalanced the relationship of forces in Europe and gave a further boost to the very process of European integration, while at the same time Germany ceased to be a 'junior political partner of France'.[5] Germany's borderland was again Poland, a country of immense strategic importance for European Germany and for the success of the EU's eastward enlargement per se. Germany began to advance a robust foreign policy in Eastern Europe and the Balkans, something which the US has always kept in check, witness the case of Germany's initiatives in Yugoslavia in the early 1990s, before the total unfolding of the Bosnian crisis.

b. The precipitation, further widening and, to a certain degree, deepening of the process of European integration are events of significant importance for what can be called the 'European project'. These events – whose origin can be traced back to the mid-1980s with the launch of the Single European Act under the auspices of Jacques Delors – are exemplified by the Maastricht (1992) and Amsterdam (1997) Treaties, the accessions of Austria, Finland and Sweden (1995), as well as by the introduction of the euro and the proposed 'big bang' eastward enlargement announced at the IGC of 1996–7. The launch, albeit reluctant and with many difficulties, of the ESDI (European Security and Defence Identity) is a further indication of Europe's process of emancipation from both the Soviet threat and US transatlantic supremacy.

c. The restructuring of NATO and its apparent transformation from a *defence* pact into a *political* organisation is another crucial indicator (see the following chapter).[6] The chief purpose of NATO's eastward enlargement is the establishment/projection of US hegemony in security zones, which during the Cold War were under the influence or direct control of the USSR and China. This purpose could not have been served on the basis of its Cold War defence posture. NATO had to be transformed into a *political* organisation with an aggressive military posture, in order to employ the 'stick and carrot' tactics towards Russia and China. This dual type of diplomacy could serve American strategic interests by preventing the formation of a geo-political European axis stretching from France to Russia and even China. The Gulf War and, more pertinently, the Bosnian and Kosovo crises provided the testing ground for the new aggressive policy of the US. The alliance, on the eve of its Kosovo campaign in March 1999, integrated three new members into its structures: Poland, Hungary and the Czech Republic. Those with an inclination to think strategically are challenged to contemplate the consequences of this type of expansion, which in effect prevented Europe and Germany from establishing a privileged geo-political partnership with Poland, Ukraine, Belarus, the Balkan states and Russia, whose energy resources, particularly gas, are of vital significance for the West. But the US has employed the 'stick' along with the 'carrot' throughout. Although NATO's geo-political type of expansion can hardly stop until after Russia itself has become a full member, and despite the inclusion into NATO of states such as the Baltic states, as well as Slovakia, Slovenia, Romania and Bulgaria, the US has always showed willingness to 'co-operate'. In the 1990s, the US championed the NATO–Russia Founding Act and established the NATO–Russia Permanent Joint Council. In 2002 the US brought Russia closer to the West. Although the US pulled out of the Anti-ballistic Missile Treaty of 1972 in order to be free to develop a missile shield, it convinced Russia to sign a treaty committing both sides to cut their 'nuclear warheads by two-thirds, to 1,700–2,000 over the next ten years'.[7] Inevitably, NATO's expansion and the US–Russia understanding limit the extent to which European and Chinese interests can increase their influence over the oil and gas 'pipeline map' of the Balkans and the greater Middle East (see below). The US is in favour of helping Russia to expand its oil industry as it wants to diversify its sources of acquiring oil.[8] At the same time, the US, being in a position of strength, will be able to remove some key parameters that obstruct its political and economic freedom of movement in Russia's peripheries and zones of influence. This is the policy framework within which regime change in Iraq, which is so vehemently supported by the US–UK even by waging a war of aggression against Saddam Hussein, can be analysed and understood.

d. The disintegration of 'really existing socialism' also had an enormous impact on the domestic politics of some Western European states. For example, the collapse of the Italian political system in the early 1990s, which had been based on the centrality of the corrupt Christian Democratic–Socialist (DC–PSI) axis of power, was mainly the result of two interconnected processes: that of the collapse of the East and of the process of European integration. In particular, the break-up of the USSR gave the 'green light' to the transformed Italian Communist Party (PCI), the PDS (Democratic Party of the Left), to compete for power with the other political parties on an equal footing. Finally, the PDS led a centre-left coalition government during the second half of the 1990s, a period of general euphoria for the parties of the 'neo-revisionist' or 'Third Way' new European Left.[9]

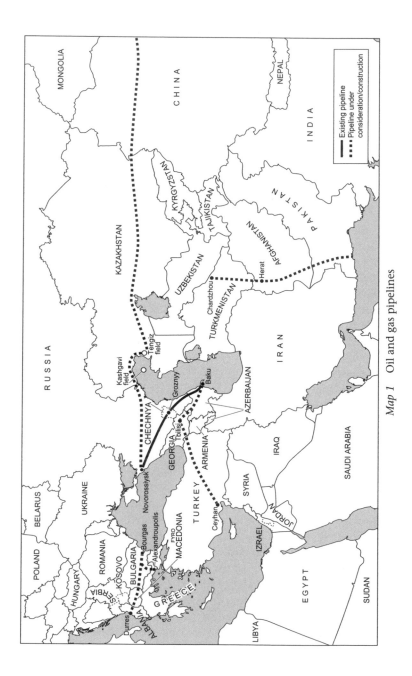

Map 1 Oil and gas pipelines

I can bring forward more cases that prove the linkages between the collapse of the East and the simultaneous 'collapse'/restructuring of the Western system of power under the aegis of the US power, the IMF and NATO. However, they would add little to the point that has already clearly emerged: namely, that the historical process of the break-up of the East produced a simultaneous 'collapse' and restructuring of the West under the hegemonic guidance of the US. We can now move on to examine some key underlying strategic factors, buttressing the US logic of power projection deeper into Eurasia's heartland. These strategic factors are related to oil and gas.

Conflicting Interests: Oil and Gas Projects in Eurasia

Eurasia as a whole accounts for 75 per cent of the world's population, 60 per cent of its gross national product (GNP) and 75 per cent of its energy resources. Moreover, '63 per cent of the world's proven oil reserves are in the Middle East [and] 25 per cent (or 261 billion barrels) in Saudi Arabia alone'.[10] Of all major oil and gas producing states and regions in the world (setting aside Saudi Arabia, Iraq, Russia, Kuwait, Libya, Iran, the Caucasus and the Caspian Sea regions), only Venezuela, Mexico, and the US states of Texas and Alaska, fall outside Eurasia's landscape.

The key point is that all major oil producing states and regions, with the exception of those in North America, are volatile and conflict-ridden.[11] Also – but now with the additional exception of Venezuela – they are surrounded by, or centred on significant Eurasian powers, all with a colonial past. These powers are Russia, China, Germany, Britain and France, with Japan in the far Eastern arc projecting significant regional and global power, which is largely driven by high-tech industries. As well as trying to accommodate Arab and OPEC (Organisation of Petroleum Exporting Countries) interests, the US today is in economic and political competition with these powers, the partial exception being Britain, with whom it enjoys a special relationship, but not at all times and not on every single matter. In the main, this story of rivalry and competition is neither a mere extension of Cold War settings, nor a post-Cold War phenomenon per se. In a way, this narrative has always been around, at least since oil, gas and other energy and hydrocarbon resources became the locomotives of modern economies and societies.

Imperial Britain and France had to subordinate Middle Eastern tribal interests, and also had to find a *modus vivendi* with tsarist Russia, when establishing their hegemonic presence in Mosul

(Northern Iraq) and the Levant respectively. As part of his Russian campaign, Hitler had planned to connect the control of the Danube and its Black Sea mouth, with the oilfields of Baku and the Caucasus.[12] After the Second World War, the US, taking over from Britain and France, also had to deal with the USSR and the Arab nationalism of the new Middle Eastern states, particularly from the Suez crisis onwards. And today, *mutatis mutandis*, the wider Middle Eastern region is equally volatile, with the US facing increased competition from EU powers, Russia and China over its energy resources. 'Our paramount national security interest in the Middle East', a 1995 US Department of Defence report stated, 'is maintaining the unhindered flow of oil from the Persian Gulf to world markets at stable prices.'[13]

Over the years, the EU has expressed similar concerns. In a 2000 Green Paper put forward by the Commission we read that: 'petrol is vital for the economy like bread' and that 'any disruption of supplies or erratic fluctuation in prices' is likely to cause social disruption leading to social demands that it may not be possible to meet.[14] The leading EU powers cannot forget the havoc caused to their economies by the oil embargoes of 1973 and 1979.

Similarly, China's economy is wholly dependent on oil and gas and the cheaper the energy the greater the likelihood of managing sustained economic growth for its population of 1.3bn. In terms of import requirements, China's need for oil is expected to rise to 40 per cent by 2010, as compared to 20 per cent in 1995.[15] In this race, Chinese giants such as Sinopec and Petrochina would have to compete with other US and EU companies as China has entered the WTO. Although the worry about oil and gas prices is only one concern among many others for the key players, it is a major one.

The 'economic miracles' of the 1950s and 1960s experienced by the West were driven by a Keynesian set of national policies based on a rationalised management of aggregate demand. John M. Keynes advocated that macro-economic state intervention was a necessary and sufficient tool for economic growth and for balancing out market disequilibria. It entailed the development of welfarism and the control of interest rates and inflation through fiscal/budgetary instruments. Increases in real and nominal wages were to be offset by an increase in the level of consumption and by investment strategies. However, this policy, whose main aim was to consolidate 'an aggregate volume of output corresponding to full employment as nearly as is practicable',[16] came to a halt with the collapse of the

Bretton Woods system (1971) and the first oil shock (1973).[17] The shock, which came in the wake of the Yom Kippur war (October 1973) between Israel and Arab states (mainly Egypt, Syria and Jordan), was exemplified by an increase of 70 per cent in the price of crude oil. Moreover, the Arab member states of OPEC stopped exports to the US and Netherlands, while reducing overall exports by 25 per cent.[18] This contributed to an increase in the rate of inflation in the West, shook up the Keynesian consensus and introduced strong pressures upon the fiscal performance of the Western states and the average (relatively high) rate of real and nominal wages.

Although the West today is less dependent on oil than it was, due mainly to the adoption of energy policies, such as the establishment of strategic fuel reserves or the diversification of fuel sources from oil to nuclear and gas, the fact remains that 'oil still has the power to shock'.[19] Since 1973, the world has experienced two other significant oil-driven crises (in 1979 with the Iranian revolution and in 1990–92 due to the Gulf War). The negative impact upon the West on both occasions was alarming. In this context, one of the fundamental policy aims of the US today is still the stabilisation of the international price of crude oil at the lowest possible marketable levels.

Yet this remains one objective among many others, simply because the US is not only interested in obtaining cheap oil or gas, nor in obtaining them from the Middle Eastern states alone.[20] The US, having won the Cold War, also wants to control, as much as possible, their production and safe transportation to Western markets by eliminating possible West European, Eastern (e.g. Russia, China) or Middle Eastern competitors. Moreover, the emergence of possible alternatives to the Middle Eastern energy resources, such as those discovered in the Caspian Sea region, has opened up new policy avenues for the US. With the disintegration of the USSR, Central Asia, together with the Caucasus, the Black Sea and the Balkans, have assumed particular geo-strategic significance, either as oil and gas producing regions or as strategic transport routes. The roots of the new geo-political game since the collapse of the USSR lie precisely here.

Among other things, the break-up of the USSR was inevitably going to lead to a politico-economic crisis over energy and pipeline networks, which were centrally administered and planned by the state authorities. Although the process of privatisation/decentralisation is far from completed in Russia, the new independent states in

Central Asia, the Caucasus and the Black Sea region, most of which were connected to the USSR's energy network, have assumed a new geo-political centrality in Eurasia, which for the US is difficult to ignore.

LUKoil, Russia's giant oil corporation, 'has discovered a field of 5 billion barrels of proven reserves in the Russian part of the Caspian shelf' and 'seismic data suggest that the field's vast size could triple the initial estimates inside the license area alone'.[21] Oilfields in Azerbaijan 'are estimated to have 3–4 billion barrels of recoverable oil reserves' and the Tengiz field in Kazakhstan in the early 1990s was 'the largest discovery of crude oil since Prudhoe Bay in Alaska with proven crude reserves of 6 billion barrels, and a possible additional recoverable reserve of 3 billion barrels'.[22] The Caspian region is also very rich in gas (Turkmenistan is the world's fourth largest gas producer), hydrocarbons and fish. In particular, it has 'the world's largest concentration of sturgeon, producer of caviar'.[23] Any oil and gas supplies that spread the political risk away from OPEC, Keith Fisher argues, 'are seen [by the West] to be a good thing'.[24] Or, as Fiona Hill put it:

> US interests [in the Caspian region] are very straightforward. Removing the stranglehold of the Middle East over the world's oil supplies through the exploitation of Caspian resources will have a positive effect on the global energy balance, and bring long-term commercial benefits for the US if US oil companies are directly involved.[25]

Thus, the Middle East, although still a key region for European and American interests, has not been the sole focus of the West since the Cold War. There is indeed an energy 'pipeline map' drafted by leading US and UK companies, such as Chevron, BP and Amoco (which merged in 1998), UNOCAL, Texaco, Exxon and Pennzoil, and it is this map 'around the oil and natural gas resources of the region that connects the Balkans to Afghanistan'.[26] It is in this respect that the Middle East, although still of paramount strategic and global importance, can be seen only in the context of a greater Middle East, which includes Central Asia and the Pakistan–Afghanistan zone, the Caspian and the Caucasus. In the event, however, US policy is forced to discipline and/or accommodate the interests of some important regional actors, while also facing competition from EU states.

All five littoral Caspian Sea states (Russia, Iran, Azerbaijan, Turk-menistan and Kazakhstan) are in fierce competition over the vast energy resources and disagreements have arisen between them over the delimitation of the continental shelf and territorial waters since the break-up of the USSR. In the first half of the 1990s, Russia and Iran insisted on a continuation of the legal status of the Caspian, which was valid during the Soviet period and consisted of treaties signed in 1921 and 1940. These treaties had stipulated the status of the Sea in the form of a condominium between Russia and Iran, but this came to be disputed by the new break-away post-Soviet republics of Azerbaijan and Kazakhstan. The new post-Soviet states argued that the treaties were imprecise as regards energy resources exploitation and continental shelf issues. Thus, Azerbaijan and Kazakhstan began claiming the oilfields of the Caspian on the basis of 'the provisions of the 1982 Law of the Sea, which assigns national sectors to littoral states'.[27] But this was unacceptable to Russia, which saw the Caspian not as a 'Sea' but as a landlocked lake, hence the irrelevance of the 1982 Law of the Sea in the Caspian case.[28] Towards the late 1990s and early 2000s, however, Russia began to change its approach, and tried to make unilateral agreements with other littoral states over the delimitation of fishing sectors and the continental shelf. This infuriated Iran, which claimed some 20 per cent-plus of the Caspian, 'although its coastline represents about 14 per cent of the total'.[29]

It should be noted that these regional disputes directly affect the US and West European interests, as well as some Middle Eastern companies operating in Central Asia. Chevron and Oman Oil are major players in Kazakhstan and the Caspian region in general, alongside 'British Petroleum, France's Total and Italy's Agip'.[30] US companies have more than 50 per cent of the stakes in the Azerbaijan oil consortium and 'Turkey had pledged more than $886 million in Exibank credits' to the Turkish-speaking states of the Caspian and Central Asia.[31] As well as the new projects under way, there were already two significant pipeline routes for oil from the Soviet years 'from Azerbaijan and Kazakhstan to the Black Sea, both of which run through Russia and Chechnya to Novorossiisk'.[32] The wars between Armenia and Azerbaijan over the Nagorno-Karabach, and between Russia and the Chechens, which triggered Turkey's and Saudi Arabia's discreet involvement on the side of the Azeris and Chechens, caused serious problems for the US as it tried to perform a balancing act between Iran, Turkey and Russia under its hegemonic mediation. The same holds true for the conflict between (pro-US)

Georgia and (pro-Russian) Abkhazia, which is a province of Georgia (the US deployed troops there in February 2002).[33] At the centre of all these conflicts was and is control over strategic territorial zones that bridge the Caspian with the Black Sea as oil and gas transport routes. Time and again, the headache for the US has been how to avoid a repetition of the Middle East volatility in the Caspian and the Caucasus; how to guarantee the safe transportation of oil to Western markets; as well as how to eliminate other regional (e.g. Russia, Iran) or global competitors (e.g. EU states).

The EU – led by Germany and France – together with Russia and China have a distinct presence in the Eurasian competition over energy resources. As early as 1990, 'Dutch Prime Minister Ruud Lubbers broached the idea of a European-wide energy community, which would capitalise on the complementary relationship between the European Economic Community, the USSR and the countries of Central and Eastern Europe.'[34] The Lubbers scheme was later evolved into an EU-led international agreement, aiming at regulating various programmes related to energy. One such programme is TACIS (Technical Assistance to the Commonwealth of Independent States), which had spawned 'two network infrastructure programmes', TRACECA (Transport Corridor Europe–Caucasus–Asia) and INOGATE (Inter-state Oil and Gas Transport to Europe).[35] Launched in 1993 and 1995 respectively, both programmes were aimed at assisting the construction of new pipeline networks, or the renovation of old ones, in the zone stretching from the Caspian and the Black Sea regions to Western Europe. The EU, under pressure from the US, tends to avoid transit routes that are under Russian influence or pass through Russian territory: this is due to US awareness that an energy axis may develop between Franco-German and Russian interests.[36] True, EU companies are also in competition with the Russian giants Gazprom (the country's virtual gas monopoly) and LUKoil (the state-run oil corporation), but this may cease to be the case when key former Soviet Republics, such as Ukraine, are integrated into the EU. The truth of the matter, however, is that there is fierce competition between the US and the EU in the greater Middle East, and this has been exemplified several times in the 1990s, either directly through the EU, or through the individual attitudes of key EU states or companies.[37]

China has its own plan for acquiring oil and gas, as it wants to diminish its dependency on Russia and Iran. Viewing the Caspian Sea region and the new Central Asian republics as key strategic zones that could serve its own energy and economic interests, China has construction plans for 'a 4,200km network of gas and oil pipelines running from China's Western province of Xinjiang to the major East coast metropolis of Shanghai'.[38] This has the potential to establish a 'Pan-Asian Global Energy Bridge', thus bringing about significant geo-strategic realignments in Eurasia and endangering the leading role of the US.[39]

The oil game is truly global. There is, for instance, harsh competition over energy production between Saudi Arabia, Russia and Venezuela. Any change of *status quo* in Iraq in the wake of the fall of Saddam Hussein would alter the geo-economics/geo-politics of oil and gas in the Middle East, not least because a number of Western companies may or may not finalise the agreements signed with the Iraqi government during the 1990s. Leading among them are France's TotalFinaElf (which agreed to exploit the development of Iraq's huge Majnoon oilfield), LUKoil (which agreed to develop the West Qurna field), Italy's Agip and China's China National Petroleum Corp. Admittedly, an opening-up of Iraq's oil market would challenge the primacy of Saudi Arabia in OPEC, thus allowing the US to rebalance its import quotas from the Middle East. Iraq is the seventh largest oil producer in the world, but its oil reserves are second only to Saudi Arabia's and its oilfields are 'badly underutilised ... because of deteriorating equipment'.[40]

Crude Oil (end of 2001 estimates)

	Reserves bn barrels	Production m barrels per day
Saudi Arabia	261.8	8.8
Iraq	112.5	2.4
UAE	97.8	2.4
Kuwait	96.5	2.1
Iran	89.7	3.7
Venezuela	77.7	3.4
Russia	48.6	7.1
USA	30.4	7.7
Libya	29.5	11.4
Mexico	26.9	3.6

Source: BP Statistical Review of World Energy (quoted in 'Don't mention the O-word', *The Economist*, September 14, 2002, p. 26).

There is also involvement of Latin American companies in the construction game of pipelines in Central Asia. For example, the

independent Argentine company, Bridas, unveiled a plan for a Turkmenistan–Afghanistan–Pakistan gas pipeline in July 1995. However,
the Los Angeles-based UNOCAL and Saudi-owned Delta-Nimir
interfered aggressively and thwarted the Argentine initiative.[41] The
US assists its companies by employing diplomatic and military
means and tries to keep this global competition over energy in check
by imposing its own agenda. In the case of US–Saudi friendly
relations over energy, the *quid pro quo* generated for each party is
rather clear-cut:

> Saudi Aramco, the state oil company, earns about $1 a barrel less
> on sales to the US than on sales to the countries of Europe and
> East Asia. That discount translates into a subsidy to US consumers
> of $620 million per year. In return, the US deploys military forces
> in the Persian Gulf, which is of course also expensive. And given
> US sensitivity to Riyadh's policy concerns on an array of issues,
> from the Arab–Israeli peace process to Kosovo and to Central Asia,
> Washington pays the additional price of being constrained in its
> own foreign policy-making.[42]

The Balkan zone constitutes a significant transport route for oil and
gas, and it is thus a strategic bridge. In this context, the Balkans can
be viewed as the geo-political gatekeeper between Western and
Eastern Eurasia, acquiring a security dimension of paramount
importance for NATO and the US.

The trans-Balkan pipeline project headed by leading US and
European oil investors (US Eximbank, the EBRD, the World Bank
and the AMBO – the US-owned Albanian, Macedonian and Bulgarian
Oil corporation), begins in 'the Bulgarian Black Sea port city of
Bourgas, crosses through Macedonia, and ends in the Albanian
Adriatic port of Durres'.[43] This pipeline, designed to transport oil
and gas from the Caspian Sea, would have to pass 'only 20 km from
Kosovo's Southern border'.[44] Various feasibility studies carried out
between 1997 and 2000 had raised the budget of the project to
$1,000,000, in view of seeing it completed by 2005. Thus, it is no
accident that NATO mounted its Kosovo campaign and that the
largest American foreign military base built since Vietnam is that of
Camp Bondsteel in Kosovo, financed by the Brown & Root Division
of Halliburton, the world's biggest oil services corporation. It is also
worth noting that the managing director of that company was Dick

Cheney, before he became the Vice-President of the US in the administration of Bush junior.[45]

Russia's policy in the Balkans is equally proactive. Russia, Bulgaria and Greece have agreed on another $600,000 underground oil pipeline project, in order to carry Russian gas and Caspian crude to the Aegean port of Alexandroupolis in Greece. Russian tankers setting off from Novorossiisk will carry the crude to Bourgas, Bulgaria's Black Sea port, and the underground Bourgas–Alexandroupolis pipeline will be 256km long.[46] This will have the additional advantage of reducing tanker traffic through the Turkish Straits, thus reducing the danger of an environmental disaster.[47] The project is administered by the 'Greek–Russian consortium Trans-Balkan Pipeline', in which Gazprom, LUKoil and Hellenic Petroleum have large stakes. In the main, this has ensured that 'the Russians maintain their grip on oil export routes from the former Soviet Union'.[48] Moreover, it has reduced the strategic weight of Turkey *vis-à-vis* that of Russia, keeping the economic competition between Russia, the EU and the US in the Balkans on a relatively equal footing. However – as a report written by the Economist Intelligence Unit argued – this type of Russian initiative in the Balkans should also be seen as an attempt to 'driv[e] a wedge' between Greece and Turkey and increase its influence in the Near/Middle East, witness 'plans to sell an air missile system to Cyprus' in 1998.[49]

In addition, in March 2002, Greece and Turkey signed a $300m agreement to build a pipeline to carry gas from Iran and the Caspian Sea region through Turkey to Alexandroupolis and thence to Western Europe.[50] To a certain extent, this should be seen as a by-product of the Baku–Ceyhan project. Although this project is supported by the US, existing feasibility studies raise concerns over its high cost and it may therefore be abandoned. The Balkans as a whole, and Turkey and Greece in particular, constitute important bridges for the transfer of Asian energy to Western markets. In this context, Greece seems to be adopting a remarkably flexible attitude, being able to strike deals with both Russia and US-sponsored energy projects.

Overall, and given the volatile character of the Balkan region and the greater Middle East, as well as the conflict between Greece and Turkey over Cyprus and the Aegean, the following propositions seem to be inescapable:

a. The Middle East has ceased to be the sole focus of US strategic thinking. Since the defeat of the USSR during the Cold War, the

Caspian and the Black Seas, the Caucasus and the Balkans have assumed a new geo-strategic prominence in US foreign policy. The principal aim of the US since the Cold War has not only been to be able to buy cheap oil, but also to control its production and transportation by eliminating key competitors, such as China, Germany, France and Russia, as well as Arab players, such as Iran. The US also aims at reducing its dependence on Saudi Arabia and OPEC and this constitutes an additional reason for wanting to overthrow Saddam's Iraqi regime, thus opening up Iraqi oil to Western competition. Efforts by the Pentagon (February 2002) to establish a military presence in Georgia under the pretext of bolstering Georgian security against terrorism may well be seen as part of a wider strategy aimed at the consolidation of US power for the purpose of supervising regional energy interests and pipeline projects that are running through the conflicting zone of Chechnya, Armenia, Azerbaijan and Central Asia.[51] In any event, the US has, since September 11, established a remarkable military presence in all Central Asian republics, the sole exception at the time of writing being Kazakhstan.[52]

b. Only NATO's eastward expansion and the US's power projection into Central Asia could provide the necessary security environment required for similar types of energy projects, a fact that constituted a key strategic motive for the US to launch its Kosovo campaign in March 1999.[53] In addition, and responding positively to the invitation of Islamic states to support the Muslim cause in the Balkans (see the following chapter), the US was able to counter-balance its pro-Israeli policy in the Middle East offering a politically reasonable *quid pro quo* to Islam. In retrospect, this policy seems to have confused matters even more since the terrorist attacks of September 11, as these attacks were attributed to the Al Qaeda Islamic fundamentalist network run by Osama bin Laden. In any event, the Balkans, due mainly to the collapse of the USSR and the importance of the Caspian region, have risen in the 1990s to become a key geo-political bridge between Western and Eastern Eurasia, between the West and the East.

c. The US is engaged in economic competition with Russia and the EU/Germany and, therefore, has to keep their influence in the Balkans and the greater Middle East in check and under constant 'supervision'. Time and again, this realist international relations game can only be dealt with in *realist* terms, that is in terms of *realpolitik*: US energy security and other economic interests can only be guaranteed by NATO's consolidation and expansion in Europe and the US's projection of power deeper into Eurasia. The Russian–American understanding of May 2002 should also be seen within this qualified context.

d. The engagement of Greece and Turkey – with the former already a key Balkan economic player in terms of foreign direct investment, small business networks and company acquisition – with oil and gas projects, underpins the US policy of a *rapprochement* between the two states. This facilitates US interests in that it creates conditions of co-operation between two important NATO allies but traditional foes in the region (see following chapters).[54] However, given the involvement of both Greece and Europe with Russian interests in the Balkans and the greater Middle East, an unstable equilibrium of compromises seems to have emerged in Eurasia between the US, the EU and Russia under the hegemony of the former. The Cold War is not really over.

End of the Cold War?

I have maintained that the primary geo-strategic objective of the US following the end of the Cold War has been the control of, or strategic influence over, the Eurasian landmass, which stretches from the EU states to Russia, Central Asia, China and Japan. I have also argued that the policy employed by the US for the achievement of that goal is multifaceted but comprehensive: it includes sound leadership over European political and military affairs, a leadership that was established during the Cold War; it is based on the conservative economic power projection of the IMF and the World Bank;[55] it promotes globalisation and free trade through the World Trade Organisation (WTO), whilst being careful to protect the US market from foreign competition; it encourages nationalistic movements in Eastern Europe and the Balkans in order to break up medium-to-large sized multiethnic states; it secured the revision of the ABM Treaty of 1972 in November–December 2001, after a long dispute with Russia; and it uses NATO and NATO members to project power in oil and gas producing regions, while at the same time trying to secure and control the transportation of energy to Western European markets and Northern America through the elimination of competition. Brzezinski used a different language in summarising these points:

[In brief] *America stands supreme in the four decisive domains of global power*: militarily, it has an unmatched global reach; economically, it remains the main locomotive of global growth, even if challenged in some respects by Japan and Germany (neither of which enjoys the other attributes of global might); technologically, it retains the overall lead in the cutting-edge areas of innovation; and culturally, despite some crassness, it enjoys an appeal that is unrivalled, especially among the world's youth – all of which gives the United States a political clout that no other state comes close to matching. *It is the combination of all four that makes America the only comprehensive global superpower* [emphasis by Brzezinski].[56]

This complex of strategic elements of post-Cold War US policy may constitute an organic whole, but things are never as clear-cut in practice as in theory. However comprehensive and cohesive it may be, every policy formulation is but an 'ideal-typical' construction that never appears in the same theoretical form during its practical–political implementation. Policy schemes encounter resistance, and have to face contingencies, imponderable factors and reactions from socio-political and economic forces, which, in turn, happen to have their own self-serving schemes and policies to implement. Thus, the results and the consequences of US policy actions, and of every policy action, are often other than those that were expected. In a way, the battle is always open-ended, and at times contradictions are inherent in the very theoretical and notional schemes of the policies employed.

The above is applicable to America's campaign in the Gulf (1991), or the 'humanitarian war' over Kosovo (1999). By presenting themselves as guarantors and disseminators of Western liberal values across the globe, and by thinking of themselves as the 'new Romans', with the Iraqis, Asians and many others being dubbed as the 'new barbarians', NATO and the US fell into an awkward policy pattern of legal, moral and political contradictions.[57] This policy pattern, revamped by Bush junior after September 11 with the use of the phrase 'axis of evil', considers that if 'rogue states' (e.g. North Korea, Iraq, Iran) or 'failing states' (e.g. Rwanda, Haiti) prove disobedient, anarchical or to have terrorist affiliations, then the US and/or NATO are entitled to use force (as in Serbia, Iraq), or the threat of it (as with North Korea), or to make the situation even more chaotic (as in Somalia, Ethiopia/Eritrea) in order to accomplish their aims.[58] But as we shall see in more detail below, this policy scheme cannot always work appropriately and bring about the desired results for NATO and the US. For the time being, it suffices to say that this is mainly because of two reasons:

a. Delivering 'justice by means of violence' is a notional contradiction that betrays the real incentives for action in the eyes of Western European publics. Such a concept borders on 'double standards', because it cannot be implemented on every occasion, thus failing to attribute universal value to a new set of principles in international law.
b. Other significant powers tend to obstruct/resist this projection of US power in state zones and regions in which they themselves enjoy certain economic privileges and political influence. Joseph Nye is indeed right: the US 'cannot go it alone'.[59] To all intents and purposes, it needs the co-operation of both Europe and Russia to establish its hegemony in Eurasia.

The aims of the US are other than humanitarian. The Kosovo campaign clearly showed that NATO and the US were interested in a strategic positioning in the region, rather than in total victory over the declared enemy – let alone in the protection of human rights of Kosovo Albanians. This strategic positioning would enable them to determine the success of NATO's eastward projection deeper into Western Eurasia. By bringing Serbia into line with mainstream NATO policy, and provided that Albania, Kosovo and Macedonia would stabilise under NATO's grip, something which, among other things, implies co-operation between Greece and Turkey, no disruption of oil and gas pipeline projects connecting the Balkans with the Caspian Sea could be conceivably anticipated. Eurasia is the key region in the US quest for world dominance. But the first stage to be accomplished in moving towards this goal is the consolidation of American power in South-western Eurasia's thick oval belt, that is the zone of conflict in which most of the US-led institutions and systems of alliances have operated since the Cold War years: the Balkans and the greater Middle East.

There are a number of interpretations of the way in which the US responded to the terrorist attacks of September 11 and handled the ensuing crisis.[60] There is also contemplation over whether or not the post-September 11 US has changed its post-Cold War foreign policy and security priorities.[61] Official US–UK policy argued that the ruthless bombing of Afghanistan in 2001–02 and the establishment of permanent US bases and listening posts there were both necessary in order to back efforts for the eradication of the Al-Qaeda terrorist network.[62] Similarly, both powers have argued that Saddam Hussein is an evil dictator who defies the UN, as he possesses biological, chemical and other weapons of mass destruction (WMD), and that, therefore, he has to be removed from office by all means available. There was also premature euphoria over the US–Russia arms reduction agreement of May 2002 and the establishment of a new NATO–Russia Council, events that have led commentators and politicians to declare the 'real end of the Cold War'.[63] These are superfluous arguments.

Our analyses so far suggest that the post-September 11 policy of the US has not been guided by the imperative of the extermination of Al-Qaeda which, if at all, could have been achieved by intelligence and other surveillance and economic means, without the use of brutal military force on poor and deprived populations. Nor has it been guided by the need to remove Saddam Hussein from power because he may use WMD against Israel and other US interests in the Middle East. Rather, the aim of the campaign in Afghanistan, or of any possible future campaign of the US–UK in the greater Middle East, has been/will be based on pre-existing schemes aimed at the gradual encircling of Russia and China, the control over oil and gas pipeline projects, the opening up of the Middle Eastern market to Western competition as well as the strategic surveillance of India and Pakistan, whose conflict over Kashmir has periodically assumed unpredictable turns.[64] A Eurasian network of oil and gas pipelines with China and Russia at their epicentre would thwart any US plan for establishing hegemony over this crucial region. In addition, the US would prefer a disengagement of the EU dependency on Russia's supply of gas, as there are always fears of a special geo-political understanding between Russia and France/Germany. The US–Russia arms reduction deal of May 2002 and the joint NATO–Russia Council are nothing more and nothing less than forms of engagement, whose continuing survival would depend on progress achieved on issues related to trade, oil, gas and Eurasian security matters.[65]

'A few days before September 11', Bulent Gokay observed, 'the US Energy Information Administration documented Afghanistan's strategic "geographical position as a potential transit route for oil and natural gas exports from Central Asia to the Arabian Sea".'[66]

During the campaign in Afghanistan, Pakistan and Turkmenistan discussed 'the development of a gas pipeline from Turkmenistan via Afghanistan to the port of Gwadar, now being built with Chinese assistance on the Baluchistan coast'.[67] Given NATO's unstoppable eastward expansion, a US presence in Afghanistan and Central Asia – which follows that in the Gulf, Yemen and Saudi Arabia – provides strategic depth to the management and control of the region's energy resources for the US and its closest allies. In this context, as we shall see in more detail below, Turkey constitutes an invaluable strategic pawn in the energy pipeline projects of the US global interests, projects that aim, if possible, at bypassing Russia.[68] Moreover, the US, by using air and naval bases in Turkey, Saudi Arabia and Kuwait, as well as nuclear-powered aircraft carriers, can employ an integrated projection of power in Central Asia and the Middle East that cannot possibly be matched even by all the other Western powers put together.[69]

This sort of interpretation of post-September 11 US foreign policy is evidenced by the pronounced links between the NATO's eastward enlargement drive and the US strategic projection of power towards the entire Western Eurasian zone, which is taking place with or without the direct involvement of other NATO powers. *The US aims at unifying the Balkans with the greater Middle East for planning and geo-strategic purposes, a hegemonic scheme that could not be put into full operation during the Cold War due to the USSR's strong politico-military posture in Eurasia and the resistance of Arab nationalism.*

Overall, the US geo-strategic imperatives in Europe and Asia, as they had been elaborated during the first half of the 1990s, have not changed since September 11. If anything, September 11 seems to have accelerated the pace, the unilateral rigour and the theoretical comprehensiveness of policies by which the US is pursuing its goal of the political mastery of Eurasia and its oil and gas producing regions. As Michael Cox has suggested, the 'new' American hegemony of which so many writers now speak in earnest is in fact not 'new' at all. Rather, 'it is the result of a combination of largely ignored trends which predated September 11'.[70] As we shall examine in more detail below, throughout the 1990s, the US was fully aware of the dangers of terrorism and of 'rogue' states possessing 'weapons of mass destruction'. Furthermore, although post-Cold War terrorism may have new clothes, it was present during the Cold War either in the form of 'red terrorism' (e.g. the Red Brigades in Italy) or in the form of ethnic terrorism (e.g. the Irish case). *In the light of this, I would*

*argue that the US's struggle for mastery in Eurasia and the eastward
expansion of NATO should be seen as aggressive geo-strategic extensions
of America's top Cold War priorities, those being the defence of Western
Europe from the Soviet threat and the destruction of the USSR.*

But once the destruction of the USSR had been achieved, the Cold
War schemes and institutions had to be reformed, extended and
revamped so as to incorporate the geo-political priorities and needs
arising from the new geo-strategic setting. The destruction of the
USSR did not entail the destruction of Russia and the market
economic reforms in China strengthened, rather than weakened the
Communist-led Chinese state. Moreover, the EU, under the guidance
of Germany and France has arisen as an economic global giant challenging the trade supremacy of the US. Japan, plays its part in the
global economic competition by consolidating a significant presence
in the fields of technology and finance.

Seen from this perspective, the 'end' of the Cold War is an epiphe-
nomenon, which may well, after all, misrepresent realities. The 'end'
of the Cold War did not mean the *end* of the old geo-political,
economic and strategic rivalries between the US, Japan, China,
Russia, France and Germany. 'NATO's purpose', Lord Ismay had
famously said back in 1949, 'was to keep the Americans in, the
Russians down and the Germans out.' In a way, it remains so today,
albeit in a renewed form with new meanings and novel strategic
dimensions expressed through powerful regional economic blocs,
such as those of the EU, China, Russia, North America and Japan. *It
is a matter of fact that the main antagonistic ingredients of the Cold War,
including economic and military institutions, are still around, the sole differences being that Russia is weaker, European Germany and Asian China
are stronger, and the US is the aggressive unstoppable global victor.*[71] More
to the point, in many ways, the twenty-first century situation
resembles the pre-1919 realist geo-political settings and Great Power
rivalries, at the centre of which lay the defence of a multitude of
competing national interests. But there is a crucial structural and
political difference: no parallel can be drawn between Britain's
imperial supremacy in the nineteenth century and the US might
today. The US has indisputably become a unique global superpower
that finds no match in any modern imperial precedent. And yet, as
Nye put it, 'it can not go it alone'.

The most distinguished geo-strategic game in this respect is that
between the leading EU states and the US. The US is in favour of the
EU's eastward and southward enlargements, led by Germany and

France respectively, but the process has to remain subordinate to the US's global strategic and economic interests. The best way to ensure this is by preventing the EU from achieving *political* integration – the so-called 'ever closer Union' project of the EU. US strategy is coupled with assistance of the UK, which favours EU enlargement along neo-liberal economic lines, something which was and is to the detriment of Europe's political cohesion.[72] I will attempt to exemplify this issue by looking at the Balkan crisis in the 1990s and the roles of external forces in it. In this context, an important actor has to assume pride of place: the US-led NATO.

3   Scarface Politics

The wave of optimism that engulfed NATO and the Western democratic states in the wake of the collapse of 'really existing socialism', was soon replaced by concerns about how to tackle the new cluster of awkward problems emerging out of this collapse. Issues such as the economic and political breakdown of state socialism, or the ethnic conflict that followed this breakdown were openly discussed at all levels of international organisations and Western national governments. However, security and defence matters were only reluctantly addressed before the US initiative to launch the Partnership for Peace project (PfP) in October 1993, an initiative which encompassed the main ideas upon which NATO was to consolidate its future reform. Broadly speaking, the genus of conundrums faced by US/UK strategists can be divided into three, strictly interlinked, categories:

a. *Political and ideological redefinition of the 'enemy'.* This was somehow NATO's 'existential' problem: the alliance had to specify a concrete framework including, if possible, all its potential new 'enemies' and 'friends' emerging from the bi-polar world. Either this, or NATO would have to wither away along with the defunct Warsaw Pact, its principal enemy during the Cold War. Yet NATO's dissolution was not possible for a variety of reasons, the most crucial of which being that *NATO had never seen the Warsaw Pact as its sole enemy during the Cold War*, witness that NATO was formed six years prior to the Soviet-led alliance. Germany's influence also had to be contained, while Europe as a whole, including the Near East (see Chapter 4), had to remain within the domain of US-imposed constraints. As NATO's first Secretary General, Lord Ismay, put it, without any diplomatic *savoir faire*: NATO's aim is 'to keep the Americans in, the Russians out and the Germans down'.[1]
b. *Redefinition of NATO's operational area.* This meant that NATO had to decide whether or not it would be wise to remain in the orbital distance of the Western and South-eastern Mediterranean at a moment when the world was changing rapidly and US interests

could be promoted further: 'out of area or out of business', the mantra went.

c. *Organisational restructuring of the alliance.* With NATO's reform approved in principle, a re-articulation of the organisational and institutional framework of the alliance had to follow suit. Following the 'iron law' of Max Weber's institutional sociology, NATO, like any other institution subject to changes, had to accompany its political and ideological renewal with organisational changes.[2]

Two diametrically opposed 'points of view' emerged out of the debate taking place within the ranks of the alliance. The first, spearheaded by Zbigniew Brzezinski and Henry Kissinger, argued in favour of NATO's eastward European expansion, to be pursued on a selective geo-political basis and on the grounds of a well-defined 'set of norms' (see below). This would take place in parallel with an institutional restructuring of the alliance, maximising its degree of flexibility and operational response in the wider European zone.[3] At the same time, NATO and the US would have to employ in the background a tactful diplomacy, seeking co-operation with Russia.

The second view – wrongly called 'isolationist' by the expansionists because it presumably deprived the US of its global role and leadership – recognised the danger of Russia's alienation and warned that NATO's expansion would overstretch the alliance, thus undermining its political and organisational cohesion. The unwanted result, Edward Luttwak and Michael Mandelbaum argued, would be operational ineffectiveness, public exposure of disagreements among the allies and, hence, the danger of fragmentation. In this context, the argument goes, the mantra 'out of area or out of business' makes no sense because 'a wise alliance must know when to retrench' so as not to provoke Russia.[4]

Unavoidably, the aforementioned divide had been dovetailed with the policies pursued by the European powers which, in the run up to the Maastricht (1992) and Amsterdam (1997) treaties, were aspiring either to construct a distinctive defence and security identity for Europe (e.g. France), or to obstruct such a process (e.g. Britain). In the end, however, both Europeans and non-Europeans accepted the constraints imposed by historical reality and by the US's superior political and military drive, lining up along the great transatlantic schism. The basis of the agreement was President Bill Clinton's doctrine that the EU was welcome to have a 'separable but not separate' defence identity from NATO.

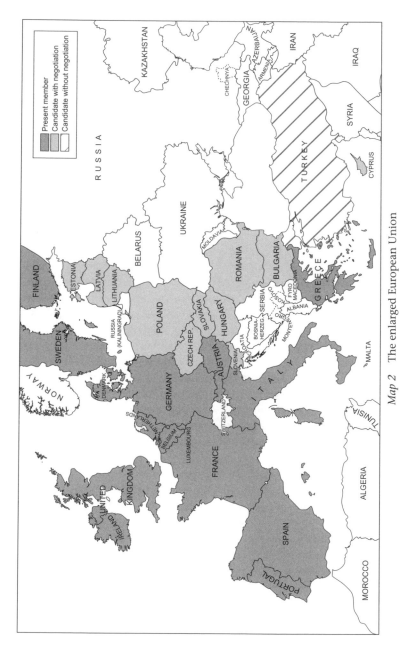

Present member
Candidate with negotiation
Candidate without negotiation

Map 2 The enlarged European Union

From the mid-1990s onwards, a vast literature on the reform process of NATO began to appear.[5] Yet no account seems to address the wider implications of NATO's transformation from a *defence pact* into a *political organisation*, a transformation that has been taking place at least since 1993. This highly politicised nature of NATO's transformation has enabled both the alliance and the US to engage themselves with broader political affairs in Eurasia, including issues such as maintaining collaborative organisational structures with Russia. At the same time the US has been able to pursue its hegemonic and aggressive policy against disobedient actors in the Balkans and the greater Middle East.

My analysis here underpins the range of arguments developed in the previous chapter. In the main, its focus is NATO's political trans-formation in the context of the US strategy in Europe and the Balkans in the post-Cold War period. In this respect, it opens up the geo-political framework of the Balkans and it attempts to show that the actual effects of the US strategy for the security of Europe, the Balkans and the Middle East are not very positive. The overall outcome of the US strategy may even be considered counterproduc-tive, reducing the role of NATO from a defence pact *producing* security during the Cold War into a political organisation *consuming* security in Europe, the Balkans and the Near East in the post-Cold War period.

Having said this, at the core of US difficulties may be neither Russia's engagement through partnership schemes with NATO, nor NATO's further expansion as such. Rather, NATO's and the US's main problem may well be their decision to engage NATO into a process of becoming a *political* organisation trying to observe a certain set of liberal ideological principles by means of violence. To illustrate my thesis and demonstrate NATO's inner and notional contradictions, I will be using the case of its intervention in Kosovo and the positioning of Greece and Turkey in the post-Cold War Balkan theatre. I will also be drawing parallels between NATO's strategy of expansion ('the expansion of a defence pact') and the European Union's eastward enlargement ('the enlargement of an economic and, potentially, political international organisation').

NATO's 'New Strategic Concept'

As outlined earlier, NATO decided to expand eastwards, a reform which, *inter alia*, entailed a restructuring of the ideological, military and administrative axes of the alliance. NATO's 'new strategic concept', put forward in November 1991, was the product of an unstable equilibrium of compromises between 'isolationists' and 'expansionists'. It emphasised 'out-of-area' missions and crisis management operations in order to protect the alliance's interests mainly in the wider Eurasian zone.[6] Moreover, and in order, partly, to appease the 'isolationists', a co-operative framework to engage Russia was envisaged. In the main, however, the 'new strategic concept' entailed an extra-territorial/European/Near Eastern revisionist reading of Article 5, which stipulates that an attack on one alliance member will be considered as an attack on all. Moreover, the alliance attempted to balance the European interests and to envisage ways in which Russia could be engaged in a 'peace partnership' led by the US. This was not a problem-free design, as the framework upon which it was based rested on highly controversial hypotheses.

Strategists in Washington and London deemed that the post-Cold War system of global actors was composed of four main groups. The first group consisted of *core partners*, that is successful and economically advanced Western European democracies that can join the US in security and defence issues. The second group was the so-called *transition states*, such as former Communist countries on whose behaviour depends the extent to which the core will grow. The third category consisted of the so-called *rogue states*. These states reject the ideals of the core, sponsor terrorist activities and are eager to acquire WMD in order to damage the interests of the US and the core (e.g. Iran, Iraq, Syria, Libya, North Korea). The fourth group was the so-called *failing states*, which are ravaged by social upheavals and wars. These states or regions impose huge humanitarian demands on the US and the core.[7]

In a way, therefore, the 'enemies' had been defined: they were the 'failing states' and the 'rogue states'. Nevertheless, the battle to win over the so-called 'transition states', which included Russia, was open. Yet NATO had to qualify further its constitutional principles on the basis of which 'transition states' could join the alliance in the post-Cold War environment. For that purpose, NATO, emulating the European Union, drafted its own *acquis communautaire*, that is to say the set of 'rules' or 'norms' which every new recruit would have to conform with and obey.

NATO's *acquis* is composed of three 'classes of norms' or 'baskets' which, it is believed, mirror the post-Cold War security environment.[8] The first basket includes norms that bolster international peace, such as the right to collective self-defence, arms control, antiterrorism covenants, respect for the authority of the UN Security Council and non-aggression. The second set is composed of rules that govern the functioning and the well-being of the global economy: those relating to freedom of trade, law of the sea, international co-operation, environmental protection. The third and final basket refers to those rules that bear on the treatment of people by sovereign states: those relating to human rights, political democracy, individual liberties and other tenets of civil societies and states.

'Transition states' that endorse this set of principles are welcome to join the alliance on the sole proviso that they must be *European* states, broadly defined. For example, when the debate over NATO's reform process was about to conclude its first phase at the Madrid NATO summit in 1997, former Secretary of State Madeleine Albright said that 'no European democracy will be excluded from the enlargement process because of where it sits on the map'.[9] However carefully worded, it is clear that this was a statement of *exclusion*, rather than *inclusion*.

Problems of 'Variable Geometry'

The phrase 'no *European* democracy' indicates that post-Cold War NATO still sees itself defined, both operationally and constitutionally, against Europe's wider geo-political security zone. Yet, its enlargement proceeded selectively with strong geographical/geopolitical considerations. Hungary, Poland and the Czech Republic were up for approval in 1997, but not the Baltic states, Slovenia, Romania or Bulgaria, which were to be included at a later stage. Russia, understandably enough, reacted because the move undermined its own geo-political zone of peripheral influence, including states such as Ukraine, the Baltic states and even Belarus.[10] In this qualified context, NATO's chosen way of enlargement in the 1990s was bound to entrench military/territorial frontiers, thus encouraging the consolidation of new 'enemy blocs' with Russia at their epicentre.

The pro-expansionist/revisionist bloc had probably thought that this way of enlargement would solve the alliance's 'existential' problem. Given that NATO's principal enemy, the Warsaw Pact, had ceased to exist since 1991, NATO had to spot a new 'enemy' in the post-Cold War period in order to justify its existence. However, this line of thought is misleading because, as we saw earlier, NATO, quite rightly, has never seen itself solely in terms of containing Communism's advance in Europe. Had this been the case, it would have reacted differently to Moscow's interventions in Hungary (1956) or Czechoslovakia (1968). If Lord Ismay's phrase is to be taken at face value, then NATO's worries are still 'how to keep the Germans down' and, therefore, how to hinder the creation of a geo-strategic and geo-economic axis stretching from France to Russia or, as General De Gaulle once put it, 'from the Atlantic to the Urals'. From this perspective, a legitimate assumption is that a US–German partnership under the NATO umbrella would increase US leverage over the EU and Eurasian affairs. This would create conditions for a more substantial engagement of both Germany and Russia under US guidance. Moreover, NATO had and has established interests in the greater Near East, with Greece, Turkey and Israel at the centre of its policy. NATO has always aimed at consolidating a working framework of peace and co-operation among the European and Near Eastern states, thus containing any form of radical difference among them: quite rightly, the US, among other things, did not want to see 'an inter-war period in Europe again'.[11] But there is more to the affair than meets the eye.

The phrase 'no European *democracy*' implies that NATO welcomes new members, and it is willing to defend them, as long as they are democracies endorsing the principles included in the three 'baskets'.[12] But Cold War NATO was *primarily* a defence pact and not a political organisation. As such, it never needed conditions of political democracy to operate effectively and advance its goals. Indeed, throughout the post-Second World War period, NATO's policy has been served and observed by non liberal-democratic regimes. Portugal was a member of NATO during Salazar's and Caetano's dictatorships, and Turkey's participation in the alliance has survived three military coups.[13] Similarly, today, NATO interests can be served and upheld by any state system or socio-political agent, regardless of their *political form*. The sole precondition is that they must be *friendly* and *co-operative* agents.

Some argue that the trouble with this criticism is that, unlike during the Cold War years, it is hard for NATO and the US today to justify their policies by supporting authoritarian political systems that pay no respect to human and civil rights.[14] Again, this is both historically and politically wrong. As Britain's Foreign Secretary Ernest Bevin argued in January 1948, and as NATO's own Treaty stipulates, one of the alliance's chief aims was to have been the 'organisation and consolidation of the ethical and spiritual forces of Western civilisation'.[15] We know that this exclusivist, if not racist, statement also failed to deliver its promise during and after the Cold War. For example, it can hardly be argued that Turkey upholds the liberal-democratic values of the Enlightenment, and it is equally difficult to justify Turkey's illegal invasion and continuing occupation of one third of Cyprus since summer 1974. Admittedly, therefore, some important ideological and political elements of NATO's 'new strategic concept' are to be found in its founding principles. But how did the NATO enlargement in the 1990s proceed?

In the event, NATO opted to expand on the basis of a peculiar version of the European Union's 'variable geometry' strategy for enlargement.[16] Seen from this angle, NATO's eastward projection was more than a geo-political jigsaw. Given that the Union has never been a cohesive bloc, none of its members could adhere to the *acquis communautaire*, which is the EU's own traditional set of legal 'norms and procedures' for the acceptance of new members.[17] In practice, economic, monetary and other inequalities and disagreements, particularly over social, defence and foreign policy matters, allowed the European Union to pursue its enlargement policies on the basis of a notion of 'variable geometry'. This canon formalises exceptions to the *acquis* principle and perpetuates, if not accentuates, the internal divisions among the member states. For example, during the Maastricht Treaty negotiations in November–December 1991, Britain was given an opt-out clause on the matters of EMU, social policy and common defence and security policy.[18] Hence the talk about a 'multi-speed', 'two-speed' or a Union with 'concentric circles'.

The 'variable geometry' approach was bolstered further in September 1994, when the German parliamentary group of the ruling CDU/CSU, prepared and circulated a paper suggesting that the core countries of the Union could move ahead with the process of integration while new applicant countries could join at their own pace and at a later stage.[19] In practice, this meant that a core of European states would go ahead with the consolidation of the monetary, economic and political union, while the others would be added on as the core of the European snowball rolled over. This outraged Britain, which could see the enlargement process only as an apolitical economic design to be pursued on the basis of neo-liberal economics without any politico-institutional cohesion.[20]

The Europeans, therefore, seemed to be struggling hard with their practice of *acquis*. However, NATO's own *acquis* principle for enlargement was destined to encounter far greater difficulties. In the main, these difficulties were threefold. First, exporting the Enlightenment values of social justice, political democracy and free market economy is not necessarily, and by definition, a bad thing. But pretending that they can become a global constitutional rule upheld by a *military* alliance on *every* occasion and imposed, if necessary, by means of violence, is quite different. As we shall see below, the transformation of NATO from a *defence* pact into a *political* organisation guided mainly by the ideological principles of the three 'baskets', is hardly convincing. It has had a very interesting trajectory though. It was discussed during the Gulf and Bosnian crises (1990–94); it saw its completion at the Madrid summit in 1997; it reached its utmost diplomatic limit in February 1999, when NATO asked the Serb delegation at Rambouillet to sign the famous 'Appendix B' (there, NATO officials demanded that Serbia not only surrender its sovereignty to the second and third classes of norms, but also let NATO have a free run not only of Kosovo, but of all of Serbia);[21] finally, NATO members turned against NATO's own policy when, after September 11, in a face-saving declaration, they pledged solidarity with the US in its war on terrorism, but nothing more than that.

Second, imposition of free market principles (the second 'basket') upon 'transition states' may produce some results other than those intended. For example, as Susan Woodward's path-breaking account on the Balkan crisis has shown, the break-up of Yugoslavia was not primarily the result of the eruption of endogenous ethnic violence caused by a mere collapse of the Communist polity and ideology. Nor should it be attributed to the lack of a charismatic leadership after the death of Tito (1980). Rather, it was the unintended consequence of the IMF's intervention, which imposed fiscal discipline and institutional centralisation: a necessary reform package that was nevertheless fiercely opposed by key constituent Republics of Yugoslavia, such as Slovenia and Croatia, a chorus that was joined by the Kosovo Albanians.[22] This IMF imposition implied an end to Yugoslavia's nearly co-federal structure and entailed that the richest of the Republics, that is Slovenia and Croatia, would have had to foot the bill for the neo-liberal led reforms. As the regional economic disparities in Yugoslavia had persisted throughout the Cold War, it was precisely this that deepened the ethnic divisions and encouraged separatist nationalist agendas to flourish.[23] The Yugoslav state was a classic case of a structured inequality among regions, in which ethnic tensions were exacerbated via a neo-liberal modernising package of economic reforms imposed from outside. Susan Woodward aptly summarised the break-up of the country as follows:

The [Yugoslav] conflict is not the result of historical animosities and it is not a return to the pre-communist past; it is the result of the politics of transforming a socialist society to a market economy and democracy. A critical element of this failure was economic decline, caused largely by a program intended to resolve a foreign debt crisis ... Normal political conflicts over economic resources between central and regional governments and over the economic and political reforms of the debt-repayment package became constitutional conflicts and then a crisis of the state itself among politicians who were unwilling to compromise ... Nationalism became a political force when leaders in the republics sought popular support as bargaining chips in federal disputes.[24]

The West, therefore, had misjudged the effects of the IMF intervention upon Yugoslavia. Equally, as I will try to explain below, NATO's claim to apply its own *acquis* (the second and third set of norms) in the cases of Serbia and Kosovo was yet another miscalculation, creating serious problems for both the alliance and the region as a whole.

Third, NATO's 'variable geometry' notion came to be seriously undermined by NATO's own actions. Guided by its geo-political map of 'friends' and 'enemies', and in order to forcefully impose the *acquis*, NATO tended to create emergency situations, accentuating existing social and ethnic tensions in Eastern Europe. The result was the establishment of non-economically viable statelets, of militarised ethnic ghettos and, hence, new kinds of prison populations, fragmenting the map of Eastern Europe and the Balkans. It could not have happened otherwise, as NATO is not primarily an economic or political institution. It used to be, and is still mainly, a military defence organisation with a rigid command structure and, therefore, discipline among its members matters a lot more than among European states on monetary or fiscal issues. From this perspective, NATO's principal fault is not that it went and goes to war. Rather, its main mistake was its decision to transform itself into a politico-military power upholding and implementing liberal ideological goals selectively and at will. It had no alternative *because its geo-political notions of expansion, and operational reach, driven by energy and other economic interests, could not make practicality and morality coincide.* Hence a legitimate accusation was levelled against the policy actions of NATO and the US, particularly after the Kosovo war (March–June 1999): that they bordered on 'double standards' politics. I will discuss here only the case of Kosovo, in order to explore further NATO's constitutional contradictions and its resulting failure to advance a coherent reform package for itself in the post-Cold War era.

Political, Moral and Legal Conundrums: The Kosovo War

Kosovo Albanian nationalists were troublemakers throughout the history of Communist Yugoslavia. Along with the Slovenes and Croats, the Kosovo Albanian authorities undermined efforts by the federal Yugoslav government in the 1980s to impose economic discipline and central authority over the regions, in order to implement the economic reforms required by the IMF and the World Bank. In addition, 'between 1966 and 1989 an estimated 130,000 Serbs left the province because of frequent harassment and discrimination by the Kosovar Albanian majority'.[25] As a result of protests on the part of Kosovo Serbs, and because of the centralisation of power at the federal level demanded by the IMF, Kosovo lost its status as an autonomous province and became part of Serbia in 1989. The Kosovo Serbs, in turn, encouraged by the nationalistic government of Slobodan Milosevic, saw this as an historic opportunity to retaliate. This reads, of course, as a vicious historical cycle, with one side taking revenge over the other at every opportunity. Having said this, however, NATO could not base its attack on Serbia solely on the grounds of Serb nationalistic aggressiveness. Furthermore, the 1995 agreement at Dayton between the rump of Yugoslavia and the West, stipulated that no Western power would interfere over the Kosovo issue. In a sense, this was 'correct' because according to international law no state has the 'outright right' to intervene in the internal affairs of another state and borders are sacrosanct. Yet it was the way in which the attack itself occurred that unleashed a whole series of ideological and political contradictions that had been running through the alliance since its foundation in 1949.

First of all – and this applies to the cases of Bosnia, Slovenia and Croatia as well – by which criteria did NATO and the West sponsor one particular nationalism against another? The theory of norms and NATO's post-Cold War map of 'friends and enemies' may suggest that Serbia was a 'rogue' state, Kosovo was a failed region and that nationalism is an evil force that hinders globalisation. But both the normative theory and NATO's own constitution make no reference as to what makes one particular nationalism more sympathetic to the alliance than another. True, there were confused views about Slobodan Milosevic, but the West basically supported him because he 'appeared to be an economic liberal (with excellent English), who might have greater authority to implement the reform'[26] required by the IMF, a reform which, as we saw earlier, demanded a strong conservative political hand to impose fiscal discipline and constitutional centralisation. Milosevic's ruling group appeared to have that strong conservative hand. As late as March 1998, he was for the West 'the right man to do business with'.[27] Moreover, on February 23, 1998, US Special Envoy to the Balkans Robert Gelbard went so far as to say that the KLA was a 'terrorist group'. In the words of Chris Hedges:

> [Robert Gelbard] gave what many had interpreted as a green light to Belgrade to go after the rebel bands by announcing in Pristina that the KLA 'is without any question a terrorist group'. He went on to add that the United States 'condemns very strongly terrorist activities in Kosovo'. Within two weeks Serb forces had turned Prekaz into a smouldering ruin, killed close to a hundred people, and ignited the uprising.[28]

There is scarcely any evidence that Milosevic's strategy was aimed at ethnically cleansing the entire Kosovo region.[29] It seems that the aim of the Serb campaign in Kosovo was 'depopulation' rather than 'extermination'. As Christopher Layne and Benjamin Schwarz argued, 'students of "low intensity conflict" will recognise the similarities between the counter-insurgency tactics of the Serbs in Kosovo and those of the French in Algeria, the British in the Boer war and the Americans in the Philippines'.[30] Thus, the only clear-cut evidence we possess is that put forward by NATO generals and defence analysts, when they warned President Clinton that an air attack on Serbia from high altitudes would be an invitation to Serb paramilitaries to start carrying out the emergency 'depopulation' plans that they had drawn-up specifically for the region.[31] Was the Serb leadership aiming at 'depopulation' in the hope that most Albanians, once out of Kosovo, would not return? We do not really know. But it is also interesting to note that NATO's bombing from high altitudes placed all the risk on civilians, while making both military actors relatively immune from risks. This very fact may well be considered as a breach of the Geneva Conventions.

As discussed earlier, NATO presented itself as a political rather than military actor trying to deliver a humanitarian agenda (the third 'basket'). In order to achieve the implementation of that agenda, NATO went so far as to ask the Serbian delegation at Rambouillet to comply with three conditions: of these, at least one of them, indeed the most crucial one, could not have been accepted by any political leadership of any modern state. The first was that within three years the Kosovars should have the chance of voting for independence and possible annexation of Albania. The second was that Serbia should accept free market economic principles. And the third – the one that no modern state could ever accept – was that NATO forces should be given permission to deploy not only in Kosovo but *anywhere* in Serbia. NATO's solution was presented as the *only* solution to the Kosovo crisis and the Serb delegation faced an ultimatum: they either had to agree with what was on the table, or their state would be bombed.[32]

Coercive diplomacy is an established practice between state officials, diplomats and political delegations dealing with economic and foreign affairs.[33] But NATO's determination reads as the worst kind of coercive diplomacy and could not have been otherwise because the negotiating body was a military alliance whose prestige, internal discipline and cohesion was dependent on the determination and ability to carry out its agenda, if need be, by violent means. Such was the situation when NATO launched its campaign against Serbia, violating its own constitutional principle as a defence pact and all existing international rules.

For the first time in post-war history – although it may be appropriate to draw a parallel with Brezhnev's invasion of Czechoslovakia over three decades ago – NATO attacked a sovereign country without the approval of the Security Council of the United Nations. Rightly or wrongly, the Charter of the United Nations drafted after the Second World War deemed that *inter-state* conflict was the major issue to be tamed in international politics, thus failing to effectively address the problem of *intra-state* violence. In this context, NATO's campaign against Serbia was *illegal* for two fundamental reasons: first, because there is no general doctrine for using military violence in cases of humanitarian need in international law;[34] second, because its campaign was not approved by the supreme organisation that regulates international relations and authorises action. This created a unique precedent both for the study of international relations and the practical conduct of foreign affairs.[35]

Were the principle of 'violent humanitarian intervention' to assume institutional status, how could humanitarian necessity conform with the practical operational conduct of military intervention across Europe and the globe? Were *morality* to become a legal component in the conduct of foreign policy, then it would have to coincide with the *operational practicality* of such conduct. Selective application of the principle can hardly convince Western public opinion because it borders on double standards and creates suspicions about Great Power neo-imperialistic designs: absurd though it seems, why not bomb Ankara for the suppression of the Kurds, or Moscow for attacking the Chechens? Yet, Western public opinion can easily understand something which the media pass over in silence, namely, that an abstract focus on human rights and nationalism obscures the primary political cause of ethnic cleansing, that is, as Diana Johnstone put it: 'the fear on the part of the sovereign authority that the presence of members of a politically organised ethnic group will be used to support *territorial* claims'.[36]

This is, of course, far from a justification of ethnic violence and atrocities that themselves constitute a breach of the Geneva Conventions. *Ethnic cleansing is in no way a legitimate tool of statecraft.*[37] However, Johnstone's clear-cut assertion is a sharp reminder, indicating the primacy of *political* over *ethical* goals in the conduct of domestic and foreign policies of modern states. In point of fact, there is no moral substance in any foreign policy discourse advocating 'protection of human rights', let alone in the case of NATO's campaign in Kosovo. For example, as we saw earlier, NATO and the US had some very specific geo-political and security interests to defend in the Balkans and the Black Sea region, as well as in Central Asia, where the 'anti-terror judgement' was used to bomb the Taliban regime in Afghanistan. In the main, these geo-political interests had to do with the safety of oil and gas pipeline projects, as well as with the eastward expansion of NATO per se, which could not occur while having a pro-Russian hostile Serbia in its underbelly.

The issue of the 'double standards' is not really a matter that can be solved. No conditions can ever be envisaged in which the US or any other hegemonic power would brush their national and geo-political interests aside for the sake of international law, justice and 'one standard' humanitarian principles. Yet there is something that can be done. Both the US and the international community may deem it appropriate to decide which definition should be adopted and enshrined in international law with regard to, for example, the concept of 'self-determination'.

The political and intellectual history of the twentieth century has provided us with several definitions of the concept: of these, however, only two have had considerable political impact, mainly because the persons who first formulated them were leading politicians of two big countries. The first stems from the Liberal Wilsonian tradition which followed the First World War. It argues that in a pluralist-democratic system the majority rules democratically and the minority controls, also democratically. In the Yugoslav context, this would mean that the ethnic components of Yugoslavia would have had ambiguous political and legal grounds for self-determination and independent statehood, because they would have entailed the break-up of a country with concrete ethnic majority elements, such as the Serbs and the Croats.

The second definition can be drawn from the work of Vladimir I. Lenin. The leader of the Russian Revolution had advanced a notion of 'self-determination' according to which not only the ethnic majority has the right to declare self-rule and independence in a given territorial area, but also the ethnic minority.[38] This entails, for example, that if the Slovenes wanted to go for an independent state, then they had the right to do so. And that if the Turkish-Cypriots wanted to split the Republic of Cyprus where the ethnic majority element is Greek (80 per cent), they had the right to do so. The same is valid for the Hungarian minority in Romania, or the Turkish minority in Bulgaria and so on.

The trouble with the US, NATO and other powers is that they do not stick, either in theory or in practice, to one principle or the other, thus paying lip service to the international community and law. But if one of the two principles were to be adopted, then the international community would, at least, be able to pronounce upon great power actions in a more consistent manner. As things stand at present, the US and other powerful actors, such as Russia and China, simply use both notions of self-rule at their convenience, that is to say, according to their geo-economic and geo-political interests.

The above are not 'normal' contradictions of an institution destined to go to war, or of a policy designed to conduct war. They are the unique contradictions of an institution and of a policy, which were structured to go to war in order to fight on the basis of *abstract* liberal-democratic principles. NATO did not win the war with Serbia because, as a first-year student in any military academy would know, a war is only won when the enemy is *smashed* and *disarmed*. One may argue that NATO also failed to win the war because it failed to accomplish its political goals set out at Rambouillet. Also, since

Kosovo is still constitutionally part of the rump of the Yugoslav Co-Federal Republic (Serbia and Montenegro), the West should have felt very uncomfortable when in the late 1990s it encouraged Montenegro to go for independence, thus artificially creating a constitutional situation in which, as Yugoslavia would no longer exist, Kosovo's *de facto* independence could be legitimised. Moreover, the uprising of Macedonian Albanians in Tetovo in the wake of the Kosovo campaign, which nearly destabilised the strategically important multi-ethnic Republic of Macedonia, can be seen as a direct spillover effect of NATO's pro-KLA intervention in Kosovo.[39]

Having said this, I would argue that the option for NATO to expand, restructure and transform itself along the lines of a political organisation upholding and imposing the ideology of Liberal Democracy was bound to create more problems for the alliance than those which such transformation was supposed to solve. The bombing of Serbia seems to have driven the alliance into a fight with itself. The continuing claim of Albanian nationalism for a 'Greater Albania', as well as the precarious situation in Bosnia and Croatia indicate failure rather than success for NATO in its effort to stabilise the Balkans and produce security in the region after the Cold War. In this context, had the US admitted openly that the whole campaign was aimed at establishing strategic control over the Balkans by encircling 'rogue enemies' and ambivalent 'transition states' in order to engage them in a subordinate relationship, it would have made the first brave step towards dissolving its own substantive policy contradictions. But what NATO cannot openly admit, Daniel Benjamin, former member of the US National Security Council (NSC), leaves us in no doubt. In criticising George Bush's pre-election theses concerning US engagement in the Balkans, he wrote:

> Mr. Bush showed a misunderstanding of a major strategic achievement of the Clinton administration ... In particular, [Mr. Bush] missed the intrinsic connections between enlargement and the conflict in the Balkans ... NATO enlargement advanced US interests in dealing with one of the country's foremost strategic challenges: coping with a post-Communist Russia whose trajectory remains in question.[40]

Yet, this affirmation which comes directly from an NSC insider represents just half the truth. As we saw earlier, NATO's eastward expansion and its attempt to engage Russia in a lasting partnership are processes bound up with concrete geo-political and geo-economic interests at the heart of which lie control over, and the safe transportation of, crude oil and gas to Western markets. The Balkan region with its Black Sea ports and strategically placed states is a key connecting route, whose security cannot be trusted to 'rogue' regimes (e.g. Milosevic's Serbia) or to 'post-Communist Russia whose trajectory remains in question'.

US Successes

This is far from a detailed presentation of the US strategy in Europe and the Balkans in the 1990s, or of NATO's reform process per se.[41] However, it provides the general framework, which enables us to consider the broader implications of US strategy in the wider European and Balkan theatres. I have argued that the logical outcome of NATO's geo-political type of enlargement in the 1990s was the bracketing of Eastern Europe and the Balkans, thus *de facto* redefining as an enemy the old enemy: Russia and its potential client states in the geo-strategic zone stretching from the Baltic states and the Balkans, to the Caucasus, the Caspian Sea, Central Asia and the Middle East. At the same time, the US had been employing the 'carrot tactics' in the background: it launched the PfP project in 1993 and offered Russia a political structure of co-operation through the NATO–Russia Joint Permanent Council. This dual project was detrimental to the pan-European design envisaged at Maastricht (1992) and at Amsterdam (1997), which included a rough timetable for the institutional consolidation of Europe's incoherent polity, on the grounds of a common social, foreign, defence, security and monetary policy.

The preservation of the French–German axis with the formation of Euro-corps and the integration of the West European Union (the 'defence pillar') into the EU, was pointing to a regeneration of Willy Brandt's *Ostpolitik* and Gorbachev's idea of Europe as the 'Common House' of its people. The French–German idea, encompassed two interrelated strategic dimensions. The first was a reform package for the economic reconstruction of Eastern Europe and the Balkans which, similarly to the post-war Marshall Plan, was to be administered by endogenous forces on the basis of a neo-Keynesian type of economic recovery, stabilisation and growth. The second was the gradual integration of the former Communist countries into the European Union and the institutionalisation of a powerful geo-strategic continental axis aiming at a common foreign and defence policy.[42]

Understandably enough, this was viewed by Washington and London as a project which was directly competing with both NATO and US influence in Europe and Asia. It was in complete contrast with the Pentagon's doctrine that the EU could have a 'separable but not separate' defence identity and a direct challenge to US interests over oil and gas producing regions. In addition, if ever realised, the French–German project would have exacerbated existing tensions in NATO's Southern flank, since the emergence of the EU as an independent political actor, particularly on the security and defence stage, would have upgraded the role of Greece in the Eastern Mediterranean and the Balkans at the expense of Turkey.[43]

To thwart the continental European plan, the US employed similar strategic means: an alternative economic design for the reconstruction of Eastern Europe based on the aggressive 'shock therapy' theory spearheaded by the work of Harvard University Professor Jeffrey Sachs in 1990–91; and a further consolidation and expansion of NATO in Western, Central and Southern Europe, without ever losing sight of the benefits that a substantial NATO–Russia partnership could bring for the US.[44] Having already dealt with NATO's reform process, I will examine briefly the economic alternative offered by the transatlantic power.

To start with, the joint French–German proposal included intensification of efforts to increase productive capacity via the creation of a Regional Development Bank to buttress a gradual process of transition to capitalism without major aftershocks. Funds and political reforms would be handled by each country's administration. But this, as we have seen, was considered by Presidents Reagan and Bush senior as a dangerous plan, for it adumbrated a new Pan-European Confederation embracing Europe and Russia, thus establishing a powerful geo-strategic axis uncontrolled by the US.[45]

Instead, the alternative 'shock therapy' model advanced the notion of the separation of Russia from the other East European countries, thus encouraging secessionism and nationalistic agendas; it privileged the countries that were more sympathetic to neo-liberal reforms and opted for an overall and immediate dismantling of the Communist administrative apparatus; it imposed a trade-led and a finance capital-led growth, coupled with *ad hoc* liberalisation of banking and industrial sectors. Perhaps most importantly of all, the 'shock therapy' alternative would have to be administered by *exogenous* forces, such as IMF and World Bank economic assessors, Western policy experts and think tanks.

In this context, it is not difficult to understand why the Bush senior administration failed to keep its promise to Gorbachev when the latter asked for a halt in NATO's expansion in Europe in return for allowing Germany's reunification. The stakes for NATO and the US were too high for them to stick to their promises. Gorbachev's mistake, in turn, was his failure to fully grasp that the Warsaw Pact was not NATO's sole enemy. During and after the Cold War NATO had no intention whatsoever of loosening its grip over Western Europe and the Near East (Greece and Turkey), two strategic zones composed of 'core partners'.

The US strategy was assisted by some other crucial factors.[46] I will list the most important of them:

a. The high degree of institutionalisation of the military dependency of the EU on the US, a dependency achieved during the Cold War.
b. Europe's failure during the Yugoslav crisis (1990–95).
c. The British opposition to a French–German–Russian geo-strategic axis.
d. The ascendancy of Boris Yeltsin in the Russian presidency, who was blatantly backed by the US and Western financial interests.
e. Germany and other European powers, including Britain, opposed the independence of Bosnia, since there was no majority nation there to substantiate the construction of a new state alongside the principle of 'national self-determination', however understood. But the US outflanked both Germany and the EU by entering the Yugoslav theatre demanding an independent Bosnia. The powerful American drive backed by NATO's overwhelming military superiority, as well as the Uruguay Round Agreement (1994) which established the regulatory framework of the WTO replacing GATT, led Germany to embrace the US perspective, brush aside its axis with France and offer, albeit temporarily, its support to the US during the Bosnian and Kosovo wars.[47] France and Britain, fearing isolation, increased their support for the alliance's new hegemonic drive and followed suit. Greece, with its eye on Turkey, insisted on strengthening the European common defence and security policy, but its influence has been confined to the issues it raised regarding stability and economic reconstruction in the post-Cold War Balkans.

The US has always been careful not to employ a one-dimensional, head-on confrontational strategy against Russia. Even during the Cold War, there were periods of *détente* and understanding between the US and the USSR. 'Holding the Russians out' by means of coercion has only been seen by the US as one policy option, which could be employed in parallel with others, witness the PfP project, which left the door open for the agreement between Russia and the US/NATO reached in May 2002. Back in 1996–7, Brzezinski himself explained prophetically:

> The stability of Eurasia's geo-political pluralism, precluding the appearance of a single dominant power, would be enhanced by the eventual emergence, perhaps sometime early in the next century, of a Trans-Eurasian Security System (TESS). Such a transcontinental security agreement should embrace an expanded NATO – connected by a co-operative charter with Russia – and China as well as Japan (which would still be connected to the United States by the bilateral security treaty). *But to get there, NATO must first expand, while engaging Russia in a larger regional framework of security co-operation* [my emphasis].[48]

Nor we can take the notion of 'keeping the Germans down' at quasi-face value. The US has developed an extremely important partnership with Germany at all levels: political, economic and regional. But it is a partnership that the US wants to keep in check and under constant surveillance.

The overall policy of the US in Eurasia since the Cold War has been aimed towards the re-establishment of a new Cold War duopoly image with Russia, under US hegemony.[49] This can discipline China, Japan and Germany to go along with the imperatives of American hegemony. The picture can be read as follows: there are economically strong Eurasian powers in the middle (Germany/France/Europe) and the fringes (Japan), which should remain so, because it is somewhat economically useful. Europe has been contributing to the reconstruction of the Balkans and has been providing economic aid to transition economies through its various programmes and initiatives. Japan is a leading global economic power, with large regional stakes in the 'tiger economies' of Southeast Asia. But in order to keep the balance of power in favour of the US, continental Europe has to be given the impression that it might be 'squeezed out' by the two geo-politically strong powers, that is the US and Russia. The US–Russia partnership is a relationship that can regulate itself in favour of the US through the established practice of NATO expansion in Europe and the presence of the US power in the greater Middle East. This may well foster scepticism among the newcomers, particularly among the Baltic states or Romania and Bulgaria, who want to disengage themselves from Russia's influence, but NATO expansion will certainly benefit the US in its relationship with China, Germany and Japan.

All in all, and given the debatable achievements of NATO, its contradictions and the present fragile situation in Bosnia, Kosovo, Macedonia and even Cyprus, one conclusion seems to be inescapable: American strategy in Europe has succeeded more in 'keeping the Germans down' than in 'holding the Russians and the Slavs out'. This may well bring about a political situation in which NATO and the US, particularly after September 11, will no longer be considered by the European powers as producers of security, but rather as consumers of it. I will attempt to further highlight this latter speculative point by looking closely at the roles of Greece and Turkey and the issues of Islam and Christianity in the post-Cold War Balkans.

Muslims, Christians and Foreign Policy

A neglected dimension of the Balkan and East European crises is the so-called 'Muslim question'. It should not be forgotten that Southeastern Europe, carrying the legacy of the Ottoman rule, is home to widely dispersed Muslim identities, which are forced to observe the authority of states prejudiced against Islam, such as Greece, with a 120,000-strong Muslim community, or Bulgaria, with a Muslim population of nearly 600,000.[50] Large Albanian minorities in the Republic of Macedonia are Muslims, not to mention those in Bosnia or even Chechnya and the Caspian Sea region. Moreover, given Turkey's achievement in assuming candidate status in its effort to join the EU in December 1999, two issues seem to be of relevance to the present discussion. First, the role of Turkey and Greece in the Balkans; second, why Europe, NATO and the US decided to partly reverse the alignments of the First and Second World Wars by sponsoring, to a significant degree, Muslim states or proto-states. Yet this took place before the tragic events of September 11, 2002. No one knows whether the US would have pursued exactly the same policy in the Balkans had the Yugoslav crises erupted after that date, or if the attacks on America had occurred before or amidst the Yugoslav wars.

Greece was increasingly sceptical of recognising the disorderly break-up of Yugoslavia for two main reasons: first, because 'important Greek trade routes pass through Yugoslavia, and Yugoslav stability was important for many economic reasons';[51] second, because any carve-up of the Western Balkans would create a precedent for Turkey to encourage Greece's Muslim population in Western Thrace to secede. To these, one might add another two critical factors that made Greece a firm opponent of Yugoslavia's dissolution.

The first goes under the name of the 'Macedonian issue', which involved almost all the Balkan forces in the past, and which was bound to re-emerge when the former Socialist Republic of Macedonia followed other constituent parts of Yugoslavia and claimed international recognition as Macedonia, the name of a Northern province of Greece. The second factor should be seen in relation to the Cyprus issue. If the ethnic components of the Yugoslav state have the right to secede, then why should the same not apply to the Turkish–Cypriot minority of the Republic of Cyprus, which since 1963–4 has vigorously, but unsuccessfully, claimed international recognition for a separate state?[52] Admittedly, the same notion is valid in the case of Turkey's Kurdish minority in the South-east of the country. It turns out that both Greece and Turkey are victims of the double-standard policy of NATO and the US, and of the lack of a coherent legal international framework concerning the issue of 'self-determination'.

It should be remembered that Turkey and Bulgaria, to a greater and lesser extent respectively, had become directly involved in the Balkan crisis from its very inception. In January 1992 Bulgaria was the first to recognise the Former Yugoslav Republic of Macedonia (FYROM) as Macedonia, although the Bulgarian authorities made it clear that they did not recognise a separate Macedonian nation.[53] Turkey followed suit. Considering the security of the Muslims in FYROM and Bosnia as a matter of priority, Turkey was eager to go along with the American-led strategy for an independent Bosnia while, taking advantage of Greece's hostile relations with FYROM, it recognised Macedonia in 1992. A military co-operation agreement between FYROM and Turkey was also signed. In February 1993, Turkey's President Turgut Ozal, visited Macedonia, Bulgaria, Albania and, later, Croatia. This, as Susan Woodward has noted, embarrassed Greece:

Active Turkish diplomacy in Croatia and Macedonia during 1993 under the late President Turgut Ozal, the arrival of Turkish troops to participate with the UN peacekeeping forces in Bosnia in the Spring of 1994, and a pattern of US policy perceived as solicitation of Muslim populations in the Balkans in general led to increasing nervousness in Greece.[54]

Turkey was quick to brush aside its inhibitions stemming from its Kurdish problem. The aim of Turkey's foreign policy was to expose Greece's irresponsible attitude in dealing with the issue of Macedonia and make clear to both the EU and the US that Turkey was highly interested in the Muslim population in the Balkans and that its strategy aimed at peace and democratic stability. Thus, Turkey joined in the chorus of other Muslim, Middle Eastern and Asian states, putting pressure on the US to intervene in Bosnia and Kosovo in order to protect the Muslim population there and in the wider Balkan zone.[55] In point of fact, Turkey's post-Cold War foreign policy pattern has been to revive its influence in the Balkans by exploiting the presence of the Muslim population there. As Hugh Poulton has perceptively shown, Turkey considers the Balkans as a 'kin-state' and some of its military circles view the Muslim minorities as *strategic enclaves* and, hence, as 'militarily useful'.[56]

Despite the fact that the 'Third Way' neo-socialist cabinet of Kostas Simitis has, since 1996, tried hard to improve the image of Greece's foreign policy and economic diplomacy in the Balkans, it is quite interesting to note the country's high degree of awareness with regard to the Muslim question. For example, when socialist diplomats visited Belgrade and Zagreb amidst the Bosnian crisis, Croat nationalist leaders explained to their Greek counterparts – who were very active at the time as Greece held the rotating presidency of the EU (1994) – the case for the creation of a Muslim enclave between Serbia and Croatia. The Greek side replied as follows:

> We are concerned about the creation of a Muslim state in the centre of Europe, as well as about the aid that Islamic states are sending into Bosnia-Herzegovina. We have a minority on our border with Turkey, and the creation of a Muslim state in Bosnia-Herzegovina would only encourage it to seek secession.[57]

Turkey has often accused the European Union of discriminating against its application to join solely because Turkey is a Muslim country, while European states have in common one of the varieties of Christianity. Turkish intellectuals and Bulent Ecevit himself, PM of the country at the time of writing, have repeatedly condemned such discrimination as a racist device, whose origins can be traced back to the intolerant cultural premises of the Enlightenment, arguing that Turkey's customs, in contrast, draw from the Ottoman pluralist tradition of religious tolerance. Although this is not an exaggeration, it nevertheless reveals the deepest political inconsistency of the Turkish Kemalist establishment, since nationalist secular factions and military elites prosecute Islamists *within* the country while championing their rights *outside* it. This policy, although it raised many doubts particularly after the ambivalent results it produced in the Turkic post-Soviet republics of the Caspian region, was bound to become much more cautious particularly after September 11.

In the same vein, one can argue that the transformation of Turkey in the twentieth century went hand in glove with a conscientious policy of ethnic cleansing on behalf of secular pro-Enlightenment elites. This took either the form of an institutionalised type of cleansing, for which Turkey is not the only power to be blamed (as with the case of population exchange between Greece and Turkey in the 1920s), or the form of a cruel military undertaking (as with the case of the Armenian genocide in 1915, when more than 1,300,000 Armenians were exterminated by Turkish troops).[58] Again, the basis of this policy of ethnic cleansing lay not with primordial hatreds or upon notions that 'the Turks are barbarians', but with political goals and geo-political considerations. Following the doctrine of Kemal Atatürk, all the military elites of Turkey in the twentieth century have had as their principal aim the preservation of the modern Turkish state on the basis of the geo-political territorial matrix of Anatolia. Also from this perspective, Cyprus constitutes a special case: for the first time since the foundation of the modern Turkish state in 1923, Turkey has violently claimed legitimacy and statehood over a Turkic-Muslim Ottoman minority lying outside Anatolia's geographical space.

Future historians may not find it difficult to bring out more evidence showing the connection between NATO's wars in the Balkans and the Muslim question in Europe. The US's foreign policy pattern in South-eastern Europe is clearly favouring Turkey and backs its reluctant demand to become a member of the EU.[59] For a variety of reasons, the US cannot embrace the Kurdish demand for independence as easily as the cause of Kosovo Albanians. In the first place, the US is using the Turkish air bases of Incirlik and Diyarbakir – the latter being a Kurdish populated city in South-eastern Turkey

– to launch its daily air attacks against Iraqi targets. Furthermore, the territorial and administrative unity of Turkey matters because of the oil and gas pipeline projects, connecting the Caucasus with the Mediterranean and the Black Sea: projects which, it should be noted, aim at by-passing Russia, Turkey's traditional rival in the Caucasus, the Black Sea and the Eastern Mediterranean.[60]

I have produced evidence and speculative/logical propositions which connect the issues of gas, oil and pipeline projects with the US's policy in the Balkans in the 1990s. I would also read the US's pro-Muslim campaign in the Balkans as an effort to strengthen the bonds with moderate Arab states, thus securing US interests over energy, while counterbalancing its pro-Israeli stance in the eyes of the Arab world. Future international relations historians should not be surprised if they dig out some formerly 'top secret' foreign policy documents proving that issues of this sort were important elements in the game acted out on Brzezinski's Eurasian chessboard, providing an additional explanation as to why NATO sponsored Bosnian Muslims and not Christian Bosnian Serbs. In this respect, and although we do not know the turns US policy would have taken had September 11 occurred not in 2001 but, let us say, in 1994, the following Editorial comment of the *Guardian* on the war in Chechnya reads with interest:

> The USA, which has the most leverage of all, should now support calls to withhold further IMF and World Bank lending to Russia, and should consider freezing its bilateral programmes. The Muslim world, meanwhile, which has belatedly taken up this issue, could help immensely by persuading Arab countries to cut oil prices. As the world's third largest oil producer, Russia is currently funding its war from increased revenues, which are the result of reduced OPEC exports.[61]

The Limits of NATO

Scarface, the 1983 film directed by Brian de Palma, draws on the 1932 Howard Hawks–Paul Muni classic that presents the story of the rise and fall of a Cuban refugee, who comes to Florida with nothing and, within a year, is making millions by laundering cocaine money. The hero, Tony Montana (Al Pacino), had previously exterminated all his enemies but one: his main collaborator. Montana is a macho Latin who beats his sister because of fear of losing control over her, but who does not hesitate to risk his life, when he refuses to blow up a car carrying a mother with her two young children.

But *Scarface* is more than a Freudian depiction. In essence, *Scarface* 'is about hubris' and over-reach, that is, 'the Greek idea that a man who thinks he can challenge the Gods is doomed to fall'.[62] Montana, refuses to recognise his limitations. He is warned not to underestimate the other man's greed and to heed the cardinal rule of drug-dealing: 'Don't get high on your own supply', Elvira (Michelle Pfeiffer) suggests. Montana knows the art of how to conquer the world, but he cannot find the right way to sustain this achievement. The rise and fall of every Empire's macho politics in the past can be read along the lines of the story of Tony Montana.

Throughout the Cold War, NATO and the US worked hard to consolidate their strategic presence in Europe and the Near East, while at the same time containing the Soviet threat and fostering the coherence of Europe. The collapse of 'really existing socialism' and the disintegration of the Warsaw Pact posed new problems but, equally, opened new and promising horizons for the expansion of American global influence. The spread of financial and security markets, followed by cohesive domestic reforms along neo-liberal lines were the linchpins of America's global economic expansion. NATO, with its huge military might, provided the indispensable coercive instrument for the punishment of disobedient actors. Given NATO's commitment to the European continent and the EU's failure to streamline developments in its own backyard, the Balkans, that is to say the geo-political gatekeeper between Western and Eastern Eurasia, had to be brought into line with the mainstream ideology of financial globalisation and NATO's geo-political type of expansion.

The Balkan region is indeed a geo-political gatekeeper of paramount importance. As I have established, a key reason for the US's aggressive intervention in Yugoslavia, as well as for the very process of NATO expansion per se, was and is the security of oil transportation routes from the Caspian Sea to Western markets. The US aims at taking the lion's share from the 'division of spoils' in the Balkans and the greater Middle East, a division that takes various forms of confrontation and co-operation between itself, Germany, other major European actors, Russia, Japan and China.

Yet the above developments might not necessarily have been negative for the EU, had the US avoided pursuing its strategy on the basis of faulty ideological and political lines. As a result, and in order to reconfirm its leading presence in Europe and the Balkans, NATO is facing severe difficulties in coping with the application of its own constitutional principles, modes of policy conduct and observance of international law. More to the point, NATO's transformation from a defence pact into an aggressive political organisation, upholding and selectively implementing liberal-democratic principles, reads as the most mistaken road of all that the alliance has taken since its foundation in 1949. The *feudal type of fragmentation* of Eastern Europe, Central Asia and of the Western Balkans, along with the emergence of a plethora of statelets with ambivalent economic and political futures is as much the work of the IMF and the World Bank as it is of NATO's mistaken politico-military strategy of expansion. The Kosovo war 'x-rayed' the entire problematic skeleton of NATO's reform process in the 1990s, unravelling a whole series of institutional contradictions and policy deadlocks. Moreover, the post-September 11 environment brought about a political situation in which the US was forced to rethink the utility of sponsoring or assisting, when geo-strategically convenient, Islamic organisations and agencies across the globe.

Although NATO institutionalises Europe's politico-military dependency upon the US, thus influencing the EU's political and economic decisions,[63] it is hard to envisage that in the future core European states and their publics will continue to endorse NATO's operations or expansion projects in Europe based on inconsistent or 'double standards' politics. It is also unimaginable that the EU/Germany would accept to be geo-politically 'squeezed' between the US and Russia. Europe's initiative to field 60,000 troops independent of the US-dominated NATO (the 'rapid reaction force' project) heralds a perspective and a defence strategy that has upset Pentagon strategists.[64]

The Kosovo war was the result of NATO's geo-political type of selective expansion on the basis of mistaken and rather hypocritical ideological–political premises. This expansion aimed and aims at guaranteeing the security of oil and gas pipeline projects in Western Eurasia, eliminating competition from Russia, France, Italy and Germany. Russia and China were firmly against the bombing campaign and the crisis itself produced – among other tragic incidents – the bombing of the Chinese Embassy in Belgrade, thus seriously alienating China. All this made co-operation between Russia and the US in the Balkans, Central Asia and Middle East difficult, and it was only under Vladimir Putin's administration that an attempt was made to reshuffle the cards under a new type of 'co-operative duopoly'.[65]

The debacle of the WTO at Seattle in December 1999 and then in Genoa (July 2001) adds to the US list of problems. Moreover, regional co-operation in South-eastern Europe with the assistance of the EU would create a powerful socio-economic and geo-political axis linking up Western, Eastern and Southern Europe. But no double standards need to apply anymore. As the Greek Foreign Minister George Papandreou has convincingly argued, having in mind the economic reconstruction of the Balkans, Europe's policy of regional co-operation in the South-eastern Mediterranean applies as much to Yugoslavia as it does to Turkey.[66]

The US and Britain are the strongest supporters of Turkey joining the EU 'as soon as possible' because, among other reasons, huge amounts of the IMF cash now pouring into Turkey's ailing economy would be replaced by Europe's regional and structural funds. But a closer connection between Turkey, the Muslim world and the EU may lead to a revival of a distinct common European foreign policy toward the Middle East peace process, similar to that experienced in the early 1970s, when the then European Political Co-operation (EPC) gave its own interpretation of the United Nations Security Council's Resolution 242, challenging the US's regional plans.[67] It is worth noting that both Turkey and the EU were sceptical about a renewal of hostilities between a US-led alliance and Iraq after September 11, as it would have created further economic and security complications for both Turkey and the EU. The entry of Cyprus into the EU reads along the same lines: the island's strategic location and strong economy in the South-eastern Mediterranean basin, including its registered shipping capacity, would increase the leverage of European politics in the Near and Middle East. As we shall examine in detail in the following chapters, Cyprus constitutes for the EU a litmus test for the affirmation of its independent foreign policy in the Near and the Middle East.

Overall, I would like to argue that NATO and the US have just begun facing their first set of serious problems in the administration of the post-Cold War global environment. At the core of these problems stands the mistaken transformation of the alliance from a military pact into a political organisation, a transformation that tends to *consume*, not to *produce* security in Europe, the Balkans and, by extension, in the greater Middle East. Having said this, I would not hesitate to read the post-Cold War transformation of NATO and the vicissitudes of the US policy alongside *Scarface*'s principal themes, those being 'hubris' and 'over-reach'. The 'hubris' of NATO and the US against Europe's ideological matrix of the Enlightenment principles is undeniable; and an 'over-reach' of NATO itself, in the wake of its failure to diagnose the crucial political and historical limits of its expansionist adventure, is also undeniable. The vicissitudes of US policy via NATO demystify the political myth of delivering justice through violence, disclosing that the world we live in is still a realist/neo-realist world dominated by power politics and conflicting capitalist economic and national interests. NATO and the US expand deeper into Eurasia in order to create such *fait accomplis* so as to force Russia to co-operate and Europe/Germany to be more flexible on trade and economic matters in the context of the WTO. The human cost has been enormous. In this context, primary responsibility lies with those policy-makers and intellectuals who a-critically supported both the alliance's eastward enlargement and its transformation into a political and coercive organisation, which instrumentally draws guiding principles from the Enlightenment's liberal traditions. The pro-expansionist argument spearheaded by Brzezinski and Kissinger is not convincing and the view that a legal framework should be constructed in order to support humanitarian intervention is deeply hypocritical, unrealistic and counter-productive – indeed it has become more so particularly since September 11.[68] The very limit of the US policy is the 'hubris' of liberal European values tried and abused on European soil.

It seems to me that Eurasia and its wealth are looked upon by America in the same way as Miami was looked upon by Tony Montana. Yet NATO and the US may not be falling into the same genus of mistakes as Montana did. The Clinton administration promised a humane society in Somalia and Haiti and left chaos and anarchy,[69] but Montana, an original Latin macho, did care about the life of women and children. It should be remembered, however, that Montana's fall was as much the work of his main collaborator – or, in NATO's jargon, 'core partners' – as a result of his own refusal to admit his limits. Be that as it may, great care should be taken by all sides to consider, with apologies to Marx, that the limits of NATO may turn out to be NATO itself.

4   Near and Middle Eastern Dilemmas

NATO's strategic mission, as a key instrument of the US containment strategy for the security and defence of Western Europe, was such that it allowed a conceivable 'stretching' of US influence into zones where Western geo-political interests were at stake. Owing to the declining influence of the British Empire, the US containment strategy, which began unfolding even before the end of the Second World War, necessarily had to be structured in such a way that it could provide for the defence and security of oil and gas producing regions. This political necessity, although impossible to materialise in full due to the USSR's powerful posture in Central Asia and the Caucasus, nevertheless had to strike a balance of force not unfavourable to the US and the West. Thus, even before the formulation of the Truman Doctrine in 1947, US policy-makers concluded that the success of the containment strategy in Europe was contingent upon the success of the balance of power in the Near and the greater Middle East.

As early as 1945–6, US strategists were paying particular attention to the struggle for power along the so-called 'Northern Tier'. This term 'describes the northernmost Near and Middle Eastern countries on the border of or Near the Soviet Union'.[1] In the immediate post-war period, Greece, Turkey, Iran and, at times, even Afghanistan were indeed deemed to be indispensable for the success of the US containment policy in Europe.[2]

On reflection, however, the notion of a 'Northern Tier' turned out to involve certain political issues that were conducive to disunity, rather than unity, between crucial regional actors and allies of the US. In the first place, the notion came to be challenged by the Greek–Turkish conflict over Cyprus and the Aegean, and also by the Iranian revolution of 1979. Secondly, the emergence of a Jewish state in 1948 reshuffled the regional balance of power in the Middle East, reignited Arab and Palestinian nationalism, thus creating an unstable equilibrium of forces in the very security underbelly of the 'Tier'. In this context, and given the influence of the USSR in the Arab world, the US could not afford to separate in real political and strategic terms, as rigorously as it did in theory, the 'Northern Tier' from the Arab–Israeli conflict and the security of oil and gas producing zones.

This chapter is an attempt to explore the significance for the US of the Arab–Israeli conflict and the problems that arose in the 'Northern Tier' mainly during the first three decades of the Cold War. Our chief focus will be the international context of the Cyprus issue and, by extension, Greek–Turkish rivalry and other security issues in the Middle East that pertained to the geo-political context of the Cold War. Through this perspective, we shall become aware of the dilemmas of US policy in the Near and the Middle East, dilemmas that were enmeshed with the antagonism of the USSR and European powers per se. Our analyses here will pave the way for the exploration, in the next two chapters, of Turkey and of Cyprus–EU relations.

The 'Northern Tier' and the Greek–Turkish Dimension

By assigning to both Greece and Turkey $400m in aid, the Truman Doctrine had set the tone for the Marshall Plan for the reconstruction of Western Europe. In addition, it initiated a process of transition of hegemony in the Southern Balkans and the Eastern Mediterranean from Britain to the US. The exception was Cyprus, where Britain insisted upon holding onto its colony. The events that prompted the US to put forward the notion of a 'Northern Tier' were all part of the regional dynamics that were emerging out of the war and taking shape within the newly formed boundaries of the Cold War.

The end of the war found Iran under the triple occupation of the USSR, Britain and the US. Due to the USSR's successful resistance, and having secured from the Germans the oilfields of Ahwaz and the refinery at Abadan (the largest in the world), the allies used Iran's facilities throughout their war effort. Post-war Soviet determination to hold onto Iran, on the one hand, and the subsequent Soviet challenge to Turkey's sovereignty on the other, prompted the US to consider both Near-Middle Eastern countries as of invaluable strategic importance. The USSR wanted to control Iran's oil and gas production, gain access to the Gulf region and also use the Kurdish issue 'as a means of making inroads to Turkey'.[3] With regard to Turkey as such, the USSR, under the pretext of pressure exercised by its Armenian and Georgian Socialist Republics, aimed at achieving control over the Turkish Straits and the Turkish provinces of Kars and Ardahan. The crises over Iran and Turkey, although they had been brewing since the war years, manifested themselves almost simultaneously (Iran: March 1946; Turkey: August 1946).

Greece, apart from its symbolic value as the 'cradle of Western civilisation', bordered three Communist countries (Albania, Yugoslavia and Bulgaria). Had the Greek Communist guerrillas been successful in defeating the Greek nationalist forces during the second guerrilla war in Macedonia (1946–9), then Greece could easily have become both the USSR's and Bulgaria's Trojan Horses for gaining access to the Eastern Mediterranean.[4] Greece's land border with Turkey across the Évros/Maritsa river thus had to be maintained at all costs. But as this border was adjacent to the bottleneck of the Bosporus and the Dardanelles, defence of the Aegean Greece and Black Sea Turkey assumed particular importance. From this perspective, US strategists saw Greece and Turkey as forming a united geo-strategic bloc able, if properly backed, to deter Soviet incursion into the Eastern Mediterranean and the Suez via the Turkish Straits and/or the Aegean. The Greek–Turkish equation was not balanced in the strategic thinking of US policy-makers in that Turkey emerged as strategically more important than Greece, a fact that was later to be taken into account when they began considering the Greek–Turkish conflict over Cyprus.

Turkey had borders with Communist Russia, and as it was situated next to oil and gas producing regions, could be used militarily by the US to starve the USSR of oil.[5] Turkey was contributing strategic depth to the containment strategy for the defence of Europe, and it could potentially act as a bulwark of deterrence in the crucial fronts of the Balkans, the Black Sea, the Middle East and even Central Asia. It had a large standing army, numbering some 460,000 men in 1946, and had the potential to become a considerable Black Sea and Eastern Mediterranean naval power. In addition, it could offer vital bases and listening posts to the US and the West, which were deemed to be indispensable for the deterrence of any possible Soviet incursion through the Caucasus. The Turkey–Iran–Afghanistan tier was thus becoming a vital line of defence in the struggle against Soviet domination of oil and gas producing regions. Iran dominated the Eastern shoreline of the Persian Gulf and Afghanistan provided a crucial, buffer type of landmass. Despite the fact that the chain was bound to become irrelevant if the Greek link was missing, the actual geo-strategic ordering put together favoured Turkey at the expense of Greece. As Bruce Kuniholm put it:

The security of Greece and Turkey were of critical importance to the United States. While both countries offered bases for operations in the Eastern Mediterranean, Turkey was strategically more important because it dominated the major air, land, and sea routes from the Soviet Union to the Eastern Mediterranean and Persian Gulf. While Greece could probably never resist an attack in force, Turkey could impose an appreciable delay on attacking forces and, supported by the United States, could offer strong resistance. Based on these considerations, the JCS (Joint Chiefs of Staff) defined the following long-range US strategic interests: (a) A Greek military establishment capable of maintaining internal security in order to avoid Communist domination; (b) A Turkish military establishment sufficient to ensure continued resistance to Soviet pressure, and able to delay Soviet aggression long enough to permit US and allied forces to deny certain portions of Turkey to the Soviet Union.[6]

This strategic reasoning formed the basis upon which the US implemented its policy towards Greece and Turkey, at least until the Turkish invasions of Cyprus in summer 1974. The US assisted Greece, both economically and militarily, basically in order to develop it into a domestic anticommunist security regime; and it also assisted Turkey in becoming a defence 'micro-giant' in order to be able to 'delay Soviet aggression'.

It is therefore no accident that, although both Greece and Turkey joined NATO simultaneously in February 1952 following their participation in the Korean War (1950), Greece had been invited to submit its application only after the positive conclusion of US–UK–Turkey consultations in 1950–51.[7] Having this order of priorities, the US soon began distributing military aid to Greece and Turkey on an unequal basis. During the crucial period between 1952 and 1959, when Cyprus was experiencing EOKA's (National Organisation of Cypriot Fighters) anti-colonial struggle for self-determination and *enosis* (union with Greece – 1955–9), Turkey received over twice as much US military assistance as Greece ($1.36 billion to $673.9 million).[8] This trend continued throughout the 1960s and, consequently, before 1974, 'Greece's forces, lacking strong air and naval components, remained little more than a trip wire in case of Soviet attack, whereas Turkey developed a well-rounded force capable of an independent offensive campaign.'[9] Although there were additional reasons for the inaction of Greece's forces in summer 1974 (e.g. the plight of the Greek military caused by the junta's seven-year administration), the fact remains that Greece had far inferior power projection capabilities than Turkey. Greek political leaders in the 1950s (Constantine Karamanlis) and 1960s (George Papandreou) complained to the US about this unequal distribution of military assistance, but their efforts proved fruitless.[10]

The Arab–Israeli Conflict

The geo-strategic terrain of the Arab–Israeli conflict during the Cold War can be defined in terms of occupying the sensitive geo-political space under the thick belt of the 'Northern Tier'. This definition assists us in deciphering the links between US policy towards the Middle East, and the regional pattern of alliances and rivalries that emerged out, or on the fringes, of this conflict, which the US had to manage successfully in order to contain the influence of the USSR.

The birth of Israel was a painful and protracted process. In the main, it was the result of a combination of events, such as the horrific experience of the Holocaust of the Jewish people, the long-standing determination of the Zionist movement to establish a state in Palestine, as well as of Britain's decision to withdraw from there. More than 6,000,000 Jews had been exterminated by the Nazis before and during the Second World War and the Zionist demand of Theodor Herzl for the creation of a Jewish state in Palestine began gaining considerable ground in Europe and the US.[11] The demand of the Jewish people 'to have a state of their own', in which they could seek refuge and shelter, was coupled with the willingness of the British to give up their mandate in Palestine, although holding onto Cyprus and their ground in the Suez Canal.

Following their failure to back Greece's irredentist aspirations in Asia Minor in 1919–22, the British and French sought to prevent Soviet influence in the Middle East, dividing the spoils between them. This was to be done by uniting their communication lines from the Suez Canal and the bridge-island of Cyprus, eastwards to the Levant and the oil fields of Iraq and India.[12] But Britain's partial withdrawal from the Near and the Middle East in the wake of the Second World War, created a power vacuum at the very heart of oil and gas producing zones, a vacuum that the victorious USSR could easily exploit to its advantage.

Britain began looking for an exit strategy in Palestine, and by doing so confused matters there even more. Britain had mixed feelings about sponsoring the creation of a Jewish state, and had several times blocked the arrival of Jewish immigrants to Palestine.[13] Yet it did not have a clear-cut policy towards the Palestinians either. The Jewish institution-building in Palestine began between the wars under the encouragement and auspices of the British. Verbally, however, Britain could not afford to call upon Jewish institution-building alone, and it was forced by the nature of things to also invite the Arab/Palestinians to set up their own proto-state structures. Thus, in 1939 a British White Paper called for an independent Palestine in ten years. This sort of 'divide and rule' policy had become untenable and created mistrust, not only between the Arabs and the Jews, but also between each of them and the British. Characteristically, an anti-Jewish and anti-Anglo-French Arab League was formed in March 1945, whilst 'by October 1947, Jewish attacks had killed 127 British soldiers and wounded 133 others'.[14]

The newly founded United Nations and the US inherited this British policy failure in Palestine. Israel's declaration of independence (May 14, 1948), which was drawn from a UN decision for a partition of Palestine into Arab and Jewish zones, meant war for five Arab states. Israel, supported by the US, exploited the disunity in the Arab alliance and won the war, which resulted in an increase in its territory of 21 per cent compared to the UN territorial allocation scheme.[15] Yet, this created a huge refugee problem that still haunts the peace talks between Israel, the Palestinian authority and the international community.[16]

The birth of Israel went therefore hand in hand with the rebirth of Arab nationalism, albeit incoherent and disunited, and with a constant security problem for both the Israelis and the Arabs. This security/insecurity problem, at least during the early stages, chiefly stemmed from the issue of refugees and Arab/Palestinian grievances over the foundation of Israel, or the way in which Israel was established. It also went hand in glove with the Cold War geo-strategic settings, as it had become clear from the beginning that the USSR was keen on supporting the Arab cause in order to expand its influence in the Middle East and the Eastern Mediterranean.

Tension in the Middle East was something that the US did not always wish for, as important security and strategic interests of the West were at stake. Clearly, the USSR was ready to capitalise, not only on the openings offered to her by the Arab states and their non-aligned movement, but also, and even more importantly, on the antagonisms that developed periodically among NATO allies themselves. Moreover, the US could not afford to sustain its first line of defence in the greater Middle East, that being the 'Northern Tier', with its soft underbelly (Syria, Jordan, Lebanon, Iraq and Egypt) in constant turmoil. Thus, US policy-makers were forced to develop a multifaceted and risky policy, by trying to reconcile conflicting regional and global interests. In the main, what at times came to be called the 'Eisenhower doctrine' (1957) or 'Carter/Reagan doctrine' (late 1970s to 1980s) during the Cold War, was in fact a careful balancing act in relation to the Near and the Middle East, trying to accommodate five key interlinked objectives:

a. The security and survival of Israel or, as Henry Kissinger put it in 1970, 'the United States is committed to defend Israel's existence, but not Israel's conquests'.[17]
b. The accommodation of divergent, rather than homogeneous, Arab interests in order to keep as many Arab states as possible – as well as Cyprus and the 'Northern Tier' – away from the influence of the USSR.
c. The elimination of differences among NATO members, including differences between the US itself and some of its key allies, such as Britain and France.
d. Contingency planning for projecting US and NATO power in the Eastern Mediterranean and the Persian Gulf, in case deterrence failed.[18]
e. And, in retrospect, as this possibility emerged during the late 1960s, the US had to prevent the Arabs from using the 'oil weapon', thus inflicting a serious economic crisis upon the West.

To these five policy objectives, one can add a sixth, which was to ensure the cohesion of the 'Northern Tier', mainly by preventing an armed conflict between Greece and Turkey over Cyprus. This objective, however, can be added onto the US priority list only after 1962–3, when the British decided to halt their involvement in Cyprus' domestic security affairs.

The US global policy balancing act in respect of the Near and the Middle East can be seen from a number of events that the region experienced in the 1950s and 1960s, most of which were directly related to the Arab–Israeli conflict and the Greek–Turkish one over Cyprus. I will deal here with the Arab–Israeli case, while dedicating a separate section to the Cyprus issue.

To start with, the foundation of Israel and the defeat of the Arabs in 1948–9 triggered major political upheavals within the Arab states themselves. Egypt's monarchy was overthrown in 1952 and a series of coups took place in Syria between 1949 and 1955. King Abdullah of Jordan and PM Riad as-Sulh of Lebanon were assassinated in 1951. The most important domestic development took place in Egypt, when two years after the 1952 revolution, in October 1954, Mohammed Neguib was replaced by Gamal Abdel-Nasir (Nasser).

Nasser, who was initially welcomed by both Israel and the US, had soon distanced himself from both the Baghdad Pact and the West and came to be overtly backed by the USSR.[19] Embarking upon an ambitious programme of modernisation via increased state intervention in economic affairs, Nasser challenged the stationing of some 85,000 British troops around the Suez Canal and decided to nationalise it on July 26, 1956, in order to raise funds for the financing of the Aswan Dam. This represented a direct challenge to Britain and France, who produced an ambiguous plan to undo Nasser's policy, a plan that first assigned to Israel the task of taking the Canal by force.[20] The Israelis did indeed take most of the Sinai peninsula, but when Britain and France, under the pretext of keeping the Arabs and the Israelis apart, began invading Egypt in order to retake Suez, the US intervened to thwart their project. Facing the US military challenge, and under a UN threat of an oil embargo, the Franco-British forces withdrew immediately. They then painfully lamented that they were second-rate powers in the Middle East and the Eastern Mediterranean, incapable of independent action.[21] But US rationale had different foundations.

The Franco-British action and the involvement of Israel broke the fragile Baghdad Pact apart, and the US found itself in the difficult position of having to build anew a coalition of the moderate Arab states under its hegemonic influence.[22] Moreover, the US wanted to prevent a spillover of the conflict into a major Cold War confrontation in the greater Middle East, all the more so since the USSR had by then managed to establish a remarkable intelligence, naval and military presence in the region.[23] In addition, the US began undercutting Europe's overall strategic position in the area, as European forces had started siding with the Arabs in their attempt to rescue their imperial privileges over oil and gas deals that they had enjoyed before the Suez crisis. Ultimately, under pressure from Arab nationalism, as well as economic problems at home, Britain and France completely withdrew from the Persian Gulf and Algeria respectively. The process of decolonisation was at its peak and in this context East Mediterranean Cyprus figured prominently.

Conflict over Cyprus

The rationale behind the inclusion of Turkey and Greece in the Western sphere of influence was drawn on the basis of a wider context. Not only were Greece and Turkey seen as forming a united line of defence, but also the Balkans and the Middle East were considered to be part of a potentially uniform geo-strategic zone. Although this should not be exaggerated since, during the Cold War, the Balkans and the Middle East were grouped separately for planning purposes, the fact remains that there was strategic potential to exploit, particularly in the Western Balkans. For instance, when Tito's Yugoslavia finally came to employ a non-aligned foreign policy in accordance with the Stalin–Churchill percentages agreement,[24] the chances for the West to influence the Balkan zone increased substantially. As Susan Woodward noted, throughout the Cold War Yugoslavia survived

> [thanks] to US military aid; US-orchestrated economic assistance from the International Monetary Fund, World Bank, US Export–Import Bank, and foreign Banks; and the restoration of trade relations with the West after August 1949. In exchange, socialist Yugoslavia played a critical role for the US global leadership during the Cold War: as a propaganda tool in its anti-communist and anti-Soviet campaign and as an integral element of NATO's policy in the Eastern Mediterranean. Jealously guarding its neutrality, Yugoslavia became an important element in the West's policy of containment of the Soviet Union. It prevented the Soviets from gaining a toehold in the Mediterranean and protected routes to Italy and Greece by providing a strong military deterrence to potential Soviet aggression in the Balkans.[25]

The success of US policy towards the Balkans and the Near East reached its apex in 1953, when Yugoslavia, Greece and Turkey signed the Balkan Treaty of Friendship and Co-operation, which was extended into a mutual defence pact the following year. But tensions between Turkey and Greece were soon to follow, when Britain included Turkey in its bilateral discussions with Greece over the future of Cyprus (1954–5). This disturbed the understanding between Greece and Turkey that had been developing since 1930 with the Venizelos–Ataturk Convention of Friendship and Reconciliation.

Greece viewed Turkey's participation in the talks as inappropriate and illegal. According to the Greeks, the 1923 Treaty of Lausanne stipulated that Turkey would no longer have the right to lay claim over any of the former territories of the Ottoman Empire where Muslim populations could be found. The Turks, however, had a different interpretation of the relevant Article of the Treaty, insisting that they had the legal right to be involved. The final version of Article 16 of the Treaty of Lausanne reads as follows:

> Turkey hereby renounce all rights and titles whatsoever over or respecting the territories situated outside the frontiers laid down in the present Treaty and the islands other than those over which her sovereignty is recognised by the said Treaty, the future of those territories and islands being settled by the parties concerned.[26]

Although this wording seems to be favouring Greece's point of view, it 'left the door open to subsequent debates between Turkey and Greece concerning which nations could legally be regarded as "parties concerned" with reference to the fate of Cyprus'.[27] The ensuing conflict between the two countries over Cyprus threatened to split NATO's 'Northern Tier' (Southern flank) at least twice in the 1960s (1963–4 and 1967), as well as, and even more seriously, in 1974 when Turkey invaded Cyprus twice (July 20 and August 14, 1974).[28]

Yet it was not Greece itself that aimed at a military confrontation with Turkey in order to assert itself in Cyprus through a policy of union. Rather, it was the Greek Cypriots who fervently pursued the goal of *enosis* (union with Greece) and demanded mainland Greek support. *Enosis* is a Greek Cypriot demand that can be traced back to Greece's own struggle for independence from the Ottoman yoke in the 1820s, a demand that has remained unaltered throughout the subsequent decades. The spark for a violent Greek Cypriot campaign against British colonial authorities was provided by Henry Hopkinson, junior Minister for Colonial Affairs in the British cabinet. When challenged by Labour opposition MPs in a parliamentary debate in July 1954, he spelled out an unfortunate statement: 'It has always been understood and agreed that there are certain territories in the Commonwealth which, owing to their particular circum-stances, can *never* expect to be fully independent' (my emphasis).[29] The word 'never' was unacceptable to the Greek Cypriots. The following year, on April 1, 1955, a number of bombs were detonated across Cyprus, aiming at British colonial installations and interests.

The EOKA struggle for self-determination and *enosis*, led by Colonel George Grivas (leader of EOKA's clandestine military arm) and Archbishop Makarios (the political–religious leader) had begun.

The US regional geo-strategic imperative, particularly from the early 1960s onwards, was to remove Cyprus as 'the Greek–Turkish bone of contention', creating conditions for solid co-operation between NATO allies Greece and Turkey.[30] To a significant degree, as in the case of Palestine, the Greek–Turkish conflict over Cyprus was a problem directly inherited from Britain's colonial policy of 'divide and rule' on the island. During the EOKA anti-colonial struggle, a considerable number of Turkish Cypriots, often of working-class origin or unemployed, were recruited by the British authorities as gendarmes and security personnel. This policy underpinned the transformation of Cypriot Muslims into Turkish nationalists, while establishing Turkey as a diplomatic party to the Cyprus question. It was therefore British strategy in the 1950s to openly pit the Turkish minority against the Greek majority, thus establishing irreconcilable differences between the two communities, differences that were bound to have a negative impact upon Greek–Turkish relations.[31]

Moreover, as early as 1955–6, and again with Britain's connivance, the Turkish strategy began to consider the Cyprus issue in the context of a wider revisionist understanding with Greece, which involved issues such as the Aegean, the Muslim minority in Greek Thrace and the Greek minority in Istanbul. Turkish policy-makers had assessed that, in the event of a war, Turkey could only be supplied through its Southern ports of Antalya, Mersin and Iskenderun, and that if Cyprus became Greek, this could no longer be guaranteed. Turkey was indeed afraid of being encircled by Greece, a traditionally hostile nation. In the words of Nihat Erim, who was acting at the time as special adviser to the Turkish PM Adnan Menderes on the Cyprus issue:

> Inasmuch as Greece wants to disturb the balance achieved in Lausanne by proclaiming enosis, Turkey should demand bilateral negotiations on all matters concerned, namely, on issues regarding Western Thrace, the position of the Patriarchate, the Greek minority in Istanbul, as well as some Aegean islands.[32]

So, whereas the US was aiming at a solution that could accommodate Greece and Turkey in order to maintain NATO's cohesion, and thus the strategic operationality of the 'Northern Tier', the Turkish policy, with the backing of Britain, was envisaging an overall plan to deal with bilateral relations. In 1958, Turkey refused to ratify the Geneva Convention on the continental shelf, and when later in the early 1970s she challenged Greece's sovereign rights in the Aegean Sea, Turkey was quick to recall that she was not one of the signatories of the Convention – Greece signed rather belatedly, in 1972.[33] Turkey's overall plan was in fact tantamount to a *revision* of the Treaty of Lausanne.

The Aegean Sea and Thrace bear strategic similarities to that of Cyprus in that the US was equally keen to avoid Greek–Turkish hostilities over regions hosting their ethnic communities. In the first place, a Greek–Turkish war would have provided great opportunities for the Warsaw Pact to expand its influence in the Eastern Mediterranean by siding either with Greece or Turkey, depending on the prevailing circumstances and on which option would be more convenient for the USSR. In addition – a factor that is equally valid today – the Black Sea trade and Flight Information Regions (FIRs) would have been disrupted or deactivated, events whose repercussions would have been felt in the Suez Canal trade and across the entire network of NATO's communication lines. In a sense, however, the case of Cyprus was different altogether because, among other things, Britain, Greece and Turkey managed to produce a parody constitution in 1959–60, which was unjust, divisive and, above all, against the very charter of the United Nations.[34] 'Even the Intelligence and Research Bureau of the US Department of State', Van Coufoudakis observed, 'in a prophetic analysis in the summer of 1959, concluded that these [constitutional] agreements were burdensome and unworkable and predicted their collapse.'[35]

Turkey bargained hard over Cyprus and pursued shrewd tactics of leaning towards the USSR after 1964, when a Turkish invasion was averted at the eleventh hour by the US President Lyndon Johnson. But even before the notorious 'Johnson letter', which warned the Turks to avoid any adventurism in Cyprus because NATO may not be able to guarantee the security of Turkey's Eastern borders, the US had taken a unilateral decision to remove Jupiter missiles from Turkey, which were destined to repulse a Soviet attack.[36] The political victory of Makarios in the UN following the inter-communal strife of 1963–4, coupled with his clever international tactics and the US–Turkey dispute over the Cuban missiles crisis

(1962), induced the US to consider Turkey's Eastern frontiers as 'out-of-area', and thus not defensible.[37]

The Turco-Soviet co-operation took the form of stronger economic ties, and reached its apex in 1967, when 'the USSR agreed to build a number of industrial plants in Turkey, including a steel mill, an aluminium smelter, and an oil refinery'.[38] Moreover, in 1967 (the Six Day War) and 1973 Turkey refused to facilitate American support for Israel in the two Arab–Israeli wars. More to the point, in the October 1973 Yom Kippur war, the US was left totally on its own as 'all other NATO members [including the Greek junta] with the exception of Portugal declined to facilitate US out-of-area involvement'.[39]

In the Yom Kippur war the US indeed felt the need to mobilise its allies to a common war effort to save Israel, as it was becoming clear that Israel could not hold out on its own against the Egyptian and Syrian surprise attack supported by the USSR. The Arab states were using Soviet military equipment, of the latest technology, and the USSR itself was amassing some eighty warships in the Eastern Mediterranean, readying troops to be airlifted into the area of conflict.[40] At this critical conjuncture, Cypriot President Archbishop Makarios – himself one of the founders of the non-aligned movement and several times dubbed by US policy-makers as 'the Castro of the Mediterranean' – refused to allow the Americans to use the facilities of the British sovereign bases in Cyprus. Britain was explicitly in concert with Makarios's stance. It was those critical events that made crystal clear to Henry Kissinger and US defence analysts the politico-military importance of Cyprus for the defence of Israel.

From this perspective, the generic framework of Turkey's geo-strategic primacy *vis-à-vis* Greece assumed a particular significance for the US in the context of the *rapprochement* between Turkey and the USSR. The ferocity of the Arab–Israeli conflict, Europe's antagonism to the US, and Cyprus' and Greece's unwillingness to back the US in the Eastern Mediterranean, led the US to reconsider Turkey's importance. More to the point, the loss of Turkey, that the US feared after the pro-USSR inclination of Turkey's foreign policy, would have caused havoc to NATO's integrated defence and com-munication lines. It would have destroyed the geo-strategic practicality of the 'Northern Tier', offering enormous advantages to the USSR and enabling her to advance further into the oil and gas producing zones of the Middle East. In the event, the loss of Turkey to the USSR might have meant the loss of Israel as the 'Northern

Tier' would have been penetrated by the joint bloc of the USSR with Arab nationalism.

This is the appropriate regional and global context within which the US partition schemes for Cyprus of the 1960s and early 1970s can be analysed and understood. These schemes, drawn up by the security and diplomatic teams surrounding George Ball and Dean Acheson in 1964–5, mainly provided for union with Greece with the concession to Turkey of a large military base on Cyprus.[41] In this way, the US had hoped to rebalance Greek–Turkish relations within NATO and strengthen the 'Northern Tier' by forging Greek–Turkish friendship through a solution of the Cyprus issue acceptable to both Turkey and Greece. However, neither Makarios nor the democratically elected government of George Papandreou in Greece, which was under the decisive influence of his son Andreas, accepted the partition schemes.[42] The strategy pursued by the Republic of Cyprus at the time was that of independence and non-alignment, and any sort of acceptance of the partition schemes would have turned the Republic into an awkward NATOland divided between Greece and Turkey. In fact, the partition schemes proved unworkable because the US took into account its own security only and not the political volition and 'interests of the Cypriots'.[43]

Having said this, the US policy of finding a solution to the Cyprus issue that might keep both Greece and Turkey 'happy', was inextricably linked with two strategic imperatives. First, to maintain the deterring and defence posture of the 'Northern Tier'; second, to maintain the balance of force in the Middle East and the Eastern Mediterranean in favour of NATO and Israel. These strategic imperatives underpinned the US strategy to rebalance Turkey's foreign policy inclination towards the USSR, a strategic need which assumed particular urgency for the US after the October 1973 Yom Kippur war.

Towards Summer 1974 and After

The imposition of a military junta in Greece in 1967, within which most of the leading officers were on the payroll of the CIA, removed any hope of a balanced and just solution to the Cyprus issue. The Athens regime was constrained by the strategic remit of the Cold War policy priorities of the US. It assumed power in order to boost anti-communism and domestic security, reverse the momentum of George and Andreas Papandreou's democratic movement, and also to facilitate a solution of the Cyprus issue according to the US partition plans.[44]

The Greek junta dislocated the anti-partition foreign policy framework of the democratic governments of George and Andreas Papandreou and pursued a head-on confrontation with Archbishop Makarios, undermining his policy for an independent Cyprus. For seven years, Makarios successfully resisted the junta's hotchpotch nationalistic plans for union with Greece, with Turkey receiving in return a large military base on Cyprus. But he failed to deter the junta's coup of July 15, 1974 in Cyprus, and Turkey's first invasion followed five days later. Within two days, and taking advantage of the military Turkish Cypriot enclave linking up Kerynia with Nicosia, the Turks managed to create a bridgehead around this enclosed zone.

Henry Kissinger and the US were not very interested in who would win in summer 1974, although the outcome of the confrontation was rather predictable. As we saw earlier, the issue at stake in July–August 1974 was neither the territorial integrity of Cyprus nor which regional NATO power the US should please. The real issue was the cohesion of NATO's Southern flank and of the 'Northern Tier' and this, albeit with difficulty, was maintained.[45] True, the US had tilted towards Turkey at the expense of Greece between 1964 and 1974, but this was the result of Turkey's successful policy, supported by the primacy of its geo-strategic positioning during the Cold War. This said, however, Turkey's strategic value alone would have been useless if it was not backed by successful foreign policy manoeuvring and favoured by the negative turn of events in the Arab–Israeli conflict.

Despite fierce opposition by Secretary Kissinger and President Ford, the US finally imposed a Congress-led short-lived arms embargo on Turkey (1975–8) and supported in the UN Greece's demand for non-recognition of the Turkish-controlled zone in Cyprus (37 per cent of the island). This decision was not the result of a moral way of thinking on the part of the US. Rather, it was the product of the bizarre constitutional arrangements of 1959–60; the ferocity of the second Turkish invasion (August 14–16, 1974), taking the Turkish-controlled zone out of the Kerynia–Nicosia enclave and extending it well beyond any preconceived partition scheme put forward by Acheson and Ball; and the need to pacify and please Greece and the Greek–American lobby in the US Congress.[46]

Henry Kissinger and Bulent Ecevit have since declared that the Cyprus issue was 'solved' in summer 1974. This is far from true. They both know that the Cyprus issue, if at all, has been *fixed*, and not *solved*. It is this 'fixing' that has since 1974 kept Greece and Turkey fighting at the diplomatic level alone; and it is this 'fixing' that has since 1974 served the US, Turkey and Israel in the Near Eastern theatre (see the next two chapters). But it is also because of this 'fixing' that, *inter alia*, the US can manipulate both Greece and Turkey at will, whenever it sees fit. At times, Great Powers find it more convenient not to 'solve', but to 'fix' problems.[47]

The establishment of the Turkish military in Cyprus not only created conditions for the partition of the island, but it also put Greece at a politico-military disadvantage over the entire security zone stretching from Cyprus, westwards and northwards to the Aegean and Western Thrace. Turkey could now openly challenge Greece's sovereign rights in the Aegean and Western Thrace, and also challenge the legitimacy of the FIR of Athens, demanding that its aviation authority be transferred to Istanbul. Turkey had also asked Greece that a median line in the Aegean be drawn, conferring Turkey the right, among others, to provide security for the Eastern Aegean islands off its coastal line.[48] In the event, Turkey demanded a reporting air aviation line in the Aegean, which coincided with the Western median edge they claimed for the continental shelf.[49] In other words, both the air and the sea of the Aegean should be divided between mainland Greece and Turkey. The issue of the Greek minority in Turkey was somewhat solved: following the pogroms of the mid-1950s and 1960s in retaliation to the Greek advances in Cyprus, no substantial Greek minority could be found in Istanbul or Izmir. This can be seen as a blatant violation of the Treaty of Lausanne and of the 1930 Ankara Convention, which provided for an approximately equal number of Western Thracian Muslims and Istanbul Greeks to be excluded from the compulsory population exchange of the 1920s.

Greece's Cyprus debacle was further complicated by the country's painful transition to democracy. Although the new political class under the leadership of Constantine Karamanlis successfully used the dictators as scapegoats, the entire polity and its bureaucratic apparatus went through a serious crisis for a variety of reasons. Greece, not having experienced any proper Keynesian policy-making in the 1950s and 1960s according to Western European patterns, was bound to adopt it at a time when welfare and redistribution policies were on the retreat everywhere, after the crisis of the Bretton Woods system (1971) and the first oil-shock triggered by the Yom Kippur war. To a certain extent, Karamanlis could afford to employ a Keynesian policy framework, as Greece had experienced a remarkable degree of growth and economic development during the 1960s and early 1970s. Thus, although harming profitability, the post-1974 political class under Karamanlis expanded state interventionism and boosted aggregate demand. This type of expansionary policy was to be followed by the PASOK (Panhellenic Socialist Movement) cabinets of Andreas Papandreou in the 1980s. However harmful in the long run, Greece's Keynesian and pro-welfare reforms under Karamanlis and Papandreou should be seen as a necessity dictated by the nature of the Greek polity and society, being, as they were, in their first stages of democratisation and politico-institutional renewal.

Karamanlis' policy decision to change Greece's defence doctrine was no 'bed of roses' either. In response to Turkey's second invasion of Cyprus (August 14–16, 1974), Karamanlis re-militarised the Eastern Aegean islands in defiance of the Treaty of Lausanne, and proclaimed that Greece's main security threat came from Turkey, and not from the Communist Northern Balkans. This later enabled Greece to support its legal demand that the issue of the Aegean should be solved at the International Court of Justice, and not bilaterally with Turkey, as Turkey's diplomacy was supported by the country's advantageous military positioning in Cyprus and the Aegean. At the same time, Karamanlis withdrew Greece from the military structure of NATO (a tactical move designed to appease popular discontent over Cyprus), and began preparing Greece's application for entering into the European Economic Communities. Skilfully separating Greece from the increasingly complex Iberian (Spanish and Portuguese) entry negotiations, Karamanlis successfully reached an accession agreement with the EEC in April 1979. Moreover, Greece, despite fierce Turkish opposition, restored itself within NATO's military command in 1980 and full membership of the EEC was achieved in 1981 leaving Turkey at a disadvantage, at least economically.[50] Papandreou's cabinets in the 1980s, despite their anti-EEC and anti-NATO rhetoric, did not reverse Karamanlis' foreign policy framework. In this context, Karamanlis might well be seen as a 'post-Cold War European politician' in the midst of the Cold War.

From then onwards, Greece responded to Turkish challenges primarily by fighting its corner within Europe's institutional framework. This has often, and at times unnecessarily, taken the form of either blocking European economic aid to Turkey and/or the country's efforts to become a full member of the EU. But at least since the mid-1990s, Greek objections to the development of EU–Turkey relations began, progressively, to wither away. Greece allowed Turkey to sign a customs union with the EU in 1995, and in return Turkey refrained from vetoing Cyprus' opening of negotiations to join the EU.[51]

5   Turkish Questions for the West

Our intention is to view Cyprus' European bid in the context of US global and regional strategic requirements. This perspective will enable us to firmly pronounce upon, among others, a key theme of this book: namely, which pivotal power figures more prominently in the US's strategic consideration with regard to Western Eurasia, Germany or Turkey? Moreover, this analytical perspective will make much clearer the antagonism between the US and the EU.

As we saw earlier while examining US strategy during and after the Cold War, these requirements render some EU states, particularly Germany and France, the chief strategic allies of the US in the Western Eurasian theatre to which Cyprus, Greece and Turkey belong. Nevertheless, we have also seen that there is considerable rivalry between the EU as a whole, and/or some key EU states, and the US. This antagonism, which was established during the Cold War over a number of defence and economic issues, has been further institutionalised in the 1990s with the political and economic development of the EU following the collapse of 'really existing socialism'. The EU–US relations indeed present some interesting features.

The EU is an economic giant but with clay military and political feet. Following its mid-1990s expansion, the EU had a larger population (370 million) and gross domestic product (GDP) than the US, while acting as the 'principal provider of Foreign Direct Investment (FDI) – both as a host economy and as a source economy'. Additionally, 'it provides 53 per cent of all official development assistance'.[1] It accounts for almost 30 per cent of the gross world product and its bilateral trade with the US in 2001 totalled around $500 billion.[2] Yet the EU is not a wholly independent actor in world politics. NATO institutionalises Europe's dependency upon the US, as the EU has failed to achieve the level of political, military and intelligence integration required in order to independently organise, administer and/or project power across the globe.

This said, however, the US cannot manipulate the EU at will, as if the latter were a mere foreign policy appendage of the former. The EU has several times raised its voice in opposition to the US over a wide range of political and economic issues. These include their different approaches to the Arab–Israeli conflict; issues concerning global trade (e.g. the 'banana war' of March 1999); protection tariffs (e.g. the US imposition of trade restrictions on Europe's steel in March 2002); or the issue of global warming.[3] In the early 2000s, the EU decided to invest some $3 billion in Gallileo, a satellite system that 'deliberately and needlessly', as *The Economist* put it, duplicates America's Global Positioning System.[4] The EU also opposes Cuba's US-led embargo, and another tension appeared between the EU and the US over the newly created International Criminal Court (ICC). At a UN Security Council session in June–July 2002, the US threatened to withdraw its troops from Bosnia, unless the Council agreed to grant UN peacekeepers immunity from the ICC. In autumn 2002, Germany stood up against a possible US-led attack on Iraq, without the approval of the UN security council.

With most of these issues the US has apparently been forced to seek compromises in order to re-establish and reconfirm its privileged partnership with the EU, and it is indeed rather impossible for the US, as Joseph Nye put it, to 'go it alone' despite its unique global supremacy. EU states may in the end 'jump on the bandwagon', but at a cost that the US has to pay. A unilateralist America leads indirectly Europe's political integration. Yet this is not always the case and the US has plenty of opportunities to play one European state off against another. This US tactic works simply because the EU is not a politically cohesive bloc itself and differences among its member states come to be crystallised in the institutional framework of NATO.

NATO, EU states and the US went to no post-Cold War military campaign or engagement completely unopposed from within. For example, France, a nuclear power, has broken (several times) Iraq's no-fly zone and Italy and Greece only reluctantly approved NATO's war over Kosovo. But not every European power agreed with Italy's or France's attitudes. Apart from the split among US strategists themselves in the 1990s over NATO's enlargement, the UK was a constant irritant to France and Germany with regard to forming a coherent and integrated European polity, which could encompass the formation of a European army outside NATO. In addition, as we saw earlier, the US military intervention in Bosnia was bound up with the strategic imperative of halting Germany's economic and political influence in the Balkans, an attempt that ended up 're-dividing' the Balkans between Germany, Russia and the US under the hegemony of the latter. A reshuffling of 'alliances within the alliance' often occurs as a result of the leverage the US can exercise upon key EU states on international economic platforms. For example, the Uruguay Round Agreement (1994), which established the regulatory framework of the WTO, induced Germany to embrace the US perspective of re-dividing the Balkans under the hegemony of the US. As a result, Germany had to discreetly brush aside its axis with France, offering its qualified support to the policy of the US during the Bosnian war.

The issue of EU–Turkey relations has generated another set of conflicting views between EU states and the US and, more particularly, between Germany and the US. This, in turn, especially during the years of the Christian Democratic coalition led by Chancellor Helmut Kohl, led to a diplomatic conflict between Germany and Turkey over a number of concrete issues concerning the nature of modern Turkish politics and society.

A Democracy Guided by the Military and Used as Such

The 'Turkish Question' is composed of a number of interrelated issues, which include – not in order of importance – the following:

a. Turkey's domestic economic, ethnic and religious problems;
b. A poor human rights record;
c. The centrality of the military in the Turkish political system;
d. Turkey's overt or covert dispute with almost any one of its neighbours;
e. The dispute over Cyprus and the Aegean with EU member, Greece.

I will examine each of these issues by raising EU and US policies towards Turkey. We shall become aware that some of the problems Turkey has been facing were not due to the incompetence of its political elite, but rather the result of its transatlantic partnership with the US. The issue is multidimensional and complicated, but, for the time being, suffice to say that Turkey has often found itself at odds with the US and in agreement with the EU over the ways in which the US attempted to use Turkey in the greater Middle Eastern theatre.

The framework I have opted to lay out and within which I would like to place my analysis is that Germany and the US share no common views on the 'Turkish Question'. This conflict has partially emerged in various EU summits, whose institutional decisions have tentatively benefited Greece at the expense of Turkey. In turn, this has had a major strategic implication for the US, because it has not been able to force Germany to adopt Turkey's positions regarding, for example, the question of Turkey's EU membership. Germany has been, and continues to be, the US's foremost strategic partner in the entire Western Eurasian zone. In this respect, Turkey loses points because the US, when forced to choose between Germany and Turkey, opts in favour of Germany. The theoretical and practical canon in international relations since the years of Thucydides is 'to go with the strongest and most important ally', and this is what the US did and does. But let us take up the thread of the story from the beginning.

Turkey was and is an amalgamation of ethnicities (e.g. nearly 16 out of 67 million of its population are Kurds), Islamic religious minorities (e.g. Suni and Alevis) and secular, pro-Western elites. As we shall establish in more detail below, this social pluralism has been badly administered by the political and military classes.[5] Turkey, since the emergence of a multiparty system in the 1950s, has always had an unstable political system overseen – to understate the case – by the military. It has often been administered by a coalition of parties. Towards the late 1990s, the second most important party in a coalition led by PM Bulent Ecevit, was the Nationalist Action Party (MHP), which is profoundly nationalistic.[6]

Contrary to what is assumed by some analysts, not every secular elite, either politico-military or economic, is pro-European.[7] Well-defined class and military interests that wish to preserve their privileges drawn from the state apparatus (e.g. administrative elites, state bourgeoisie and some military factions) are implacably against the country's entry into the EU. Ian Lesser put it as follows:

> The Turkish military and the bureaucracy have been more resistant to reforms, including economic reforms, which they view as threatening to the security, integrity, and welfare of the state. Ironically, these two institutions have been pillars of the modern Republic and staunch supporters of an Ataturkist vision of modernity. As many Turks will now admit, the economic dimension of this vision, with its emphasis on statism and cen-tralisation, no longer looks very modern in light of liberalisation and decentralisation elsewhere. The evolution of the Turkish debate on these issues will shape the outlook for Turkey in the 21st century, as well as the continued viability of US and European views of Turkey as a developmental 'model'.[8]

Powerful factions within the secular military have indeed opposed Turkey's European perspective on the grounds that any democratisation/federalisation of the country on the basis of the *acquis* would lead to the eventual fragmentation/partition of Turkey (a similar view is also adopted by some hardcore factions of the MHP). This view is often presented through suggestions that the EU is not serious about accepting Turkey as a member, and that therefore Turkey should contemplate altering its pro-Western alliance system, by shifting it toward Iran and Russia. Although this may be mere rhetoric, testing the nerves of the EU–US, it is nevertheless an indication that leading military factions do not wish the Turkish EU membership to take place on Europe's terms alone.[9] In sum, the Eurosceptic stance of some powerful factions in the Turkish establishment is exemplified by the assertion that 'it is the EU that should change in order for Turkey to become a member, and not vice versa'.[10]

Islam dominates social attitudes, customs and mores and it is barely tolerated by the secular military and political elites. However, because it is deeply-seated, not only in Turkey's social identity, but also in the country's political system, both the EU and the US have vigorously opposed any pro-Islam turnabout in Turkey's domestic arena.[11] This imposes additional stress on the military – which is not a coherent bloc itself – to increase its authoritarian grip on the Islamic parties, not least because some EU leaders themselves, mostly Christian Democrats, have used Turkey's Muslim identity as a pretext to deny the country EU membership. But the issue is far more complicated.

In the first place, Islamic political parties and agencies, on the one hand, and Turkish nationalists on the other, tend to emulate and 'compete' with each other about who is more nationalistic. Turkish Islamists have over the years at times been more nationalistic and patriotic than some factions of Turkish nationalism itself. For example, during the 1974 Cyprus crisis, the bizarre coalition cabinet led by socialist Bulent Ecevit and the Islamist Necmettin Erbakan was not only fully supportive of the invasions, but it also discussed Erbakan's firm proposal that Turkey should consider taking the whole of Cyprus.[12] In the post-Cold War era, Turkey's Islamic parties and agencies have advanced an educational and economic policy aiming at regenerating Turkey's influence in the post-Soviet Turkic/Islamic republics of the Caucasus/Central Asia. Yet certain hardcore secular nationalist factions go beyond even the Islamic patriotic horizon: under the ideological influence of the pan-Turkism of Ziya Gokalp, they envisage the recreation of a greater Turkey, which resembles the Ottoman Empire and extends from the Balkans to China. According to this set of pan-Turkic ideas, the Turkic territorial zone should be called Turan, after the mythical perception of the Turanian land, which extended from the Balkans to China, Northern Africa and the Middle East.[13]

The bizarre socio-political mix of the two competing nationalisms of Islam and pan-Turkism has been one of the circumstances that has caused Turkey to present a rather inconsistent and confusing pattern of foreign policy toward Islamic/Turkic states in the Caucasian region and the various Muslim minorities in the Balkans. The Turkish military has invariably been trying to perform a balancing act between the secular and Islamic nationalist branches, by prosecuting Islamists *within* the country, while, albeit selectively, championing their rights *outside* it.[14] For instance, as we saw earlier, and in concert with other Muslim states, a firm ingredient of Turkish foreign policy projection in the Balkans after the end of the Cold War, has been the promotion of the rights of Muslim minorities. Yet, even this policy scheme has not been politically consistent and thus fully successful, and the reason, at a first sight, is very simple. The Turkish government itself has been somewhat reluctant to forcefully demand minority rights for the ethnic Turks or Muslims of the Balkans, as it has been unwilling to grant those minority rights to the Kurds of Turkey. Admittedly, this set of contradictions that cut across the political–cultural linkages between Turkey's domestic and foreign policies is just one factor that tends to contain the country's regional influence. In reality, Turkey's projection of authority in the Balkans and the Caspian region has been contained for a number of other complementary and far more important reasons.

First, the Russian and Iranian factors in the Caspian and the Caucasus and the way in which the US viewed Turkey's role in the greater Middle East prevented Turkey from increasing its influence there. Second, and perhaps more importantly, the Turkish economic problems per se thwarted any coherent advance of Turkish pro-Muslim foreign policy. To these two reasons one may, paradoxically, add Turkey's alliance with Israel. While it is true that the Turkish–Israeli axis strengthens Turkey's hand in foreign affairs, at the same time it disconnects the country's religious link with the Arab and other Islamic states. We shall deal with the Turkish–Israeli axis in the next chapter. For the time being, it is sufficient to look at the limits of Turkish power by examining briefly three issues: first, the clash between Turkish and Russian interests in the Caspian region; second, how the US is inclined to use Turkey in the greater Middle East; third, how Turkey's economic problems affect the country's general performance and image projection.

To start with, we should make it as clear as possible that Turkey's interest in the post-Soviet republics surrounding the Caspian, or in the Balkans, was not, and is not, based simply on the linguistic or ethnic affinities it enjoys with those republics. In point of fact, Turkey has tried to capitalise on the ethno-linguistic factor in order to exploit the region's resources, thus meeting 'its increasing energy requirements',[15] or as Bulent Aras put it:

> [Turkey has hoped] to find guaranteed access to vital energy resources, lucrative oil transport revenues, and new markets for Turkish goods, especially in Azerbaijan, Turkmenistan, and Kazakhstan. It has been estimated that Turkey will have to import roughly 55 million tons of oil annually by the year 2010 to maintain the present course of its economic development.[16]

Thus, with regard to the Caspian region, the country's policy has been straightforward. As well as wanting to construct and make economically viable the Baku–Ceyhan pipeline, Turkey has viewed the building of a gas pipeline between the Caspian littoral state of Turkmenistan and Anatolia as of paramount importance. This project aims at bypassing 'alternative routes such as the Russian "Blue Stream" project – dubbed "Blue Dream" by critics – to transport natural gas to Turkey underneath the Black Sea'.[17] In this context, Turkey did not hesitate to antagonise the Russians in the 1990s, by supporting the Chechens, and also by siding with the Azeris in their conflict with Armenia for control over energy resources and Nagorno-Karabach. In this, the US offered Turkey no assistance, as it could not jeopardise its developing relationship with Russia for the sake of the projection of Turkish influence in the Caspian region. Moreover, Turkey received support from the US in the mid-1990s regarding the Baku–Ceyhan project, but not in its conflict with Moscow over the Turkmenistan–Anatolia gas pipeline.[18] But even in the case of the Baku–Ceyhan project, the US could not throw its whole weight behind Turkey, because that would have entailed alienation of Russia. Meliha Altunisik has commented on the issue as follows:

After intense diplomatic efforts, in January 1995, the US government declared its support for a 'pipeline through Turkey' [the Baku–Ceyhan project]. However, this idea was presented in a general framework of US policy of 'multiple pipelines'. The US government did not want to alienate Russia altogether. On the other hand, for economic and political reasons Washington did not want one country to control the tap. This became the cornerstone of US policy throughout the 'pipeline politics'. At times the US government put pressure on the Turkish government to negotiate with Russia as well.[19]

Admittedly, there is much more to the issue of Turkey–US relations, which induced Turkey to produce an uninspiring and confusing foreign policy. For example, BP's new role in the operation of the pipeline in autumn 2002 and the determination of the US to assist the project and the three countries involved (Azerbaijan, Georgia, Turkey), served the need of the US to win over Turkey against Saddam's regime in Iraq. At the same time, the US was offering an alternative source of energy for Georgia, which is heavily dependent on Russia. In the end, the way in which the US has used Turkey and other regional and ethnic actors in the greater Middle Eastern theatre has created several grievances on the part of both Turkey and the EU.

Turkey has vested interests in developing good relations with both Iran and Iraq, an attitude viewed very positively by the EU.[20] Iraq is Turkey's third largest trading partner and its largest oil supplier. Yet the US put pressure on Turkey to accept a possible American-led bombing of Iraq after September 11. Moreover, the US, in its effort to liquidate Saddam's regime, renewed its contacts with Kurdish political factions in Northern Iraq in order to use them against Saddam. In return, the US promised guaranteed autonomy to the Iraqi Kurds, but Turkey strongly opposed this and it would probably have little choice but to deploy troops in Northern Iraq in order to prevent the possible formation of a breakaway Kurdish state, following Saddam's fall. Understandably, Turkey fears that the autonomy of Iraqi Kurds would encourage the Kurds in Turkey to unite with their Iraqi brethren, breaking up Turkey and creating a greater Kurdistan. Turkey had also raised objections to the US suggestion to lead the International Security Assistance Force (ISAF) in Afghanistan, in case the force was to be established there permanently. Turkey's attitude in this instance has greatly upset the US. The US tends to see post-Cold War Turkey as no more than a 'key front-line state'[21] in the project of aggression against clerical Iran and Iraq, in order to secure influence of, and control over undisciplined oil-producing states and subregions in the greater Middle East. This Turkish 'front-line' role might be negated if Iran and/or Iraq adopted a pro-American posture, but this is not the case for the time being.[22] All in all, the US balancing act between Russia and Turkey, coupled with the pressure the US has exercised on Turkey in relation to Iran and Iraq, has induced Turkey to produce an inconsistent foreign policy output, which is arguably confusing and causes embarrassment to the EU. But there are also some other issues that cannot be ignored.

Turkey is viewed by both the EU and the US as having a constantly ailing economy: witness endemic inflation; a huge public debt and deficit; a weak banking sector; high interest rates; negative rate of industrial production; and an unstable current account. Furthermore, nearly 45 per cent of its population is employed in agriculture and the economy is still predominately run by the state. Turkey has been in constant need of IMF injections of funds in order to stave off economic and monetary crises. These economic constraints put a huge strain on Turkey's resources and have made it enormously difficult to provide the aid she promised to the Turkic states of the Caucasus and the Caspian.[23] In addition, the IMF imposes further neo-liberal conditions on Turkey to carry out the reforms required (e.g. increase the pace of privatisation) and this widens the gap between the bulk of the poor masses of Anatolia and the middle-to-upper-middle classes.

Yet it is not quite right to talk of Turkey as being a homogeneous socio-economic zone, with the class cleavages somewhat proportionally spread out in Anatolia. Western Turkey and Eastern Turkey are two different worlds, much more so than is the case, for example, *mutatis mutandis*, in the split between Italy's industrial North and underdeveloped South. In particular, and because of the predominately Kurdish character of the region, Turkey's South-east has been wholly neglected by the state's social and economic policies.[24]

The EU's concern with regard to Turkey's poor human rights record is partly rhetoric, disguising Europe's and Germany's strategic calculations, and partly reality, reflecting a serious problem of the Turkish polity. In any case, it is an issue inextricably linked to those of Liberal Democracy and security: the Turkish military elite's way of handling those issues creates more problems for Europe and Turkey itself than it solves.

The prevailing view within the Turkish Kemalist establishment is that the country's unity can be preserved through the prevention of the expression of social, religious and ethnic pluralism at the political, legal and ideological levels. Beyond the fact that this runs against the EU's 1993 Copenhagen political criteria, the EU has no vested interest in accepting a semi-authoritarian Turkey in its ranks, as it might endanger its internal security balance. By extension, the US, under Germany's influence, seems to be reluctant also to accept the possibility of a critical destabilisation of the EU on the way to its eastward enlargement, by pushing the EU to incorporate the problematic mosaic of Turkey. The EU/German position has been a straightforward Liberal Democratic one: Turkey's democratisation prior to accession would peacefully defuse domestic tensions; as a democratic polity it would be able to absorb class, ethnic and religious cleavages, thus politically integrating the pronounced post-Cold War dynamism of Turkish society. The EU has assessed that by admitting Turkey, as it is, or with minimal improvements, it might put in jeopardy its political and economic security. Moreover, EU member states have not agreed to the transfer of the IMF's obligation towards Turkey onto the EU's regional and structural funds, and France in particular has objected to the dismemberment of the Common Agricultural Policy (CAP), which is bound to happen with the entry of Turkey. Furthermore, accepting Turkey as it is, or 'on its own terms', would create a wholly negative precedent in the conduct of the *acquis*.

The EU's 'democratisation stance' in the 1990s was primarily led by Germany, mainly because of the conflicting nature of German/Turkish interests in the Balkans and the Black Sea region. In addition, there were/are certain, rather unfounded, fears that a European Turkey would exacerbate the strain on Germany's economy via labour-driven immigration from Turkey.[25] To these two reasons, one could add the reluctance of the ruling CDU–CSU coalition under Helmut Kohl to accept Turkey as a member of the EU, a reluctance that the post-1998/99 cabinet of the SPD-led coalition under Gerhard Schroeder did not share.

In any event, the Turkish military, at times backed by anti-modernising class factions dependent on the state machine, has tended to resist the EU's and Germany's 'democratisation stance'. This, *inter alia*, has been due to a self-serving assumption that Turkey's military might, fully assisted by the US, possesses such capabilities that it could successfully conduct wars, if need be, on two and one-half different fronts.[26] The army has thus been able to take risks by undertaking independent and even provocative actions, either in order to create *fait accomplis* and/or to restore domestic stability, and/or to legitimise the political position of specific elites. In this context, the military can be seen as a player that not only anchors the cohesion of the Turkish polity, but also as a body that directly exercises foreign and domestic policies, without the democratic and deterring mediation of political classes and diplomatic services.

From this perspective, it is no accident that Turkey has been eager to resort to a display of power and determination towards Greece and Cyprus in order to defuse organic domestic crises. For example, PM Tansu Ciller, in an attempt to reinforce her political position after inconclusive elections in December 1995, appealed to Turkish nationalism by disembarking Turkish journalists and commandos on the Greek Aegean islets of Imia, who took down the Greek flag. Both countries swiftly began amassing their fleets in the Aegean, and the crisis was finally defused after personal intervention from the US President Clinton, with both parties agreeing to leave the islets without a national symbol (the drawing of 'grey zones' in the Aegean). On the one hand, this episode, the worst between Greece and Turkey since 1987, was a troubling reminder of Turkey's domestic problems, rather than a bad foreign policy test for the newly formed Greek cabinet under the 'Third Way' Social Democratic leadership of Costas Simitis (January–February 1996). On the other, it irritated the US leadership, because a Greek–Turkish confrontation in the wake of the Dayton accords, which had just stopped the war in Bosnia, was rightly viewed as nonsensical.[27]

The US and the 'Turkish Pivot'

Despite the fact that the US seems to be officially supporting the main tenets of EU and German policy towards Turkey, it nevertheless adopts an essentially different approach on how to solve the 'Turkish Question', particularly with regard to the issue of democratisation of the Turkish polity. According to the US, the democratisation of Turkey is a matter of it becoming an EU member, and not of it being left outside the 'club', achieving Western standards of Liberal Democracy prior to membership. As Turkey is America's fundamental geo-political pivot in the Near East, the US maintains that it is the EU institutional framework that should resolve Turkey's problems, and not Turkey itself. 'Turkey is a critical geo-political pivot', Sbigniew Brzezinski observed, but at the same time it 'confronts serious domestic problems and its capacity for effecting major regional shifts in the distribution of power is limited'.[28] This strategic assessment fosters the US notion that EU membership for Turkey would enhance US leverage over Turkey's and Europe's affairs and, by extension, over the greater Middle East. Sabri Sayari, Executive Director of the Institute for Turkish Studies at Georgetown University in Washington, saw it as follows:

> From Washington's perspective, Turkey remains an important ally with a strategic role in a number of regional problems that concern American national interests. These include the Gulf and Eastern Mediterranean contigencies, stability in the Balkans and the Caucasus, and Caspian energy development. As a result of the perceived continued importance of Turkey for US national interests and foreign policy objectives, Washington supports Turkey's bid to become a full EU member, promotes Turkey's desire to have one of the main pipelines for the transport of Azeri oil to the Western markets [the Ceyhan–Baku project], and seeks to expand investment and trade ties with Turkey.[29]

Yet there are some other important reasons why the US wants Turkey to become an EU member 'as soon as possible'.

Turkey's EU membership is considered by the US to be a way of decoupling Islamic fundamentalism from mainstream Turkish politics. As the Turkish ethno-linguistic zone extends from the Caucasus to China, Turkey, *inter alia*, can project a modern and secular image of Islam that helps the US to isolate Islamic fundamentalist notions, particularly after September 11. However, as we saw earlier, this policy takes on confrontational geo-political dimensions with regard to clerical Iran and Iraq, and both Turkey and the EU are reluctant to endorse it. There has already been an understanding between Turkey and the EU against the US stance of seeing Turkey as a 'front-line state' of aggression. Thus, Graham Fuller's assertion that, in their relations with Turkey, 'Washington is driven nearly exclusively by geo-political and strategic considerations' whereas Europe 'by several more concrete considerations', is mainly correct.[30]

However, a strengthening of US–Turkey ties through Turkey's EU membership is only one strategic aspect among many others. Along broad lines, in fact, two scenarios might possibly unfold. In the first place, and with Turkey as a member, the US might be in a position to play both Turkey and the UK off against Germany/the EU in Middle Eastern and Central Asian matters. This may well be combined with the use of the Israeli pivot, turning realities in Western Eurasia and the Mediterranean against a possible German/French/Italian stance. In such a scenario, the Russian and the Chinese factors would hold the key, as they would be tempted to endorse either a US-led alliance or a continental/European one. In any event, however, the US would do everything possible to ensure a stronger policy card against a possible Franco-German front if Turkey becomes an EU member. But there is a counter-scenario to this.

A European Turkey may well weaken the Turkish–Israeli axis and induce a closer partnership between Germany, France and Turkey, thus disqualifying the leverage of the US over Turkey. The creation of such a bloc may also draw Israel into the equation, swiftly producing an even more positive understanding between the EU and the Arab states. This understanding, coupled with the economic projection of the euro in Middle Eastern deals over oil and other energy resources, would completely undermine US economic power there.[31] The US is the world's biggest debtor, but its debt is denominated in dollars. The US economy would be very vulnerable 'if a significant proportion of Middle East oil revenues were switched to another currency'.[32] In this context, the EU–US battle for influence over Turkey must be viewed as truly open and of paramount importance, with an outcome that cannot be predicted.

The special understanding between the US and Turkey with regard to the Near and the Middle East has always been based on the principle of *unbalanced reciprocity*. Turkey offers ample rewards to the US for the latter's economic, military and political support. Turkey's backing of the US war policy in the Gulf in the early 1990s cost Turkey the 'closure of the oil pipeline from Iraq, together with the loss of Middle East trade, [which is] estimated to have cost Turkey up to $9 billion in lost revenue'.[33] Throughout the 1990s, the US used the Turkish air bases of Incirlik and Diyarbakir for its daily military operations against Iraqi targets. The US also used these air bases, together with the UK's bases in Dekhelia and Akrotiri/Episkopi in Cyprus, during their campaign in Afghanistan in 2001–02. Nevertheless, and despite the initiation at the Baku–Ceyhan project, Turkey, along with Jordan and other Middle Eastern States, was reluctant to endure a new fully-fledged campaign against Iraq.[34] Given that a major US attack against Iraq should not be excluded after September 11, Incirlik, Diyarbakir, as well as the UK's Cyprus bases assume particular military and intelligence significance. There are also various joint economic ventures between Turkey and the US, and Turkey is one of the largest recipients of US military equipment.

The special understanding between the US and Turkey also concerns the balancing and the containment of Russia in the Caucasus and the Caspian. Although the US has been reluctant to extend support to Turkey's anti-Russian policy in Chechnya and Azerbaijan, Turkey acts as a deterrent to possible Russian projections, which may threaten American interests in the Caspian and the Caucasus. Moreover, encouraged by the US, Turkey has managed to strengthen ties with Ukraine, a key country in the very security zone of Russia that the US wants fully on its side. In June 1997, Turkey signed an agreement with Ukraine 'for the construction of a pipeline between the port of Ceyhan on Turkey's Mediterranean coast and its Black Sea port of Samsun'. Among other things, this 'pipeline could help Ukraine reduce its dependence on Russian oil'.[35] The US indeed views the post-Cold War Turkey as a country with a multi-dimensional 'front-line' role covering the Caspian–Middle East–Balkan arc. But partly because of the geo-political weight Russia and China carry for the US, and partly because of Turkish economic sluggishness and/or Turkish interests in Iraq, Iran and Middle Eastern trade, this Turkish role is severely constrained.

This set of constraints notwithstanding, the post-Cold War multidimensional 'front-line' role assigned to Turkey by the US appears to have benefited the co-operation between the two countries on the basis of the same principle of 'unbalanced reci-procity'. Since the early 1990s, US–Turkey relations 'have been increasingly de-coupled from Greek–Turkish relations'.[36] For example, the US no longer links military aid to Turkey with a viable and lasting solution to the Cyprus issue. Moreover, in 2002, Turkey completed a successful agreement with the US and the UK over the EU's Security and Defence Identity (ESDI). To Greece's chagrin, Turkey has managed to exclude from ESDI operations the tension zones of Cyprus and the Aegean.[37] In return, Turkey agreed to let the EU use NATO assets based in Turkey. The US has thus achieved a major objective, that is the dependence of the EU Rapid Reaction Force on NATO assets, while at the same time Turkey has safeguarded its own national interests at the expense of Greece.[38] Although the whole affair remains unresolved at EU level at the time of writing, the fact is that the decoupling method tends to disfavour Greece and the EU's political role in Central Asia and the Middle East.

Summing up the Realist Game

It is appropriate now, before entering into a discussion of Cyprus' EU prospects, to reinforce and expand the set of concluding remarks put forward in the previous chapters. The US pursues its policy in the Balkans and the Middle East by aggressively expanding its Cold War strategic framework of security and defence principles. A great achievement of US policy since the Cold War has been the 'reunification' of the Balkans and the Near East for planning, strategic and economic purposes. However, this 'reunification' was achieved through the 're-division' of the Balkans and the new post-Soviet republics of East-Central Europe between Germany, Russia and the US, under the aegis of the latter. Hence the US support to Germany's eastward drive via the enlargement of the EU.

The Cold War notion of a 'Northern Tier' tends thus towards becoming Western Eurasia's thick strategic belt surrounding Russia and China. Although Iran has been absent from the chain's rattling equation since 1979, Afghanistan and other crucial Middle Eastern states and subregions have been fully restored to American interests, at least since the Gulf War. True, there are also other disobedient actors in the greater Middle East, such as Iraq, Syria and Libya, but substantial progress has already been made towards achieving the key objectives: the encircling of Russia and China; the control over energy pipeline projects; and the elimination of hostile competitors. The US is aiming at achieving a settlement in the greater Middle East similar to that achieved in the Balkans: namely the 're-division' of the region between itself and the key Eurasian actors under US hegemony. During the Cold War, particularly when encountering the nationalism of Nasser, the Arab–Israeli conflict, Europe's pronounced antagonism, the Cyprus conflict and the USSR's military might, the US experienced far greater problems in controlling the Middle Eastern game than it does today.

In the light of this, European Greece and NATO Turkey are still significant pawns on the Near Eastern chessboard and they continue to be considered by the US as a united geo-strategic bloc. Similarly, both countries are viewed as factors of stability in the wider zone stretching from the Black Sea and the Balkans, to the Eastern Mediterranean and the Caucasus. The Aegean remains a key international sea route and Greek–Turkish friendship is seen by the US as a vital precondition for the avoidance of hostilities, and thus the avoidance of the disruption of sea trade, pipeline projects and FIRs (flight information regions).

In continuity with its Cold War policy, the US wants a permanent and lasting solution to the Cyprus issue, as long as this solution satisfies both Greece and Turkey in the framework of NATO and the EU. In the same vein, however, Turkey continues to be seen as strategically more important than Greece, a conclusion which can be drawn from a number of factors. These factors include the US attitude towards episodes of confrontation between Greece and Turkey in the Aegean and Cyprus since 1974; continued IMF and World Bank support to Turkey, despite various Turkish defaults; and the US backing of Turkey in various European fora pressing the EU to offer Turkey full membership (see next chapter). In addition, post-September 11 events have upgraded further Turkey's pivotal geo-political role.

But Turkey's regional geo-strategic primacy, today as in the past, is not a quasi-unaltered structural condition. As we have seen, and as we shall establish in more detail below, there have been serious disagreements between Turkey and the US, on the one hand, and between the EU and the US over Turkey's geo-political role and domestic problems, on the other. Moreover, in the institutionalised framework of NATO and the EU, the US tends to see Germany as more important than Turkey in the overall Western Eurasian chessboard. In this respect, Turkey is forced to refine its foreign policy according to changing political circumstances. Similarly, the outcome of the Greek–Turkish antagonism can only be seen as a result of successful pursuance of economic, political and defence diplomacy by all parties concerned, as well as of other regional variables in Western Eurasia, rather than as a predetermined result based on abstract geo-strategic considerations. I would argue that Greece has diagnosed Germany's importance for the US in Western Eurasia and, because of this, it plays the Cyprus game in the EU very cleverly and tactfully.

When balancing Turkey's problematic linkages between domestic and foreign affairs, on the one hand, with the country's strategic contribution to the US Eurasian policy on the other, the superpower opts in favour of supporting the Turkish pivot in the Near East. Time and again, this should be seen as a result of successful bargaining at politico-military and economic levels between Turkey, EU states and the US, and not as an *a priori* set decision based solely on Turkey's structural geo-strategic primacy in the greater Middle East. Furthermore, as it will become clearer below, Turkey is not more important than Germany, both in Western Eurasia and in global terms. Turkey is thus forced to make a number of compromises, most of which reflect the power and political volition of the EU states and Germany in various international fora. For example, under pressure both from the EU and US, Turkey agreed to launch a courageous process of political and economic reforms. Although wholly incomplete by European standards as, for example, broadcasting in Kurdish was actually forbidden by the existing broadcasting law, the reforms launched in 2001–02 were definitely a sign of good will and are bound to deepen during the course of the next decade.[39] Moreover, and despite the fact that Turkey's political class is rather careless about regional and class cleavages, Turkey bargains successfully with the US over IMF handouts.

The primary objective of the US pro-European stance regarding the accession of Turkey is *geo-strategic*. Turkey has the second largest standing army in NATO and manages to strengthen its military position in the neuralgic zone of the Balkans and the Middle East. Additionally, by bringing Turkey into the EU 'as quickly as possible', the US would be able to exercise additional pressure on Turkey for the support of its policies against 'rogue states' in the Middle East. Although the US has not supported Turkey at the expense of Russia in the Caucasus and the Caspian regions, the fact is that the Turkish Eurasian East can still be used as a crucial deterrent against any unwanted pro-Russian or even pro-Chinese developments in the area.[40] In this respect, *mutatis mutandis*, it is not an exaggeration to assume that the US seems to be considering Turkey as the Germany of the Middle East.

The secondary, but equally important, objective of the US is *economic*. As outlined earlier, the US and the UK are the strongest supporters of Turkey joining the EU as huge amounts of IMF cash now pouring into Turkey will be replaced by the EU's regional and structural funds. No matter that Turkey's entry will totally destroy the EU's crippling Common Agricultural Policy (CAP). This is a worry of the French, the Greek and, in the context of eastward enlargement, of the Polish farmer, but not of the US or the UK. After all, the US has been arguing since the early 1960s against the CAP, as it has created a protection shield against American exporters, restricting their access to Europe's agricultural market.

EU states, led by Germany and Greece, have since the mid-1990s emphasised the imperative of Turkey's democratisation prior to its accession. This demand has been bound up with the issues of Turkey's poor human rights record, the leading position of its military in the political system (a 'military democracy')[41] and other matters of economic (a developing economy) and political (the Kurdish issue, the Cyprus issue) security, all of which are interlinked. It appears that the EU wants to standardise Turkey's economy and polity in accordance with its norms, and then accept Turkey as a member, thus facilitating the incorporation of a large country into its structures without major aftershocks. On the contrary, and in order to serve its geo-strategic purposes, the US has declared Turkey's EU membership as a condition *sine qua non* for its democratisation.

Having said this, I would argue that the US struggle for mastery in the Balkans and the greater Middle East today, as well as the particular strategic importance attributed to Turkey, should be seen as an extension of the US's victorious Cold War strategy. This assessment, however, is subject to periodical revisions according to the changing diplomatic and geo-political balance of force. *In this rounded equation Turkey cannot and does not supersede Germany's geo-strategic importance in the overall West Eurasian belt.*

We can now shed further light on the issue of Cyprus–EU relations viewed in the wider strategic context of Eurasia, thus exemplifying, among other things, the strategic primacy of Germany in comparison to Turkey.

6 Eurasian Gambles Over Cyprus' EU Prospects

Over the years, a plethora of strategic analysts and historians, with or without expertise on the Cyprus issue, have arguably recognised the crucial role of international factors on the Cypriot domestic political stage. By and large, their rationale has been based chiefly on the geo-political location of the island in the Eastern Mediterranean, overlooking the Middle East and the Suez Canal. Myriad top secret declassified documents have shed light on the linkages between the island's strategic site and the geo-political considerations of foreign and security analysts of superpowers in the greater Middle East.[1] The ruling classes representing the (majority) Greeks and the (minority) Muslims – later Turkish Cypriots – on the island were periodically, and rather cleverly, manipulated by far more powerful, exogenous actors. Thus, in modern history, if Cyprus came to be under the grip of the dominant power in the Eastern Mediterranean, this was mainly so because it was seen as a launching pad towards the domination of oil and gas producing regions. Had the declining Ottoman Empire been fully aware of the long-term strategic significance of this oil potential, it would perhaps have never leased Cyprus to Britain in 1878. Greece had its chances between 1912 and 1922, but its warships, although good at laying a grip on the Aegean islands, could not project power deeper into the Eastern Mediterranean. Had Greece been able during the Balkans wars, or soon thereafter, to do so, guaranteeing the security of Britain's communication lines, Lloyd George's Britain would not have objected to this as long as a reasonable *quid pro quo* was offered on the part of Greece.[2]

Arguably then, bar the study of Soviet policy toward Cyprus,[3] we do indeed possess a remarkable number of scholarly works on the international and strategic aspects of the Cyprus issue focusing on the period stretching from between the wars up to the 1970s. Regrettably though, despite the widely held view that the Cyprus issue remains perhaps one of the most intractable politico-strategic affairs in international relations today, this has not led contemporary students of

Cyprus–EU relations to seriously advance their analyses beyond a mere acknowledgement of this fact. What do we mean by that?

There is a lack of published material focusing on the international dynamics and strategic aspects of Cyprus–EU relations. At best, contemporary analysts of Cyprus–EU relations peripheralise the Eurasian and even the Near Eastern dimension of the issue, focusing instead on institutional aspects of the discussion and/or on themes concerning the 'structural adjustment' of Cypriot economy and society according to the norms of the EU.[4] At worst – unfortunately, this is the largest group of commentators – they tend to become hostage to describing scenarios and contingencies applicable in the event of either Greece or Turkey turning out to be dissatisfied with the EU's policy in solving the Cyprus issue via the island's accession.[5] In sum, when we engage ourselves with analyses concerning EU–Cyprus relations, we usually come to realise that they brush aside crucial geo-strategic dimensions of the Cyprus issue, dimensions which occupy a key position in the US's and EU's economic, foreign and security policies.

I argue that we need to have a sound understanding of the strategic context within which Cyprus' European gamble is located in order to pronounce confidently upon its EU prospects. I thus locate Cyprus in the global dynamic context of US and EU policies in Eurasia and in the regional context of the greater Middle East, mainly focusing upon the post-Cold War period. The requirement is to decipher the parameters and the linkages of the balance of power in the Eurasian region, and in its Near Eastern subregion, to which Cyprus belongs. The analytical framework I attempt to construct on this issue, in order to situate Cyprus' multidimensional geo-politics, is that the US considers its strategic partnership with Germany and France as more important than that with Turkey. Further, that if the US were forced to choose – in terms of their functional primacy in the Western Eurasian theatre – between an Atlantic Germany leading the EU's eastward enlargement and Turkey, then the superpower would opt for Germany. Although never officially declared, I am inclined to believe that Greece's gamble that it would block EU enlargement if Cyprus is not admitted to the EU, is almost entirely placed within the remit of this strategic assessment.[6]

Subsequently, I examine more closely Cyprus' European perspective by focusing on the political positions of both sides, Greek and Turkish Cypriot alike, and trying to diagnose the strategic reasoning that underpins their positions. I argue that Greece and the Republic of Cyprus have employed the EU/Germany diplomatic card in the background and the legal card up front, as Turkey has lacked legitimate grounds since 1963–4 to defend its claims and politico-military position in Cyprus. Turkey, on the contrary, has counted on its own regional geo-strategic primacy and military superiority, with almost all other arguments put forward being epiphenomena of its strong geo-political dimension, in order to buy time. My overall tentative assessment is that Cyprus' European membership was bound to hang on a positive diplomatic and strategic balance in the 1990s and early 2000s, meaning that Cyprus' European gamble may well produce a final settlement on the island. This would represent a major achievement for the EU, in that it would reaffirm a strong foreign policy stance, which differs in substance from that of Turkey and the US.

However, the perspective of a just and lasting solution to the Cyprus issue via the EU factor may be thwarted, because in current affairs we cannot predict the degree of tactful defence, economic and political diplomacy that each party will pursue. Nor can we forsee the ways in which the Iraqi crisis would impact upon the diplomatic bargaining power of all actors concerned, that is to say, first and foremost, Turkey. Thus, *ceteris paribus*, and as things stood in the early 2000s, Cyprus' EU membership was to take place with or without a solution to the island's *de facto* division. This much we know. Going beyond that, entails falling into line with conjectures that are wholly alarmist and highly speculative. But stepping backwards, means confining ourselves to an analysis of the official reports and statements of the parties involved, thus remaining on the surface of things.

EU–Cyprus Relations and Germany's Primacy

Our analyses so far indicate the geo-strategic primacy of Turkey in respect of the position of Greece and Cyprus, but not with regard to that of the EU and/or Germany and Greece put together. As Brzezinski argues authoritatively, Germany, in the first place, and France are 'the Eurasian bridgehead(s) for American power and the potential springboard for the democratic global system's expansion into Eurasia'.[7] We have also argued that the US post-Cold War policy and strategic evaluation of the Near East are but an extension of its Cold War notions. No major strategic break between the US Cold War and post-Cold War policy occurred with regard to Eurasia and its Near and Middle Eastern subregions. All geo-political actors have behaved within the remit of the transfiguration of the new balance of power in the 1990s and the US has proceeded with a necessary revision of its guiding Cold War strategic principles. But this revision was neither a break with the past nor a radical U-turn marked by events, such as would be, for instance, the abolition of NATO. The new post-Cold War setting was thus as follows: the US was the victor, united European Germany and China became stronger, and Russia was the loser. In the 1990s, the Balkans were to be 're-divided' not between the USSR/Russia and the US/West as in the 1940s, but between the US, Germany and Russia under the paramount supremacy of the former. The US is seeking to achieve a similar settlement in Central Asia and the Middle East, efforts that have been intensified, particularly after September 11. The US has extended/expanded its Cold War hegemonic policies, it has not abandoned them.

Germany has been the driving force behind the EU's eastward enlargement and France behind its southward Mediterranean and Middle Eastern projection. First proposed by the Italians in 1989, a Conference on Security and Co-operation in the Mediterranean (CSCM) was modelled on the Conference/Organisation of/for Security and Co-operation in Europe (OSCE) and was placed under French leadership. Other South European countries joined in the French–Italian chorus, as well as 'North African countries, Turkey, Jordan, the PLO [Palestine Liberation Organisation] and the Labour Party leadership in Israel'.[8] This project evolved into the Euro-Mediterranean Conference in Barcelona in November 1995, which produced a more concrete partnership programme, providing for a 'Euro-Med' free trade area by 2010 and an increase in EU aid to the region.[9] Overall, the French idea is that 'free trade and more aid will enhance stability and prosperity on the Southern and Eastern Mediterranean rim, foster cross-border trade within that region, underpin the Middle East peace process, and help advance pluralism in a region where authoritarian government is the norm'.[10] The 'Euro-Med' project created another point of friction between France/EU and the US. The Americans were not invited to attend the Barcelona Conference and they had 'organised almost at the same time a Middle East/North Africa economic summit in Amman, Jordan (which Syria refused to attend), to which an impressive mix of industrialists, financiers and officials were invited'.[11]

Brzezinski concedes that as a percentage of overall budget Germany's contribution to the EU is 28.5 per cent, to NATO 22.8 per cent and to the UN 8.93 per cent. In addition, Germany is the largest shareholder in the World Bank and the EBRD (European Bank for Reconstruction and Development) – the latter being substantially involved in the EU's Stability Pact for the reconstruction of the Balkans.[12] Germany is a global economic power and the politico-economic locomotive of the EU. Strategically positioned at the heart of Europe, Germany's Southern flank is safeguarded by the position of friendly Austria and their joint influence in the Balkans; its Eastern rims through Poland, Hungary, Romania and Ukraine; and its Western zone through its on-and-off partnership/understanding with France. Germany's leadership of the EU's eastward enlargement is bound up with concrete geo-strategic considerations and is based on a notion of political federalism modelled after Germany's own. It is this notion of political federalism that the US wants to deter.

Britain is not a major geo-strategic player in Europe, but it is of great significance in the context of its Commonwealth position and its military attachment to the US concerning military operations and energy business in the greater Middle East. The geo-strategic positioning of Greece, Turkey and Cyprus has remained structurally unaltered for the US in the Near Eastern theatre. More to the point, Cyprus' geo-strategic significance has not been downgraded since the end of the Cold War and its merchant fleet enjoys the sixth largest registry in the world. 'The accession of Cyprus to the EU', Communications and Works Minister Averof Neophytou pointed out in April 2002, 'would boost the EU's shipping fleet by 25 per cent, increasing the EU's share of world shipping from 16 to 20 per cent.'[13] Moreover, in 2001–02, Cyprus and Syria advanced the construction of an under-sea natural gas pipeline. Although the $200 million project was delayed due to problems in the construction of a pipeline from Egypt to Syria, through which gas supplies destined for Cyprus would be pumped, the construction of the pipeline would enable Cyprus to export surplus gas to West European markets.[14] Cyprus is a real asset and an invaluable geo-strategic bridge connecting Europe and the Middle East. The EU has both political and economic interests in allowing an independent and united Cyprus to enter its ranks.

But all the points made above amount to saying that the Turkish pivot is disqualified in the face of Germany's and France's eastward and Mediterranean drives respectively, and that the US has no intention whatsoever of jeopardising the EU's enlargement in Western Eurasia for Turkey's sake. But this is conditional upon the

US–UK logic of enlargement, that is 'enlarging the EU without fed-
eralising it'. Yet as every strategic assessment is subject to changes
according to shifting diplomatic, economic and power relations, we
can only put forward and examine the practical validity of the
following proposition. *The terms under which the Cyprus issue may be
solved by the EU factor are conditioned by the changing strategic and
diplomatic terrain between EU states and the US in Western Eurasia, that
is the area stretching from Turkey's Caucasian borders to Germany's Baltic
and Ukrainian frontiers.*

We cannot afford to discuss here the possibility of Cyprus being
left *outside* the next EU enlargement. Nor we can confine ourselves
to predicting scenarios about the possible reaction of Greece or
Turkey in case one of them turns out to be dissatisfied over Cyprus'
European prospects. As made clear earlier, we cannot limit our
discussion to this sort of exercise. This is primarily because a politically responsible decision has been taken on the part of the EU, that
the internationally recognised Republic of Cyprus will join the 'club',
regardless of whether a solution to the island's *de facto* division is
found before accession. And the US, although it put forward some
important qualifications, has acquiesced in this. Let us give a brief
historical summary of EU–Cyprus relations by raising aspects of the
relational cleavage between Germany/EU, on the one hand, and the
US/Turkey on the other. In doing so, we shall also become aware of
the fact that the EU/Germany are not mere foreign policy pawns in
the hands of the US, particularly when important geo-political
interests affecting Eurasian postures are at stake.

When Britain – Cyprus' largest market – joined the EEC in 1973,
Cyprus managed to establish an Association Agreement with the
Economic Communities in the same year. The Agreement was
instrumental in providing for a customs union, which was to be
accomplished in two consecutive stages. However, due to the
disruption caused by the Turkish invasions, the second stage
commenced only after 1988. This stage was in turn split into two
phases and the whole process was scheduled for completion by 2003.

On July 4, 1990 the Republic of Cyprus submitted its formal application to join the Communities as a full member. The Europeans,
aware of the problem, nominated an observer to register possible
problems and issues raised during the talks between the Greek and
Turkish Cypriot leaderships. At the European Council meeting in
Corfu in June 1993, when Greece was holding the EU's rotating
presidency, the EU took a further step, putting on an equal footing

the membership of Cyprus with that of East-Central European states. This alarmed Turkey and the US, but they were both somewhat mollified soon after that, as a customs union agreement between Turkey and the EU began to loom large. In a masterly deal crafted between the EU, Greece and Turkey under the auspices of the US (February–March 1995), the EU went much further and declared that entry negotiations with Cyprus could commence six months after the Amsterdam IGC of 1996. At the same time Turkey signed a customs union agreement with the EU.[15]

But perhaps the most important of all decisions taken, was that at the Luxembourg summit of December 12–14, 1997, resulting in the near humiliation of Turkey and forcing the US to accept Germany's determination not to offer Turkey candidate status. From our analytical perspective, the Luxembourg summit was important in that it conferred candidate status on Cyprus, but not on Turkey, and because these developments took place under the auspices of Germany and Greece and despite US/Turkish disapproval.[16] The most galling thing for Turkey was that the EU announced two groups of candidates, but Turkey figured in neither of them. Moreover, most of the candidates were former Communist countries, that is to say 'enemies'. The first 'fast track' group consisted of the Czech Republic, Slovenia, Cyprus, Poland, Estonia and Hungary, and the second – which needed more preparation before joining – of Bulgaria, Lithuania, Latvia, Slovakia and Romania. The EU produced a conciliatory statement intended to placate the Turks, pledging to bring them closer into the ranks of the Union, but to no avail.

'This overall set of circumstances', Alan Makovsky wrote, 'and the growing Turkish conviction that Germany and Greece were intent on keeping them out of the EU at all costs ... convinced the Turks that the solemn pledges in the summit communique, including the emphasis placed on an accession strategy to bring Turkey "closer to the EU in every field", could not be trusted.'[17] In this context, it is interesting to note that although US officials did not disagree with the EU's decision and had publicly stated that Turkey should be treated like any other candidate country, in private they had criticised 'European "shortsightedness" and "lack of political ingenuity"'.[18]

The EU further consolidated its relationship with the Republic of Cyprus, and in April 1998 it formally opened discussions with it over the *acquis*. A month earlier, the Greek Cypriot President of the Republic, Glafkos Clerides, had officially asked the Turkish Cypriot leadership to join the Cyprus accession negotiating team, but the

Turkish side refused to do so. At the EU's summit of June 1998, Mesut Yilmaz had 'a sharp exchange of words with German Foreign Minister Klaus Kinkel', asserting that 'Germany's EU strategy in Central and Eastern Europe was merely a continuation of its Nazi-era *Lebensraum* policies'.[19]

The US was directly involved in every negotiating phase. It is no accident that at the historic Helsinki summit in December 1999, 'the EU agreed – under intense pressure by the US – to accept Turkey as a formal candidate for EU membership', while committing itself to parallel negotiations over Cyprus.[20] A 'road map' was drawn up by the EU, monitoring progress in Turkish political, economic and social affairs, and it was believed that this would steer Turkey towards adopting political norms that pertain to Western Europe and the *acquis*. In November 2000, also under intense pressure from the US, the European Commission proposed an accession partnership for Turkey, which came to be adopted in March 2001. However, Turkey was the only one of the 13 candidate members with whom accession negotiations over the *acquis* were considered premature.

US Qualified Support to Germany and Greece

This protracted process of EU–Cyprus relations and the cleavage between Germany and the US that emerged further support our proposition of the EU/Germany primacy *vis-à-vis* Turkey, but it also exemplifies the point that that US strategic leaning toward the pair is likely to be highly qualified and balanced. In addition, it proves that the Greek–Turkish conflict has global dimensions, not only because of its energy security dimension (oil and gas pipeline projects), hence its geo-political significance, but also because it is internationally institutionalised mainly by NATO and the EU. From this perspective, powers such as Germany and France may periodically, and for their own reasons, support Greek positions in the EU, in spite of their declared wish to 'stay clear of Greek–Turkish disputes'.[21] The EU could not back down with regard to Cyprus' accession and the US could not put pressure on Germany/EU to do otherwise, except by asking them to qualify their position in favour of Turkey. Henri Barkey and Philip Gordon commented perceptively on some of these issues as follows:

> A crisis over the island's EU accession could dramatically raise regional tensions, undermine Turkey's difficult but steady evolution toward Europe, and create fissures among EU members.

All this would leave the US caught between its desire to promote a wider and more prosperous Europe and its inclination to stand by its Turkish friends. *In the face of these risks, trying to dissuade the EU from fulfilling its promise to accept Cyprus is tempting, but it is not a realistic option* [my emphasis]. Given the EU's commitments and interests, such an American intervention is unlikely to succeed – which EU member would or could agree to carry Washington's water on this issue? – and thus would lead only to needless tensions with Europe, Greece and Cyprus. An American attempt to block the Cyprus accession would also mean reversing the long-standing position of Democrats and Republicans that Cyprus should be eligible to join the EU; it would remove any remaining pressure on the Turkish side to accept a political settlement; and perhaps more importantly, it would lead to Greece's certain veto of EU enlargement to any of other pending candidates. That would create a crisis within Europe, which is the last thing the US needs or should care to be blamed for.[22]

The most important qualification the US put forward had to do with the entry of Turkey into the EU 'as soon as possible'. We also know that, in parallel with this, the US aimed at drawing Greece and Turkey closer, developing closer economic, political and strategic ties, a locomotive that has been at work since the mid-1990s, and not only since autumn 1999, following the devastating earthquakes in both countries.[23] At the same time, both the UK and the US appeared to be supportive of the Turkish position concerning the ways in which the *acquis* could be implemented in Cyprus. In the main, this thorny issue is linked to the allowance of extensive derogations, meaning the imposition of certain limitations to the implementation of freedom of movement of persons, capital, payment and settlement for some 180,000 Greek Cypriot refugees.[24] It would also mean that the refugees, the sole possessors of the legitimate title deeds since 1974–5, might be asked to seek compensation instead of returning to, resettling in, and having economic use of their land and properties. In January 2002, soon after the two Cypriot leaders, Glafkos Clerides and Rauf Denktash, resumed talks under EU and US pressures, an authoritative Editorial comment in the *Financial Times* stated:

> The shape of a likely settlement is already clear. Cyprus will need to become a bizonal federation, with a single executive and shared

presidency but maximum autonomy for the two parts. The North must be flexible over its territorial claims on parts of the South. While a settlement should include a right to return for Greek Cypriots, in practice they should be encouraged to accept compensation. Nor can there be completely free movement of people and capital across the island. The EU should allow the necessary derogations.[25]

Seen from this angle, the implementation of extensive or even permanent derogations would, at least in theory, allow Turkey to maintain significant, ethnically cleansed, territory on the island for political and military purposes, a design whose origins can be traced back to the old schemes of partition of the 1960s and early 1970s. Moreover, the establishment of permanent derogations with such enormous political implications would create a unique precedent in the implementation of the *acquis*. In any event, the issue of Cypriot refugees seems to be inextricably linked to the Turkish security posture since the mid-1950s, according to which either an independent Cyprus dominated by the Hellenic element, or a Cyprus united with Greece, would be a severe blow to Turkey's geo-political and strategic interests in the Near East. The US and the UK had to go along with the Turkish notion somewhat, not least because they were the main inventors of the various separatist plans between 1957 and 1974. Van Coufoudakis put it as follows:

[The] US with support from Britain has managed to turn the issue of [Cyprus] accession into one more instrument of pressure in order to advance another burdensome political settlement that essentially legitimises the conditions created by Turkey's invasion and occupation. If this gambit is allowed to succeed, an agreement between the government of Cyprus and the Turkish Cypriot community prior to the Cypriot accession will pre-empt the applicability of European norms and will provide major derogations from these norms in the case of Cyprus.[26]

The discreet position of the US–UK bloc over the question of derogations notwithstanding, the issue of Cyprus–EU relations as such induced the Greek and Turkish sides to put forward interesting arguments.

Greek and Turkish Arguments

To begin with, the EU could not easily acquiesce in the US–UK wish for permanent derogations, because Turkey made the mistake of transferring to Cyprus over 100,000 Anatolian settlers, most of whom have been lodged in abandoned Greek Cypriot properties. This Turkish move, which was basically aimed at altering the demographic composition of the island, has become a real political and moral obstacle to the implementation of derogations on the part of the EU. Although somewhat eager to compromise on the grounds of a limited implementation of the *acquis* for a certain 'transition period' which would satisfy both sides, the EU was left with no option but to acquiesce in authoritative legal opinions, which confirmed the illegality of these sort of population transfers.[27] In any event, the EU aimed at bringing a united Cyprus into its ranks or, as was characteristically said: 'with one voice, so as to be able to perform its obligations'.[28]

The problems with the Turkish strategy have indeed been legal. An argument put forward by Turkey in support of its separatist position in Cyprus was that the two ethnic communities could not live together, witness the ethnic strife and anomalous situation before 1974 and the nearly impeccable peaceful order on the island since. This argument, rather overlooked by the Greeks, was often presented in the wider historical context of Greek–Turkish relations, whose degree of peaceful coexistence as separate states has been due to the exchange of populations between them in the 1920s. In this context, the Turkish side saw the international recognition of the self-styled Turkish Republic of Northern Cyprus, recognised only by Turkey, as a condition *sine qua non* for a solution to the Cyprus issue inside or outside the EU. However, this Turkish stance, which was based on the creation of a *fait accompli* in 1974, complicated matters, as the EU could not go against the resolutions of the UN Security Council, which has denied recognition of the Turkish military enclaves since 1963–4, and of the Turkish occupied zone since 1974. If the opposite ever occurs, then this (a) would deprive the UN of any seriousness and (b) would mean legitimising the ethnic cleansing of some 250,000 persons, both Greek and Turkish Cypriots, by the Turkish invading forces of 1974, and by the Greek paramilitaries in 1963–4 and 1974.

Another argument put forward by Turkey was that Cyprus could not assume membership of any international organisation, i.e. of the EU, if Turkey itself was not a member. Turkey attempted to draw legitimacy for this argument from the 1960 Treaty of Guarantee, namely Articles I(2) and II(2).[29] However, the argument was turned down by authoritative legal opinions, which claimed that those articles were not concerned with membership of regional economic associations, but with *union with another state*. Indeed, as James Crawford, Alain Pellet and Gerhard Hafner put it, the purpose of these articles was to prevent union of Cyprus, or of any part of it, with Greece or Turkey, as well as to forbid the partition of the island.[30] The EU supported this legal opinion, and the US–UK went along with it, whatever their private reservations. Thus, in a recent FCO (Foreign and Commonwealth Office) document made available in public on March 12, 2002, we read:

> The British Government does not accept the Turkish Government's assertion that Cyprus's application to join the European Union is illegal. In the Government's view there is no legal obstacle to Cypriot membership of the EU, since EU membership does not constitute 'union with another State' and is therefore not ruled out by the Treaty of Guarantee. The Government subscribes to the legal analysis in the joint Crawford/Hafner/Pellet opinions on this point. The Government's view of the legal position is also supported by the actions and statements of other EU member States, the European Commission and the UN Security Council.[31]

Having said this, Greece's tactful diplomacy in the 1990s in support of Cyprus' European bid, as well as its tendency to acquiesce in the US–EU demand for *rapprochement* with Turkey, seemed to have placed Turkey with its back against the wall. Turkey was thus left with no serious diplomatic option, other than to dig into a self-entrenched policy, threatening to annex the zone it occupied in 1974 if the EU admitted the Greek Cypriot recognised state prior to a political settlement. Greece's predictable response was that it would block not only Turkey's European efforts, but also the very process of EU eastward enlargement. But Turkey had a bullish Turkish Cypriot negotiator, Rauf R. Denktash, whose 'walk out' attitude in the bi-communal talks during the 1990s 'has strengthened the Greek Cypriots' hand, relieved them from having to negotiate, and made it difficult for the EU to do anything but include Cyprus in its ranks'.[32]

I would like to argue that Turkey's threat to annex its Cypriot occupied zone was backed by its strong military posture in Cyprus more than in the Aegean, and by its key geo-political importance for the US. I would also like to maintain that Greece's threat to block the EU eastward enlargement is based on the understanding of Germany's primacy in Western Eurasian *vis-à-vis* Turkey's, a primacy supported by the US.

Military Diplomacy by the 'Turkish Pivot'

Turkey's strongest trump card was, and indeed is, military and strategic. Turkey knew that the post-1974 *status quo* in Cyprus served not only its own national interests (e.g. exclusion of Greece from the Eastern Mediterranean, pressure on Greece to draw a median line in the Aegean) but those of the US also. The Turkish presence in Cyprus attributed strategic and intelligent depth to the Turkish–Israeli axis, while overseeing Turkey's Hatay province – which is claimed by Syria – from the Karpass peninsula of Cyprus. Additionally, it facilitated control over air and sea routes critical for the defence of Israel and the advancement of US interests in the South-eastern coastal strip of the Mediterranean. As far as its Eastern Mediterranean positioning is concerned, Turkey's strategic role today runs indeed on the same Cold War track.[33] Thus, Turkey is a key guarantor for the US, not least because its Anatolian landmass provides for the integrated security of possible crude oil transportation from the Caspian and the Caucasus to the Mediterranean, such as the Baku–Ceyhan plan.[34]

The US apart, Turkey, somewhat more than the UK or Greece, had the potential to be defined as a real sovereign power on Cyprus, irrespective of whether or not it kept its infantry on the island. As we know from the political and legal philosophy of Carl Schmitt, sovereignty is less related to a legal notion, than to a political one. According to Schmitt, *political sovereignty is not a constitutional or legal matter, but a matter of power. That is to say, it belongs to those who can bring about a state of emergency.*[35]

True, Turkey's politico-military grip over Cyprus is restricted by the US's far superior posture in the Eastern Mediterranean, as well as by the UK and/or Greece. Turkey's real sovereignty is also limited by the EU, due to the institutional and political framework of relations between the EU and Cyprus that has been developing since the 1990s. However, the point at issue is that we have been presented with several examples which illustrate Turkey's primacy when it has chosen to stake out maximalist positions backed by the threat of force. If this primacy exists, then the argument developed by Turkey concerning the formation of two sovereign states (the co-federal solution or 'the partnership state') in view of protecting the Turkish Cypriot community from Greek nationalists, does not make much sense. It could only make legal sense which, in turn, could impact positively on the political and economic status of the occupied zone, which has been refused international recognition. In fact, by recognising the occupied zone as an independent state via a co-federal solution, or what the Turkish Foreign Minister Ismail Cem called in 2002 a 'partnership state',[36] Turkey could legitimise its strategic positioning in Cyprus reversing all negative political and international consequences stemming from the invasions of 1974. But let us look at two examples, one in relation to Turkey's tactics toward Greece and Cyprus, and one concerning the UK, both of which show the gains Turkey received when putting forward maximalist positions.

In 1998, when Turkey found out that the Greek Cypriot government was ready to import the Russian-made SS-300 ground-to-air missile system, it threatened to destroy the missiles on their way to Cyprus, by using military force.[37] In order to defuse the tension, both the EU and the US urged Greece and the Republic of Cyprus to abandon the idea of deploying the system in Cyprus. The Greek Cypriot government, under enormous pressure from Greece – at the time striving to reach the EU criteria for monetary integration – backed down. The missiles, although purchased, never arrived in Cyprus and it is believed that they were stored somewhere in Crete. Thus, thanks to Turkey's tough line, the deeply unequal balance of force on the island between the Greek and the Turkish sides remained unaltered.[38]

At times, Turkey attempted to outflank/undermine even the UK's position in the region. It should be remembered that Turkey's longer-term aim since the mid-1950s has been the strategic control of the whole of Cyprus, and one way to achieve this would be by acquiring a form of shared political sovereignty with the Greeks over the South, while at the same time remaining in full control of the North.[39] In the main, this is the reason why Turkey has opposed the 'double union' solution since 1974, even if this would mean legitimising its presence over the whole of the Cypriot territory it occupied with the invasions. In point of fact, Turkey does not wish to have Greece in its underbelly, because this cannot exclude either a strategic partnership between Greece and Israel, nor Turkey's actual encirclement by Greece. But beyond this, control over the Southern zone is blocked by some significant powers.

The two British sovereign bases in Akrotiri/Episkopi and Dekhelia, the Greek air base at Paphos – which was created within the framework of the united defence doctrine between Greece and the Republic – as well as France's presence in Cape Gkreko, constitute a serious obstacle to the Turkish strategy.[40] Yet, Turkey has disregarded several times the British sovereign posture, as well as the UN buffer zone. In summer 2000, the Turkish forces moved the ceasefire line some 300 metres into the UN buffer zone, bringing under their control the small Greek Cypriot village of Strovilia, which was situated there. This was immediately denounced by the UN, but the real issue lies elsewhere. By creating a new checkpoint in the UN zone, Turkey established a common border with the British sovereign base of Dekhelia, as Strovilia was the sole buffer preventing this from happening. This enhances Turkey's bargaining power and further paves the way for an eventual takeover, if Britain ever evacuates its base or part of it. Another blow to Britain was the abduction by Turkish forces of a Greek Cypriot from a UK sovereign base area on December 12, 2000. Allegedly, this was done because the Greek Cypriot was in possession of 1.1 kilos of cannabis, but the UK police on the base admitted that no trace of drugs had been found on the Greek Cypriot.[41]

From this perspective, Turkey and the Turkish Cypriot leadership were not quite sincere when they argued for two sovereign states on Cyprus in order to safeguard their security in the face of the threat posed by the Greek Cypriot majority. Rather, and having in mind the conditions of social and economic security generated in a European demilitarised Cyprus, this argument seemed to be covering up the real intention of Turkey, which was the strategic control of the entire island via a 'partnership state', and not the security of the Turkish Cypriots from Greek nationalists. In any event, Turkey can be one of the *politically* sovereign powers in Cyprus without even bothering to have a military presence on it (for example, as opposed to Greek air power, Turkish warplanes can reach Cyprus' airspace almost instantly after taking off). Greece could not create a state of emergency in Cyprus with a fair chance of success, and the UK has no conceivable economic or political reason to do so. Thus, time and again, it appears that the argument for the maintenance of Turkey's troops in Cyprus is not connected with the security of the Turkish Cypriots, but with Turkey's long-term strategy of gaining strategic control of the whole of Cyprus.

Turkey's strategic position owes much to its military alliance with Israel, an alliance officially declared on February 23, 1996 in Tel Aviv, and reluctantly signed (December 1996) by Turkey's Islamic Premier at that time, Necmettin Erbakan.[42] This alliance, which the US has encouraged, guided and participated with in full, seems to be a serious stumbling block for the EU's distinctive strategy in the Middle East. Nevertheless, the issue is not so simple. The US, Israel and Turkey have, since 1996, been holding regular joint military exercises in the Eastern Mediterranean, and have increased intelligence co-operation and exchanges of military personnel for training purposes.[43] Israel has become an established contractor for Turkey's sophisticated weaponry, and a security forum discussing strategic issues between the two states has been formed.[44] Furthermore, the Turkish–Israeli alliance benefits the Turkish cause in the US, as Turkey can count on the powerful Jewish lobby there countering the Greek and Armenian ones. It should be pointed out, however, that the Turkish–Israeli axis has Janus-faced strategic implications.

In the first place, it certainly tends to weaken the Greek/Greek Cypriot geo-strategic posture in the wider strategic site of Western Eurasia and the Mediterranean, where Germany and France have a strong leverage, both through the EU and independently. But at the same time it tends to downplay Turkey's bid to join the EU, since the EU's foreign policy position, for its own reasons, is clearly in favour of the Palestinians.[45] However, this does not mean that an eventual entry of Turkey into the EU would not be to the detriment of the Turkish–Israeli axis, as Turkey may be forced to choose between Israel and the EU on contentious policy and economic issues. Similarly, and even brushing aside the EU factor, the Turkish–Israeli alliance, together with its pivotal role, may fall into abeyance if the Mullahs of Iran decide to re-enter the US-led alliance in the greater Middle East and/or if Iraq adopts pro-US positions – either by US force or otherwise. Time and again however, Greece and Cyprus appear in the equation, since they are the sole gateways to European politics and economic prosperity for both Israel and Turkey.[46]

In the light of this analysis, the following tentative concluding remarks seem to be unavoidable. Turkey played the diplomatic card of military tension as it counted on its military superiority and regional geo-strategic primacy. The Republic of Cyprus and Greece played the EU and legal cards as they counted on Germany's pivotal role in Western Eurasia and on France's positioning in the Mediterranean and the Middle East. Additionally, Greece's EU and NATO memberships and its stabilising politico-economic role in the Balkans, have enabled Cyprus in the late 1990s and early 2000s to place its EU membership on a secure footing. It remains to be seen to what extent constitutional and other modalities (e.g. the issue of derogations, the Turkish military presence in Cyprus) will place the EU in a position to advance the common Cypriot cause of the island's political reunification.

7 Conclusion

US Policy in Eurasia: An Assessment

Any state's foreign policy, including America's, is constrained by a complex combination of external and domestic factors, which constitute the sources from which the political classes elaborate their international and domestic strategies. Foreign policy per se is, or should be, the balanced refinement and combined diplomatic projection of four fundamental components: the economic, the military, the ideological and the juridical/legal. Each component is relatively autonomous, a fact that enables both an independent development of its ramifications (e.g. 'economic diplomacy', 'defence diplomacy', 'coercive diplomacy', and so on) and, if need be, a robust projection of integrated power, accompanied by an attempt to incorporate all four elements. This is basically what Carl Von Clausewitz meant by his famous phrase 'war is the continuation of politics by other means'. It is the weakness and/or lack of combination of the four main components of foreign policy that make NGOs and other non-state organisations (e.g. the UN) – albeit successful in some humanitarian issues, charitable work and light peacekeeping – unable to project influence as coherently and dynamically as the modern state does.

It is also interesting to note that the last two components, the ideological and juridical/legal, involve a distorted image of reality, inasmuch as they were formed by the dominant classes in order to be manipulated by them and to legitimise actions based on their self-interests. 'The task of political hegemony', Terry Eagleton wrote back in 1990, 'is to produce the very forms of subjecthood which will form the basis of political unity'.[1] Law and ideology are, in the last analysis, reified commodities that tend to 'regulate' reality in order to mystify the real profile of forces operating along the lines of national and class interests. At times, the forms of law available happen not to satisfy these specific interests. Therefore, those who make the laws are often those who fail to abide by them.

Since 1945, the US has been overplaying all four components. But since the late 1970s, when the West began recovering from the economic crisis, under the guidance of Thatcher's and Reagan's neo-

116

liberal administrations, and since the collapse of the USSR, we have been witnessing a rampant expansion of the military, economic, ideological and juridical parameters of US foreign policy projection. In economic terms, the US has championed, more than ever before, free trade policies and globalisation, relaunching GATT as the WTO, although she does not seem to obey her own rules, when domestic class interests dictate protectionism and restraint. In military terms, the US has advanced the reform and expansion of NATO in Eurasia, asking EU powers to spend more on defence in order to share the burden of NATO expenses and not of a federal Europe. In legal/ideological terms, she has elaborated and experimented further (e.g. the Kosovo war) the ethical/legal/democratic elements of its Cold War foreign policy, although the real motive has been to camouflage the national and class elements of its military action.

The Clinton administration in the 1990s attempted to present the four main components of US foreign policy as an integrated whole that underpinned and promoted the expansion of democratic values, creating free societies and/or a 'global village'. In this respect, the new *pax Americana* under construction resembles very much the Kantian/idealistic notion of 'lasting peace', according to which democracies and free market societies do not go to war: how can you have war between two countries that host Coca Cola industries and Arthur Andersen? This is utterly nonsensical.

Over the last two hundred years, liberal democracies, including France, Britain, Italy and the US, have gone to war to preserve, promote and expand their respective national interests in order to accomplish state/bureaucratic and class objectives. In this respect, America's globalisation strategy today is the most nationalistic of all nationalisms, and the notion of an 'ethical foreign policy' tried out in Yugoslavia has backfired: democratic stability, human rights and free markets cannot be delivered by means of violence. And if the US-led 'anti-terror coalition' in the Middle East and Central Asia fail to deliver stability and democracy there, it should be to nobody's surprise. The post-September 11 global environment has outdone America's pro-Islam ideological posture in the Balkans, broken up the fragile consensus between the Palestinians and America–Israel achieved in the Oslo accords (1993) and brought to the fore the real post-Cold War issues in Eurasia: competition between US and other Western financial interests, and competition over energy resources and political influence in Eurasia and the globe. In short, this is a game that tends to resemble pre-1919 Great Power international politics and 'division of spoils' rather than the formation of a peaceful 'global village'. The only significant difference with the pre-1919 or, for that matter, pre-1939 international order seems to be the huge paramountcy of US power today.

During the Cold War the US had three or four brave and legitimate political reasons to be in Western Europe and the Mediterranean: the defence and security of Europe and the Near East from the USSR; helping the economic reconstruction of Europe; and fostering collaboration between France and Germany, and between Greece and Turkey. But with the Soviet threat gone and with Europe as economically united and strong as America, what is the fundamental reason for still having a hegemonic and expanding America on Europe's soil?

I argue that the generic framework upon which the US has based its policy in Europe/Eurasia since the end of the Cold War contains the following interlinked strategic objectives:

a. The military bracketing of Russia and China in order to obtain their subordinate co-operation.
b. The continuation of the strategic partnership with key EU states, while preventing the emergence of a federal Europe (the 'fortress Europe' project).
c. The prevention of the formation of an alternative powerful coalition in Eurasia, that would be capable of challenging the supremacy of the US.

The 'Grand Chessboard' assumption of Brzezinski is that without the fulfilment of this set of objectives, the US will not be in a position to dominate Eurasia, and this will result in its global dominance withering away. Yet, these objectives are long-term 'fixed' strategic goals and in no way prescribe the avenues that the US has been, or will be pursuing in order to fulfil them. Nor has US strategic and contingency planning been always in a position to predict or design everything in detail: US actions can be reactive rather than proactive.

As we have seen, in the wake of the collapse of the USSR, intermediate policy clusters have been employed in order to politically weaken the central institutions of the former Communist states. At the same time, the US has had to keep an eye on the process of economic and political integration of the EU. Preventing Europe from achieving a federal form of governance modelled on Germany's own would facilitate the US's globalisation strategy: no organised interests would be in a position to challenge its political/ideological/ military influence in Eurasia, thereby guaranteeing it control over oil and gas producing zones.

The collapse of the USSR and its satellites, which involved the participation of US-led institutions, generated a new geo-strategic environment in Eurasia and impacted severely upon the political arrangements of EU states. Under the guidance of Germany and France, the EU's Eastern and Southern rims were opened up to new economic and political opportunities. The creation of the Euro-zone competed directly with the dollar in world markets and the new geo-political reality that emerged promised the safe transportation of energy to the West via new geographical avenues. The energy map had to be redesigned with the construction of a complex network of new pipelines connecting the Balkans and the greater Middle East. With it, the political map of these two strategic zones has also undergone dramatic changes, as some regional actors proved to be disobedient. Nothing has been stabilised in the Balkans, Eastern Europe or the greater Middle East, and everything is likely to remain in a state of flux for the foreseeable future.

Projects around energy resources, coupled with competing financial and military interests of Western states have impelled the US to launch its robust battle to secure the upper hand. The war against Iraq in 1990–91 was directly linked to energy interests, as will be any future US intervention in the Iraq–Iran–Syria–Kurdistan zone. The US intervention in Yugoslavia was to test the first phase of NATO's eastward expansion, placing Russia's and Germany's influence in the Balkans under US security structures. The US intervention in Central Asia after September 11 is linked to a wide network of oil and gas pipeline projects connecting Eurasia's heartland with the Black Sea and the Balkans. *I argue that a key underlying element of all the three major theatres of war since 1990 (Iraq/the Persian Gulf, the Western Balkans and Afghanistan/Central Asia) has been the new geo-political environment centred on oil and gas pipeline projects, an environment that has opened up with the collapse of the USSR.* None of these three war theatres, nor NATO and EU expansion can be analysed and understood in depth, without coming to grips with the new strategic dimensions of oil and gas in Eurasia. The great potential of the EU to become an independent global actor, rivalling the US, will depend on who politically controls oil and gas producing zones and the new energy transit routes.

Energy interests have also been behind the local wars in the Caucasus area, including the war between Russia and Chechnya, the war between Armenia and Azerbaijan over Nagorno-Karabach, and the tensions between Georgia and Russia over Abkhazia. In this regional setting, Turkey, Georgia and Azerbaijan have been working together on the proposed Baku–Tbilisi–Ceyhan oil pipeline. The smokescreen, or what I like to call 'the juridical/ideological layer', has been provided by the 'anti-terrorist pact' signed between the three states in summer 2002. The US lends discreet support to the project either because of the Kurdish issue, or because of Russia's opposition, or because it may prove uneconomical and eventually lead to general unrest in the West.[2]

All in all, the construction of pipelines, the elimination of competitors and the safe transportation of energy to Western markets at stable prices are key drivers of US foreign policy towards the Balkans and the greater Middle East. NATO's eastward expansion and the fragmentation of the political map of South-western Eurasia neatly support the security dimension of US policy, mainly at the expense of European, Russian and Chinese strategic interests. The primary worry of the US, since 1990, in all three theatres of war has been the containment of German/EU, Russian and Chinese influence, the aim being their subordination to US state objectives and national interests.

A Trans-Eurasian Convention Underwritten by Eurasian Powers

Thanks to their geographical/continental proximity, Russia, Germany and China enjoy a geo-strategic positioning in Eurasia's chessboard that the US cannot ignore. Closer trade links between them and Japan, greater co-operation over energy projects and an intimate political understanding may become a real threat to America's interests. Thus, the US has felt bound to drive a wedge between all three, by alternating a policy of co-operation/ confrontation with them: witness the PfP project, or the NATO/US–Russia agreement of May 2002 (selective co-operation) and the NATO war over Kosovo (an example of confrontation).

Yet, none of these Eurasian actors is giving up the battle over energy resources and political influence: Russia is determined to hold its ground in the Caspian Sea area, Iran/Iraq, the Balkans and the Caucasus, and continues to be a major supplier of sophisticated weaponry to Balkan and Middle Eastern states; China is struggling to become economically and militarily robust to substantiate its stakes in Asia and its involvement in the WTO. As far as Germany is concerned, Ludger Volmer, state secretary in the Ministry of Foreign Affairs, stated openly in June 2002 that 'Asian countries clearly want a wider choice of partners other than the US, and see us [Germany] as a core country within the EU.' Volmer went on to say that the world is multi-polar, not uni-polar around the US, and that 'Berlin would be ready to mediate in regional flash-points, such as the Kashmir conflict between India and Pakistan'.[3]

This statement bears a resemblance to foreign policy positions advanced by Russia and China and 'many Chinese strategists openly worry about what they regard as the encirclement of China by American power in the wake of the September 11th terrorist attacks'.[4] Thus, the question arises: what policy avenue should be pursued by Russia, Japan, China and EU/Germany/France in order to counter-balance America's powerful presence in Eurasia? The obvious answer would be the formation of a strategic partnership, guaranteed by a high-level convention and underwritten by the four major Eurasian actors. However, this would be difficult, given the number of obstacles that would need to be overcome.

In the first place, as we saw earlier, key EU states such as Britain and France do not recognise Germany's lead in the EU, and Britain and Denmark are more committed to a strategic partnership with the US than the EU. For its part, the US is good at playing the 'divide and rule' game, contributing to the divisions within the EU, and NATO Turkey, along with the UK, is used extensively by the US for this purpose. The EU has no integrated military assets to speak of and lags far behind America in terms of intelligence capabilities, sophisticated weaponry, heavy airlift capacity and overall military power. Furthermore, US–Japanese political relations are regulated by a security pact under the aegis of the US and the US enjoys a strong military presence in Japan and South-east Asia. Students of European politics have also noticed that a tension exists between some of the institutional structures that the EU has over the years built for itself. John Vogler observes:

> The EU is a political entity of enormous complexity. In its external relations it is a multifaceted and 'variable geometry' actor, which can change its form during a single negotiation as competence passes from the Community to the member-states, represented by the Presidency and back again. The principal tension in the Union's emergent foreign policy is between Pillar One and Pillar

Two. Pillar One, the European Community, comprises trade, agri-culture, fisheries and development aid. It is here that the Union appears most clearly as a single actor, given the leading role of the Commission and the extensive trade and aid instruments that may be deployed in support of EU objectives. Pillars Two [CFSP] and Three [Justice and Home Affairs], established at Maastricht are, by contrast, inter-governmental and the CFSP is led by the member-state holding the rotating Presidency of the Council of Ministers. Effective external action often requires that Pillars One and Two work together, for example in the imposition of economic sanctions in support of the political objectives of the CFSP. This is not always easy, given the ambitions of the Commission to defend and extend the competence of the Community, and the countervailing suspicion of member-states over potential losses of sovereignty, not to mention the constant variations between the national interests of the member-states. In the diplomacy immediately following September 11, the require-ment for inter-pillar co-operation was manifested in a four-person 'Troika'. It comprised the Belgian Presidency, the High Represen-tative for the CFSP (Xavier Solana) and the Commissioner representing the Community (Chris Patten).[5]

It is very important to highlight this dimension of the EU bureau-cracy, simply because the degree of political integration across the EU depends largely on the capacity of its institutions to integrate and co-ordinate the Community Pillar with the requirement of a firm, single political voice on defence and security matters (the Second Pillar). Yet, this institutional dysfunction, or clash of com-petencies, does not supersede existing tensions between the EU's key member-states, tensions that are themselves inscribed in the prob-lematic institutional skeleton of the Union. In fact, these tensions are the historical and political result of the divergent national interests of its member states. Given the impossibility of integrating these divergent interests in the foreseeable future, what are the inter-mediate objectives to be pursued by the EU in order to lay the ground for a lasting strategic partnership with Russia and China?[6]

Some European powers such as Germany, Italy and France grasped the issue long ago and, soon after the collapse of the USSR, began elaborating strategies that could, potentially, emancipate the EU from America's strong grip. For instance, as we saw earlier, a discreet 'division of labour' has been envisaged and applied between

Germany and France over the conduct of EU enlargement: Germany carefully leads Europe's eastward projection and France provides guidance for Europe's Mediterranean economic programmes along the lines of a free trade area. France also directly challenges the US on Middle Eastern matters, while the EU, with Germany's backing, took the significant decision in 1997 to attribute candidate status to a *de facto* divided country, the Republic of Cyprus. Integrating Northern Africa and the Eastern Mediterranean rim into the EU could potentially deliver a serious blow for the US, not least because the countries that compose these two zones of conflict could hardly be integrated into NATO's structures. Turning the Mediterranean into a Northern African and Southern European sea, and the Mediterranean airspace into a civilian, disarmed zone of air navigation should be a strategic aim of the EU and of all African and Near/Middle Eastern states.

For a variety of reasons, the balance of power that could arise from Europe's economic and political dominance of the Mediterranean or Germany's paramountcy in its Eastern geo-political orbit would be of great strategic significance. First, if successful, these designs would alleviate tensions between key European states, building a high degree of political confidence and strategic cohesion between them. Moreover, and this is equally important, they would provide smaller EU states with an incentive to jump on the bandwagon behind Germany and/or France/Italy, according to their long-term interests.

The Mediterranean basin is an area whose geo-strategic importance is wider than its actual boundaries. Apart from its islands and air navigation routes, its territorial waters have corridors, such as the Gibraltar, the Turkish Straits and the Suez, and its coastline waters touch the shores of Israel, Syria, Egypt, Algeria and Libya. In this respect, Spain, Italy, Greece and Turkey, with the assistance of Russia, China, Japan and Northern Europe can act as catalysts, balancing out America's influence in the Mediterranean. An understanding between Portugal, Spain and Britain could facilitate a new transatlantic relationship between the EU and Latin America. Similarly, Britain and France should together elaborate a new and visionary framework of co-operation with Canada. In this respect, Britain also has much to gain by restructuring its Commonwealth structures, bringing Australia and other Commonwealth countries closer to Europe. *Instead of riding the bandwagon behind America, Britain should seek a major role in Eurasia by supporting a strong, united EU.* In short, a careful and politically fruitful 'division of labour' between EU states will be an important step for the advancement of EU cohesion, which will eventually lead to its political emancipation from the US.

However, the projection of a united EU 'from the West' will not be successful without co-operation between China and Russia and without their joint projection 'from the East'. This would alleviate fears on the part of both Russia and China about EU aspirations to rule Eurasia and then the globe. A lasting pact between the EU, Russia, Japan and China should be based on a shared and non-hegemonic set of economic, political and social principles. Moreover, if Russia, China and Japan could co-operate in Central Eurasia and the Pacific on the basis of the EU's principle of 'division of labour', then a convergence of their national interests may not prove impossible. In this respect, a framework of economic and free trade co-operation between Russia, Japan and China should be drafted, and an economic and political council regulating this co-operation should be established. Other Eurasian powers should be given strong incentives to follow Russia, China and Japan. European powers may be invited to join this structure and they should reciprocate by inviting China, Russia and other Eurasian powers such as India, Pakistan, Iran and Saudi Arabia to work with European decision-making institutions.

Admittedly, these first steps of co-operation should be based on strictly non-hegemonic attitudes and on the principle of reciprocity. For instance, the US/NATO–Russia agreement of May 2002 should not induce Russia to back a policy of exclusion towards Germany and India, both of whom wish to assume a permanent role in the UN Security Council.[7] East European, Balkan and Middle Eastern states, which constitute the middle geo-political ground between Asia and Europe, will have to be convinced that American support and/or NATO membership provides no permanent guarantees of security for them. NATO membership of Greece and Turkey has not secured their peaceful coexistence and NATO membership for Hungary and Romania is unlikely to prevent friction between them over the Hungarian minority in Romania. The EU has powerful instruments of conflict management and resolution that the US lacks: it has the means of advancing civilian and economic integration that, with proper Russian assistance, could assimilate former Soviet satellites, absorbing and resolving threats arising from ethnic conflicts. These instruments and mechanisms go beyond the reach of the US: the US and NATO lack the geographic advantages of

France, Germany, Russia and China and the EU is a truly global economic power.

The 'fusion' between Eastern (China, Japan and Russia) and Western (Germany and France) Eurasia has to be non-hegemonic and social, not only to offer an alternative to America's dominance, but also to avoid the emergence of a new European imperialism and construct a socio-political alternative to America's global neo-liberal order. This demanding project should draw on the strong European socialist traditions, as well as the Christian, anti-nationalist and anti-fundamentalist movements. These are the social and ideological components of a potentially new European/Eurasian social democratic class that is yet to emerge, consolidate itself and provide leadership and vision for a trans-Eurasian convention. *The ultimate goal should be the creation of a non-hegemonic, social democratic Eurasian administration under the aegis of Eurasian powers.*

Re-conquering America

It is true that America has created a 'technologically peerless military establishment, the only one with effective global reach'.[8] However, it is also true that American intelligence failed miserably to predict and prevent the terrorist attacks of September 11. America has '725 military installations outside its territory, of which 17 are fully-fledged bases'. Moreover, 'of its 1.4m active servicemen' some '250,000 are deployed overseas'[9] and it is in a position to exercise substantial influence and control over strategic alliances and pacts forged by regional actors. America's military might is coupled with its leading role in key international institutions and organisations such as the UN, the IMF and the World Bank, NATO and the WTO. Moreover, particularly after the collapse of the USSR, the US cultural values of individual success, ambition and self-accomplishment, what Christopher Lasch in the 1970s called *The Culture of Narcissism*,[10] tend to dominate the globe, the sole exception being at extreme nationalistic and religious fringes.

Yet, America cannot rule the world without dominating over a set of co-operative structures of rivals and competitors. These contenders have chosen not to challenge America's hegemony in a confrontational way, inasmuch as they know that rivals of the sort of Milosevic have no chance. I am referring to those parties that accommodate their interests by riding the US's bandwagon and by doing so achieve a better politico-strategic and economic position-ing for their domestic, regional and global circumstances. This sort of rivalry suits US interests, because it reproduces the economic and political conditions of existence of the US itself, while at the same time renewing its hegemony over the ensemble of powers it leads. It also profits those who are on the bandwagon.

Balanced economic competition between the US, the EU and Japan keeps world markets in a state of manageable equilibrium. Political micro-competition with Turkey over Middle Eastern and Central Asian matters boosts America's arms sales to Turkey. The same applies to other areas of the Middle East. For example, it should be understood that America is less concerned with Russia's selling of weaponry and military know-how to a pariah state, Iran, than with the fact that Iran refused to make military deals with her, thus freeing Iranian military technology from American inspection. *In this context, my central thesis is that America cannot and does not want to rule the world without rivals that co-operate with her.*

In essence, this is an axiom that derives from the very conditions of modern politics and economics. The political terrain of modernity is conducive to class democracy and conflicts and is determined by the existence of 'enemies' and 'friends'. Similarly, the setting of modern economics is conducive to monopolistic competition, mergers and acquisitions, which is tantamount to saying that it is determined by the 'enemy–friend' structural game in the market. There can never be a single and quasi-functional economic monopoly, be it global or 'state–national', as (monopolistic) prices cannot be regulated without a certain degree of competition, that balances out the demand/supply curves. Similarly, in political terms, the experience of dictatorships, fascism and totalitarian socialism has been an utter failure, not least because no free competition of political forces was allowed to take place by those holding and exercising power. And precisely because competition is an inherent feature of modernity, all forms of authoritarian regimes inculcated sharp class and bureaucratic contradictions within them, contradictions that contributed to their bankruptcy and ultimate collapse.

So, if it is true that 'America cannot and does not want to rule the world without rivals that co-operate with her', then Brzezinski's thesis, featured in the closing lines of his *Grand Chessboard*, that 'America is the first and last truly global superpower', is wholly metaphysical. Empires have risen and fallen and their fall has been the combined result of imperial 'overstretch' and of the 'co-operation' established between the Empire's ruling faction and its subordinate socio-political forces. As long as there are considerable powers within

America's sphere of interest, then the emergence of an alternative hegemonic alliance to challenge America's supremacy cannot be excluded. And there are further issues that Brzezinski and other Anglo-Saxon strategists, wittingly or unwittingly, pass over in silence.

They fail to tackle important domestic issues that make America anything but an ideal society to project abroad: racial and ethnic tensions, high levels of criminality and drug abuse, large prison populations, ethnic ghettos, poverty and an increasing underclass, and endemic corruption in corporate business, accounting and finance. A detailed analysis of the impact of those issues on general US policy matters falls outside the scope of the book and of this concluding chapter. However, I have made reference to them in order to point out that America is as corrupt as any other country could be and that it is undergoing a profound identity crisis, which is leading to an unmanageable social environment.[11]

Having said this, I would argue that America's military might and global reach notwithstanding, it can never violently confront a politically united Europe/Eurasia, for American national identity does not really function as a unifying element of America's social order. In the main, America's modernity is a by-product of Eurasia, that is to say, of its ethnic identities and industrious peoples.

Despite the shortcomings of the European Enlightenment and the regressive/divisive aspects of Europe's nationalisms, it is worth reminding ourselves that national identities across Europe are so well embedded that they need no further artificial boost from their political elite. If a concerted effort were made to advance notions of European citizenship and European social and political order, then Europe's national identities could coexist peacefully, projecting an image of fraternity, solidarity and social justice.

It is also worth reminding ourselves, that it was Europe and the Europeans that conquered America and not vice versa. Over the centuries, huge waves of emigration from Eurasia, Africa and the Latin World to America created a unique mixture of race and ethnicity. Most emigrant communities in the US, Canada and Australia have maintained strong ties with their countries of origin or their customs and traditions. America is a fragmented amalgamation of Eurasian, Latin, African and Pacific ethnic groups, with strong Irish, Hispanic, Indian, Italian, Greek, Jewish, Chinese, Dutch and Armenian communities. Given the influence of ethnic lobbies over America's foreign policy, it would be unthinkable for the US to formulate a lasting and coherent policy of confrontation towards a *politically united* Eurasia/Europe.

For their part, Eurasian powers should see this ethnic and cultural pluralism of America as an important bridge, over which to cultivate and consolidate the ties between the generations of emigrants settled in America and the emerging European/Eurasian citizenship. Eurasia should not be reluctant to project its political traditions and social values on America, a country that has never really experienced socialism (e.g. Europe's welfare state) or collectivist traditions, that is what Marx used to call, rather euphemistically, 'Asiatic mode of production' (e.g. the pre-1917 Russian populist revolutionary movement and the agrarian communities of *obscina*).[12]

With this in mind, the Europeans must first unite politically. But after the failure of 'Third Way' socialism in the 1990s, Europe's political unification can only be the work of a new democratic political class, which should seek a permanent understanding with all Christian and anti-nationalist forces. The UK will have to be convinced to participate in this grand Eurasian and non-hegemonic social democratic project and Russian and Chinese co-operation is of paramount importance.

These opportunities for Eurasia are the most serious alternative to American power. 'Re-conquering America' may be wishful thinking, but it is well to remember that 'whatever is thinkable is possible'.[13]

Notes

Chapter 1

1. Zbigniew Brzezinski, *The Grand Chessboard: American Primacy and its Geostrategic Imperatives*, New York, Basic Books, 1997, p. xiii.
2. Ibid., p. xiv.
3. Diana Johnstone, 'Humanitarian war: making the crime fit the punishment', in Tariq Ali (ed.), *Masters of the Universe? NATO's Balkan Crusade*, London, Verso, 2000, p. 153.
4. Among others, Kenneth N. Waltz, 'Globalisation and American power', *The National Interest*, N. 59, Spring 2000, <http://www.nationalinter est.org/issues/59/Waltz.html>. Waltz's classic neo-realist statement is his *Theory of International Politics*, New York, Random House, 1979. Waltz espouses some key tenets of the realist school in international relations spearheaded by Hans Morgenthau after the Second World War (see Hans Morgenthau, *Politics Among Nations: The Struggle for Power and Peace*, New York, Alfred A. Knopf, 1948). For a good discussion on the realist and neo-realist theories in international relations see Jack Donnelly, *Realism and International Relations*, Cambridge, Cambridge University Press, 2000. I do not imply here that realism/neo-realism constitutes a theoretical *corpus* without any problems or 'grey' areas. In particular, I should make clear that I use this approach in a descriptive/analytical manner, rather than as a prescriptive theory.
5. I define as 'Western Eurasia' the peripheral thick belt stretching from the Baltic states down to East-Central Europe, the Balkans, Turkey, the Middle East and the Caspian region. I define as 'greater Middle East', the classic geographical locus of the Middle East and its oval-cyclical extension, including the Caucasus, the Caspian region, North-Central-East Africa and Central Asia (Kazakhstan, Uzbekistan, Turkmenistan, Tajikistan and Kyrghystan), which Brzezinski calls 'Eurasian Balkans'; see also Alexei Vassiliev, *Central Asia: Political and Economic Challenges in the Post-Soviet Era*, London, Saqi Books, 2001.
6. Brzezinski, *The Grand Chessboard*, p. 199.
7. Peter Gowan, *The Global Gamble: Washington's Faustian Bid for World Dominance*, London, Verso, 1999, p. 313.
8. Helen V. Milner and Robert Keohane, 'Internationalisation and domestic politics: An introduction', in Robert O. Keohane and Helen V. Milner (eds), *Internationalisation and Domestic Politics*, Cambridge, Cambridge University Press, 1996, p. 4, passim.
9. I have discussed these subjects and the relevant bibliography in my *The Internationalisation of Economic Relations and the State*, Herts, Business School, University of Hertfordshire, Working Paper Series 5, 1998.
10. During the nineteenth century, modern capitalist economies experienced high levels of internationalisation under the aegis of Britain's free

trade global policies. This phenomenon was seen and analysed by Karl Marx, particularly in the third volume of his *Capital*. Neo-Marxist discussion in the 1960s and 1970s shed further light on these issues. For example, in 1973, and in line with Marx's own analyses, Christian Palloix demonstrated what scholarly research confirms today: that neither the finance capital nor multinational firms are confined to the twentieth century. In the words of Palloix: 'Firms like Singer, International Harvester and Westinghouse Electric were operating in Tsarist Russia, and Gillette, Otis, Park Davis and Ford by this time all had plants elsewhere than their countries of origin. There have none the less been changes in the way multinational firms develop. Whereas in the 19th century it was the rising value of raw materials and agricultural products that provided the basis for such firms as Unilever, Penarroya, Shell and Standard Oil, today's firms rely essentially on the so-called "mass" commodity production'; Christian Palloix, *Les Firmes Multinationales et le Procès d'Internationalisation*, Paris, François Maspero, 1973, p. 137. Cf., among others, Paul Hirst and Grahame Thompson, *Globalization in Question*, Cambridge, Polity Press, 1996 and Gowan, *The Global Gamble*.

11. See John Feffer, 'Globalisation and militarisation', *Foreign Policy in Focus*, V. 7, N. 1, February 2002, <http://artel.co.yu/en/izbor/us>.

12. Milner and Keohane, 'Internationalisation and domestic politics', p. 10.

13. The European Commission's President, Romano Prodi, in a speech delivered in London in April 2002, openly attacked the UK's 'special relationship' with the US, arguing that the UK deludes itself if it believes that that relationship gives Britain more political and economic leverage in world affairs; see, 'Presidential pique', *The Economist*, May 4, 2002, p. 42.

Chapter 2

1. Gowan, *The Global Gamble*, p. 143. Gowan offers an informed critique of liberal theorising on the Gulf crisis in the early 1990s.

2. See in particular Alex Pravda, 'Introduction: linkages between Soviet domestic and foreign policy under Gorbachev', in Tsuyoshi Hasegawa and Alex Pravda (eds), *Perestroika: Soviet Domestic and Foreign Policies*, London, Sage–Royal Institute of International Affairs, 1990, pp. 1–25, and Julian Cooper, 'Soviet resource options: civil and military priorities', ibid., pp. 141–55.

3. Brzezinski himself put it as follows: 'A clear choice by Russia in favour of the European option over the imperial one will be more likely if America successfully pursues the second imperative strand of its strategy towards Russia: namely, reinforcing the prevailing geopolitical pluralism in the post-Soviet space', in his *The Grand Chessboard*, pp. 202–03.

4. See the following statement: 'The West became deeply involved in Russia's domestic economic and political transition at the end of the Cold War, when the West's worst fear was that domestic weakness would breed political extremism and disorder in the nuclear superpower. A successful transition to a market democracy was seen as the best guarantor of a benign and stable partner. And so a strategy of economic advice and assistance emerged, its many strands including bilateral, mul-

tilateral and private institutions' assistance in the areas of trade, debt management, investment, credit and aid. However, the IMF soon emerged in a leading role'; Nigel Gould-Davies and Ngaire Woods, 'Russia and the IMF', *International Affairs*, V. 75, N. 1, 1999, p. 1. The authors accept the West's involvement in Russia's affairs, but they fail to consider: (a) the degree of the West's transformation via its participation in the Eastern transition; (b) the extent to which this involvement was conducive to peace and regional security; and (c) whether the mode of the West's participation was appropriate from an economic point of view, as *ad hoc* transition realities were wholly ignored. For example, as we shall see below, the break-up of Yugoslavia was not primarily the result of the eruption of endogenous ethnic violence, but rather the unintended consequence of the IMF intervention, which imposed fiscal discipline and institutional centralisation on Yugoslavia's federal government, a reform that was opposed by Slovenia and Croatia.

5. Brzezinski, *The Grand Chessboard*, p. 66.

6. In the relevant literature, this is usually presented as 'NATO's new strategic concept'. NATO has presumably evolved from the pre-eminence of Europe's territorial defence to the predominance of crisis and conflict management across the globe, when NATO/US interests are at stake (the 'Article 5' strategic debate according to which an attack on a NATO member constitutes an attack on all).

7. 'Old friends and new', *The Economist*, June 1, 2002, p. 26.

8. Cf., among others, Nick Mikhailov, 'Russian oil pipelines set for expansion', *Oil and Gas Journal*, March 25, 2002, pp. 62–8; 'Don't mention the O-word', *The Economist*, September 14, 2002, pp. 25–7.

9. I have elaborated these points in my *Italy, Europe, the Left: the Transformation of Italian Communism and the European Imperative*, Aldershot, Ashgate, 1998. Cf. Donald Sassoon, *One Hundred Years of Socialism: the West European Left in the 20th Century*, London, I.B. Tauris, 1996 and Anthony Giddens, *The Third Way*, London, Polity Press, 1999. Sassoon's massive *One Hundred Years of Socialism* draws from the work of Edward Bernstein and elaborates the concept of 'neo-revisionism', which envisages a new pan-European role for the parties of the Left, beyond the old narrow policy perimeter of the Keynesian nation-state. According to Sassoon, 'neo-revisionism is not a finite doctrinal corpus' and its main tenets in the 1990s were that 'markets should be regulated by legislation and not through state ownership ...; that regulation of the market will increasingly be a goal achieved by supranational means; and that national – and hence parliamentary – sovereignty is a limited concept'. Neo-revisionism entails accepting important aspects of the conservative critique of socialism and it has many variants 'because it is compelled to build on specific national contexts and political environments'. However, Sassoon's argument goes, 'a national road to social democracy – or even modernisation – was no longer possible: here lies the authentic neo-revisionism of the 1990s', ibid., pp. 734–5, 739.

10. Edward L. Morse and James Richard, 'The battle for energy dominance', *Foreign Affairs*, March–April 2002, <http://www.foreignaffairs.org/articles/Morse0302.html>, p. 3.

11. Venezuela's oil output capacity has declined sharply in the early 2000s, due to governmental instability and left-wing social uprisings. Venezuela is the world's fourth largest crude exporter, and any time it 'faces a grinding capacity squeeze' tends to threaten the interests 'of its key customers, including the US'; see, Bhushan Bahree and Marc Lifsher, 'Venezuela's capacity crunch threatens key crude partners', *Wall Street Journal Europe*, April 18, 2002, p. A10.

12. See Gabriel Gorodetsky, *The Grand Delusion: Stalin and the German Invasion of Russia*, New Haven, Yale University Press, 1999; Fiona Hill, 'Pipeline politics, Russo-Turkish competition and geo-politics in the Eastern Mediterranean', *The Cyprus Review*, V. 8, N. 1, Spring 1996, pp. 83–100.

13. Office of International Security Affairs, *United States Strategy for the Middle East*, Washington DC, Department of Defence, May 1995, p. 6.

14. Commission of the European Communities, 'Towards a European strategy for the security of energy supply', Green Paper, COM (2000), 769 final, November 29, 2000, p. 77, passim.

15. See Bulent Gokay, 'Introduction: oil, war and geo-politics from Kosovo to Afghanistan', *Journal of Southern Europe and the Balkans*, V. 4, N. 1, May 2002, p. 8.

16. John M. Keynes, *The General Theory of Employment, Interest and Money*, London, Macmillan, 1973, p. 378. Keynes' book appeared in 1936, but its impact upon Britain and Europe was felt after the end of the Second World War.

17. In August 1971, the American President Richard Nixon declared the end of the Bretton Woods system, by suspending the gold convertibility of the dollar and by introducing an extra import tax of 10 per cent. Thus, the IMF, set up at a mountain resort in Bretton Woods, New Hampshire, in 1944, was requested to make new proposals regarding a new international monetary system. In the end, the dollar was devalued and the whole framework of American proposals, in spite of France's objections, was ratified by the group of the industrialised countries in their Smithsonian Agreement, reached in Washington on December 18, 1971. The resulting international financial uncertainty was coupled with the 1973 oil shock, and with the unsuccessful attempt by the EEC to challenge the dollar, when in March 1972 EEC currencies moved 'inside the dollar tunnel, that is the 2.25 per cent bands on either side of their parity against the US currency', Loukas Tsoukalis, *The New European Economy Revisited*, Oxford, Oxford University Press, 1997, p. 141; see also, Herman van der Wee, *Prosperity and Upheaval: The World Economy, 1945–1980*, London, Viking, 1986, pp. 347–8, 472–94.

18. *Inter alia*, Kirsten E. Schulze, *The Arab–Israeli Conflict*, London, Longman, 2000, p. 49; P.R. Kumaraswamy (ed.), *Revisiting the Yom Kippur War*, London, Frank Cass, 2000.

19. See 'Flaring up?', *The Economist*, April 13, 2002, p. 81; Keith Fisher, 'A meeting of blood and oil: the Balkan factor in Western energy security', *Journal of Southern Europe and the Balkans*, V. 4, N. 1, May 2002, pp. 78–9.

20. See Johnstone, 'Humanitarian war', p. 156.

21. Morse and Richard, 'The battle for energy dominance', p. 8.

22. Hill, 'Pipeline politics', p. 84.
23. Andrew Jack and David Stern, 'Caspian states discuss resources', *Financial Times*, April 24, 2002, p. 8.
24. Fisher, 'A meeting of blood and oil', p. 80.
25. Hill, 'Pipeline politics', p. 93.
26. Bulent Gokay, 'Oil, War and Global Hegemony', unpublished paper, Keele University, February 28, 2002, pp. 3–4.
27. Hill, 'Pipeline politics', p. 88.
28. See also Meliha Altunisik, 'Turkey and the changing oil market in Eurasia', in Libby Rittenberg (ed.), *The Political Economy of Turkey in the Post-Soviet Era*, Connecticut, Praeger, 1998, p. 161.
29. Jack and Stern, 'Caspian states'.
30. Hill, 'Pipeline politics', pp. 85, 88, and Altunisik, 'Turkey and the changing oil market in Eurasia'.
31. Graeme P. Herd and Fotios Moustakis, 'Black Sea geo-politics: a litmus test for the European security order?', *Mediterranean Politics*, V. 5, N. 3, Autumn 2000, p. 125.
32. Hill, 'Pipeline politics', p. 89.
33. See in particular Michael Griffin, *Reaping the Whirlwind: the Taliban Movement in Afghanistan*, London, Pluto Press, 2001, pp. 105–27.
34. Fisher, 'A meeting of blood and oil', p. 84 ff.
35. Ibid., pp. 86–7. In July 2002, INOGATE pushed for the construction of an $800 million oil pipeline connecting the Romanian Black Sea port of Konstantsa with Serbia's Pancevo refinery on the Danube river and Omisalj in Croatia. The deal was signed in November of the same year.
36. 'Since the fall of the Berlin Wall', David Buchan and Andrew Jack argue, 'Europe has been trying to strike a special energy relationship with Russia' (in their 'A return to Russia', *Financial Times*, April 25, 2002, p. 20).
37. In the mid-1990s, for instance, conflicting EU–US policies over Iran took the form of competition between the French company Total SA and the Houston-based Conoco, particularly after President Clinton blocked US oil projects in Iran; see in particular, Leon T. Hadar, 'Meddling in the Middle East? Europe challenges US hegemony in the region', *Mediterranean Quarterly*, V. 7, N. 4, Fall 1996, pp. 44–5.
38. Gokay, 'Introduction', pp. 8–9.
39. See Richard K. Betts and Thomas J. Christensen, 'China: getting the questions right', *The National Interest*, N. 62, Winter 2000–01, <http://www.nationalintercst.org/issues/60/Brzezinski.html>.
40. Neil King Jr et al., 'Iraq war would alter the economies of oil and politics of OPEC', the *Wall Street Journal Europe*, September 19, 2002, p. A10.
41. 'In June 1996', Michael Griffin wrote, 'three months before Kabul fell to the Taliban, Bridas filed a suit in Houston, which alleged that it had been prevented from developing its investment in Yashar because of UNOCAL's interference. Company lawers claimed $15 billion in damages, equivalent to the company's share of the estimated gas reserves', *Reaping the Whirlwind*, p. 125.
42. Morse and Richard, 'The battle for energy dominance', p. 6.

43. Free Republic,
    <http://www.freerepublic.com/forum/a393d8c6e4303.htm>, p. 3.
44. Fisher, 'A meeting of blood and oil', p. 79.
45. See Gokay, 'Oil, War and Global Hegemony'. Key members in the government of Bush junior had a long standing association with oil and gas cartels, and the Bush family itself has links with the Carlysle Group, which specialises in global investments and oil and gas, and UNOCAL. National Security Adviser, Condoleezza Rice, worked for the oil giant Chevron. Zalmay Khalizad who, at the time of writing, is the American special envoy to Afghanistan, was earlier a chief consultant for UNOCAL; see the informed article by Gopalaswami Parthasarathy, former Indian High Commissioner to Pakistan, 'War against terrorism and the oil and gas dimensions', <http://www.rediff.com/news/gp.htm>.
46. See, *inter alia*, Stefan Wagstyl, 'Profile: LUKoil; Process of growth is the main target', *Financial Times* ['Russia', special insert], April 15, 2002, p. VII.
47. See in particular Ahmet Ozturk, 'From oil pipelines to oil Straits: the Caspian pipeline politics and environmental protection of the Istanbul and the Canakkale Straits', *Journal of Southern Europe and the Balkans*, V. 4, N. 1, May 2002, pp. 57–75.
48. Kerin Hope, 'Russia to reap benefits of Balkan oil pipeline', *Financial Times*, September 30, 1994, quoted in Fisher, 'A meeting of blood and oil', p. 88–9.
49. The Economist Intelligence Unit, Country Forecast, London, *Russia*, 3rd Quarter 1998, p. 12.
50. See 'Turkey and Greece', *The Economist*, April 13, 2002, p. 44.
51. Russia opposes this, not least because it suspects that the US force will be used to bolster Georgia's forces against the pro-Russian breakaway region of Abkhazia; see Patrick E. Tyler, 'Abkhazia hastens break with Georgia', *International Herald Tribune*, March 1, 2002, p. 3; Robert Cottrell et al., 'Russian unease as US war on terror shifts to Caucasus', *Financial Times*, February 28, 2002, p. 8; Robert Cottrell, 'Closer ties with the West attracts muted criticism', *Financial Times* ['Russia', special insert], April 15, 2002, p. III.
52. See Mikhail Khodarenok, 'Russia surrounded with US military bases and Moscow still do not know if this is good or bad', *NATO Enlargement Daily Brief*, CDI Russian Weekly, April 8, 2002.
53. Given Russia's energy and geo-political interests in the Balkans, the Kosovo war saw something of a revival of its influence in the region, but in military terms this was to be limited to the episode at the Pristina airport, which was occupied by Russian commandos before the arrival of the US marines. As regards the issue of Chinese influence in the Balkans, the NATO bombing of China's Embassy in Belgrade amidst the campaign speaks for itself; see, among others, Peter Gowan, 'The NATO powers and the Balkan tragedy', *New Left Review*, N. 234, March–April 1999, pp. 83–105; Ali, *Masters of the Universe?*.
54. Free Republic, p. 1.
55. It is interesting to note that the US resists EU pressures to revamp its representation at the IMF, in terms of voting rights and procedural

guarantees. The US is the largest shareholder in the institution with 17.2 per cent, but it is also the only power who has enough votes for a veto; see Paul Hofheinz, 'EU urged to revamp voting at IMF to counterbalance US', *Wall Street Journal Europe*, April 19–21, 2002, p. A3.

56. Brzezinski, *The Grand Chessboard*, p. 24.

57. In this respect, it is interesting to read the account by Joseph Nye, 'The new Rome meets the new barbarians', *The Economist*, March 23, 2002, pp. 23–5. Nye's full statement on the issue is *The Paradox of American Power: Why the World's Only Superpower Can't Go it Alone*, Oxford, Oxford University Press, 2002.

58. See the interesting leading comment, 'George Bush and the axis of evil', *The Economist*, February 2, 2002, pp. 13–14.

59. Nye, *The Paradox of American Power*.

60. For a good summary of those interpretations and a sustained criticism, see Gokay, 'Oil, War and Global Hegemony'.

61. See, among others, Ivo H. Daalder and James M. Lindsay, 'Nasty, brutish and long: America's war on terrorism', *Current History*, December 2001, <http://www.brook.edu> and Steven A. Cook, 'US–Turkey relations and the war on terrorism', Analysis Paper 9, November 2001, <http://www.brook.edu>.

62. See International Affairs & Defence Section, *11 September 2001: The Response*, Research Paper 01/72, London, House of Commons, October 3, 2001.

63. Among others, Judy Dempsey and Richard Wolffe, 'In from the Cold', *Financial Times*, May 15, 2002, p. 16.

64. See also Dennis Kux, 'The Pakistani pivot', *The National Interest*, N. 65, Fall 2001.

65. Dempsey and Wolffe, 'In from the Cold'.

66. Gokay, 'Oil, War and Global Hegemony', p. 7.

67. Parthasarathy, 'War against terrorism'.

68. Vladimir Putin, Russia's new President, is tactful towards the US, as he thinks that by cajoling the superpower a greater share in the lucrative deals over Middle Eastern oil may be achieved jointly with the US. As Quentin Peel put it ('Putin plays a weak hand well', *Financial Times*, March 18, 2002, p. 23): 'Russia is owed some $8bn by Iraq, and several Russian oil companies have lucrative contracts to export Iraqi oil for food under United Nations auspices. Moscow certainly does not want any action that leaves the country ruled by fundamentalists, or stokes the conflict between Kurds and Arabs.'

69. For example, the nuclear-powered aircraft carrier USS Enterprise, which patrols the Indian Ocean, 'has a crew of 3,200 to run the ship alone, plus 2,400 pilots and aircrew who fly and service the 70 state-of-the-art aircraft'. It is 1,100ft long and its flight deck is 250ft across and it never patrols on its own. It is always accompanied by an 'Aegis-type cruiser, a large surface ship designed to shoot down incoming missiles; by a bevy of frigates and destroyers to protect it from enemy submarines; by a lurking hunter-killer submarine or two; and by some supply vessels and other specialised craft'. The US possess 12 such carriers patrolling across the global oceans; all quotations are taken from Paul Kennedy, 'The

Eagle has landed', *Financial Times*, February 2–3, 2002, pp. I–IV (FT Weekend)

70. Michael Cox, 'American power before and after 11 September', *International Affairs*, V. 78, N. 2, April 2002, p. 263.

71. Germany's foreign policy in the 1990s evolved from funding the coalition war effort during the 1990–91 Gulf War to military participation in Kosovo and Afghanistan. Recasting 'Germany's place on the international stage', Chancellor Gerhard Schroeder, on October 11, 2001, declared that 'the country's post-war role was "irrevocably over"'; see The International Institute for Strategic Studies, 'Germany's "new" foreign policy', *IISS Strategic Comments*, V. 7, N. 9, November 2001.

72. See Maurice Fraser (ed.), *Britain in Europe*, London, Strategems Publishing Ltd., 1998. For a sustained criticism of neo-liberalism from Social Democratic and pro-European positions, see Donald Sassoon, *Social Democracy at the Heart of Europe*, London, IPPR, 1996.

Chapter 3

1. To my knowledge, there is not a single specialist working on the history of NATO and international relations that has avoided the temptation not to comment on this famous phrase; see, *inter alia*, Ronald Steel, 'Instead of NATO', *The New York Review of Books*, January 15, 1998, pp. 19–21.

2. See Max Weber, 'Legitimate authority and bureaucracy', in D.S. Pugh, *Organisation Theory*, Harmondsworth, Penguin, 1971, pp. 15–29.

3. On the organisational restructuring of NATO and the creation of new regional and subregional administrations see, among others, 'Your command is my wish' (special insert: A Survey of NATO), *The Economist*, April 30, 1999, p. 13.

4. Michael Brown, 'Minimalist NATO: a wise alliance knows when to retrench', *Foreign Affairs*, N. 3, 1999, pp. 204–18. It is interesting to note that Luttwak, amidst the Kosovo crisis, wrote an extensive piece in the *Sunday Telegraph* (April 11, 1999, p. 31), arguing that NATO's campaign was severely damaging its cohesion and genuine scope.

5. Among others, Ronald D. Asmus and Robert C. Nurick, 'NATO enlargement and the Baltic states', *Survival*, V. 38, N. 2, Summer 1996, pp. 121–42; David S. Yost, *NATO Transformed*, Washington DC, United States Institute of Peace Press, 1998; Ted G. Carpenter, *NATO Enters the 21st Century*, London, Frank Cass, 2001; Michael C. Williams and Iver B. Neumann, 'From alliance to security community: NATO, Russia and the power of identity', *Millennium*, V. 29, N. 2, 2000, pp. 357–87; Martin A. Smith and Graham Timmins, *Building a Bigger Europe: EU and NATO Enlargement in Comparative Perspective*, Aldershot, Ashgate, 2000.

6. NATO's emphasis on, and elaboration of a 'new strategic concept' was agreed by the Heads of State and Government that took part in the North Atlantic Council meeting held in Rome as early as November 1991. However, the concept and the main ideas surrounding it had not been elaborated in a coherent manner; see, among others, Yost, *NATO Transformed*.

7. See The Global Environment, *1998 Strategic Assessment*, <http://www.ndu.edu/inss/sa98/sa98ch1.html>, pp. 3–7.

8. Ibid., pp. 6–9, passim.

9. Madeleine Albright quoted in Michael Dobbs, 'US indicates preference for just 3 new NATO states', *Washington Post*, May 30, 1997, p. A30.

10. See Leszek Buszynski, 'Russia and the West: Towards renewed geo-political rivalry?', *Survival*, V. 37, N. 3, Autumn 1995, pp. 104–25; also John Lewis Gaddis, 'History, grand strategy and NATO enlargement', *Survival*, V. 40, N. 1, Spring 1998, pp. 145–51.

11. See, among others, the perceptive account by John Lewis Gaddis, *The United States and the Origins of the Cold War*, New York, Columbia University Press, 2000, pp. 1–32, 95–133.

12. In an article discussing a new enlargement of NATO incorporating the Baltic states, Antony J. Blinken, former Senior Adviser to President Clinton for European Affairs, stated: '[NATO] Aspirants know that strong democratic structures, respect for minority rights and free markets are necessary for inclusion in the club; just as important, they are necessary to remain members in good standing', 'New mood threatens NATO enlargement', *International Herald Tribune*, April 3, 2001, p. 6.

13. 'Heirs of Pericles' (special insert: A Survey of NATO), *The Economist*, p. 10.

14. See for instance William Hale, *Turkish Foreign Policy 1774–2000*, London, Frank Cass, 2000, pp. 1–11, passim.

15. Ernest Bevin quoted in Michael Howard, 'An unhappy successful marriage: Security means knowing what to expect', *Foreign Affairs*, N. 3, 1999, p. 164.

16. In the run up to the Amsterdam Treaty, European Union officials debated harshly the way in which the European Union should proceed with its eastward expansion plans. See, *inter alia*, Neill Nugent, 'Redefining Europe', *Journal of Common Market Studies*, Annual Review Issue, V. 33, 1995, pp. 5–10, passim.

17. The *acquis* principle asserts that every new member must accept all that has been approved so far: the Treaties, the entire corpus of legislation, the case law of the Court of Justice, all resolutions and all international agreements of the EU: in all, some 136,000 pages of official texts. See Sassoon, *Social Democracy*.

18. This decision was the result of informal bargaining between Germany and Britain, with Germany agreeing to support the British request for opt-outs in return for Britain's support 'for the German position on the EC's diplomatic recognition of Slovenia and Croatia'; see Michael J. Baun, *An Imperfect Union*, Oxford, Westview Press, 1996, pp. 74–5; also, Gowan, 'The NATO powers', p. 92.

19. Baun, *An Imperfect Union*, pp. 161–8.

20. Sassoon, *Social Democracy*, pp. 51 ff.

21. See the Editorial of *The Economist*, 'Messy war, messy peace', June 12, 1999, p. 17, which raised *in toto* the main issues that Michael Mandelbaum explored in his perceptive essay 'A perfect failure: NATO's war against Yugoslavia', *Foreign Affairs*, N. 5, 1999, pp. 2–8. The full text of the Rambouillet peace accord, which includes the 'Appendix B', can

be found in Luciana Castellina (ed.), *La Nato nei Balcani*, Rome, Riuniti, 1999, pp. 99–51.

22. See Susan Woodward, *The Balkan Tragedy*, Washington DC, The Brookings Institution, 1995; Marjan Setinc (Ambassador of the Republic Slovenia in the UK and Ireland), 'Slovenia and Europe: Whatever happened to the enlargement of the European Union?', speech delivered at Kingston University, European Research Centre, London November 21, 2000, memo.

23. See also the perceptive article by Iraj Hashi, 'The disintegration of Yugoslavia: Regional disparities and the nationalities question', *Capital and Class*, V. 48, Autumn 1992, pp. 41–88.

24. Woodward, *The Balkan Tragedy*, pp. 15, 380.

25. Chris Hedges, 'Kosovo's next masters?', *Foreign Affairs*, N. 3, 1999, p. 38.

26. Woodward, *The Balkan Tragedy*, p. 106.

27. See Martin Woollacott, 'How the man we could-do-business-with is becoming the man we must destroy', *Guardian*, April 3, 1999, p. 20.

28. Hedges, 'Kosovo's next masters?', p. 36. Peter Gowan gave exactly that interpretation in his 'The twisted road to Kosovo', *Labour Focus on Eastern Europe* (single issue), N. 62, 1999, pp. 44–9. Gowan's analysis implies that this tactic was a well-orchestrated design, also tested before the Gulf War in 1991, when the US gave the signal to Saddam Hussein to take Kuwait by affirming that the US had no vital interests in the region.

29. As Mandelbaum argued: 'Precisely when Belgrade decided on the tactics it employed in Kosovo after the bombing began, and indeed just what it decided – whether the displacement of almost 1,5 million Albanians was its original aim, simply a byproduct of a sweeping assault on the KLA, or a response to NATO's air campaign – are questions that cannot be seriously addressed without access to such records as the Milosevic's regime may have kept', 'A perfect failure', p. 3.

30. Benjamin Schwarz and Christopher Layne, 'For the record', *The National Interest*, N. 57, 1999, p. 13.

31. See Ben Macintyre, 'Clinton rejected warnings of fiasco', *The Times*, April 2, 1999, p. 10. This was particularly the concern, among others, of George Tenet, the CIA Director.

32. As Robin Blackburn wrote in 'Kosovo: the war of NATO expansion', *New Left Review*, N. 235, 1999, p. 111: 'The Kosovo war was unleashed, and was allowed to become a protracted assault on the whole social infrastructure of Yugoslavia, for one reason, and one reason only: that nothing less than a "NATO-led" solution and NATO-protectorate status for Kosovo was acceptable to the US and Britain, and that other alliance members went along with this, whatever their public or private reservations.'

33. For an informed discussion of the concept, see Alan George and William Simons (eds), *The Limits of Coercive Diplomacy*, New York, Westview Press, 1994.

34. For an opposite view see, among others, Catherine Guicherd, 'International law and the war in Kosovo', *Survival*, V. 41, N. 2, Summer 1999, pp. 19–34.

35. Obviously, the US did not take the issue to the UN Security Council, as it was certain that China and Russia would have opposed its strategy.

For an argument in favour of institutionalising the principle of 'humanitarian intervention' see, *inter alia*, Michael J. Glennon, 'The new interventionism: the search for a just international law', *Foreign Affairs*, N. 3, 1999, pp. 2–7.

36. Diana Johnstone, 'Notes on the Kosovo problem and the international community', *Labour Focus on Eastern Europe*, N. 63, 1999, p. 18.

37. For a comprehensive proposal of 'preventive civilian intervention' as opposed to NATO's 'military intervention for humanitarian reasons', see Julianne Smith and Martin Butcher, *A Risk Reduction Strategy for NATO: Preparing for the Next 50 Years*, London, British American Security Information Council – Basic Research Report, 1, 1999.

38. Unlike the Austro-Marxists, such as Otto Bauer and Karl Renner, Lenin 'does not reduce the right to self determination to a simple "cultural autonomy", but extends it to right of nations to establish their own state'. For an informed discussion, see Nicos Poulantzas, *L'État, le Pouvoir, le Socialisme*, Paris, Presses Universitaires de France, 1978, pp. 102–33 (the extract is from pp. 103–4). It is worth noting that Lenin's dramatic break with Stalin in 1923 was caused by disagreements between the two over the issue of nationalities and self-determination.

39. See 'Kosovo: State in embryo', *The Economist*, December 3, 1999, pp. 46–51. Admittedly, the fall of Milosevic has somehow been to the detriment of Albanian irredentism and of pro-independence Montenegrins, since it deprived them of a good bargaining chip in their diplomatic negotiations with the West.

40. Daniel Benjamin, 'US troops must stay in the Balkans', *International Herald Tribune*, December 28, 2000, p. 9.

41. For an analysis of NATO's constitutional reform proposals and its general global strategy in the context of American foreign policy see, among others, William G. Hyland, *Clinton's World: Remaking American Foreign Policy*, New York, Praeger, 1999; Anton A. Bebler (ed.), *The Challenge of NATO Enlargement*, New York, Praeger, 1999; Howard, 'An unhappy successful marriage', pp. 164–75.

42. See in particular Jacques Attali, 'A continental architecture', in Perry Anderson and Peter Gowan (eds), *The Question of Europe*, London, Verso, 1997, pp. 345–56. From 1981 to 1991 Attali was Special Adviser to François Mitterrand.

43. On this subject in particular see 'Knights in shining armour?', *The Economist* (A Survey of NATO), pp. 3–5.

44. See in particular Ian O. Lesser, *NATO Looks South: New Challenges and New Strategies in the Mediterranean*, Washington DC, Project Air Force–RAND, 2000.

45. The best statements in this vein are Peter Gowan's 'Neo-liberal theory and practice for Eastern Europe', *New Left Review*, N. 213, 1995, and 'The dynamics of "European enlargement"', *Labour Focus on Eastern Europe*, N. 56, 1997. Both can now be found in his *The Global Gamble*. It is interesting to note that the development strategy for Eastern Europe launched by the German Deutsche Bank President Herrhausen was dropped, following his assassination in autumn 1989, ibid., pp. 306–07.

46. See in particular James Petras and Morris Morley 'Contesting hegemons: US–French relations in the "New World Order"', *Review of International Studies*, N. 1, 2000, pp. 49–67.

47. On this shift in Germany's foreign policy and the role of the economic agreements between Germany and the US in the WTO foundation forum, see in particular the perceptive essay by Mary M. McKenzie, 'Constructing European security: Security conceptions, institution building, and transatlantic relations', paper presented for the 38th Annual Convention of the International Studies Association, Toronto, Canada, March 18–22, 1997, pp. 3–17, passim; also, Hanns W. Maull, 'Germany in the Yugoslav crisis', *Survival*, V. 37, N. 4, Winter 1995–6, pp. 99–130.

48. Brzezinski, *The Grand Chessboard*, pp. 208–09.

49. I draw here my speculative argument from William Pfaff, 'For Europe, a tough call on defence co-operation', *International Herald Tribune*, May 18, 2002 and Jeffrey Gedmin, 'The alliance is doomed', *Washington Post*, May 20, 2002, NATO Enlargement Daily Brief, <http://groups.yahoo.com/group/nedb>.

50. See, *inter alia*, Hugh Poulton, *The Balkans: Minorities and States in Conflict*, London, Minority Rights Group, 1991.

51. See James Pettifer, 'The new Macedonian Question', *International Affairs*, N. 3, 1992, p. 481; also James Pettifer (ed.), *The New Macedonian Question*, London, Macmillan, 1999.

52. Following the inter-communal strife of 1963, the Turkish Cypriots, enveloped in militarily protected enclaves throughout the island, claimed international recognition as a separate state entity. This was denied by the UN, but following the Turkish invasions of Cyprus in 1974 and the establishment of a Turkish-controlled zone in Northern Cyprus, the Turkish Cypriots proclaimed a 'Turkish Republic of Northern Cyprus' (TRNC) in 1983, which was recognised only by Turkey. We deal extensively with the Cyprus issue in the following chapters.

53. See, *inter alia*, Sophia Clément, *Conflict Prevention in the Balkans: Case Studies of Kosovo and the FYR of Macedonia*, Chaillot Paper 30, Paris, Institute for Security Studies, Western European Union, December 1997, pp. 22 ff.

54. Woodward, *The Balkan Tragedy*, p. 372.

55. Among others, Shawaluddin W. Hassan, 'The response of Muslim countries to the Bosnian crisis', paper presented to the 40th annual convention of the International Studies Association, Washington DC, February 16–20, 1999. The author examines the influence of the Muslim states, such as Saudi Arabia, Pakistan, Turkey, and the pressure they put on the US to intervene in Bosnia. Similar pressures on the US were also exercised by the majority of Muslim states during the Kosovo crisis, with Turkey and Saudi Arabia taking the lead. Turkey had also participated in the bombing campaign, while Saudi Arabia headed large humanitarian missions.

56. Hugh Poulton, 'The struggle for hegemony in Turkey: Turkish nationalism as a contemporary force', *Journal of Southern Europe and the Balkans*, V. 1, N. 1, 1999, pp. 15–31. Also, during the Kosovo war, Leyla Boulton wrote in the *Financial Times* ('Turkey Aims to aid Moslem brethren',

Financial Times, April 8, 1999, p. 2): 'Emotion aside, the [Kosovo] conflict is pregnant with strategic and political significance for a country [Turkey] that is not only home to 5 million ethnic Albanians but sees the Balkans as its backyard.' Boulton went on to quote Bulent Ecevit, who said that 'the people of Kosovo are our brothers; their pain is our pain ... No country has done as much as Turkey to help the people of the region.'

57. See *Bosnia Report*, series 8, London, The Bosnian Institute, January–March 1999, p. 12.

58. The genocidal decision was taken by the Committee of Unity and Progress (CUP), the highest level of the Yttihadist (Young Turk) movement; see Mark Mazower, 'The G-Word: Review of *The Treatment of Armenians in the Ottoman Empire, 1915–16*, (Document Series edited by Ara Sarafian, Gomidas Institute, December 11, 2000)', *London Review of Books*, February 8, 2001, pp. 19–21; Michael Mann, 'The dark side of democracy: The modern tradition of ethnic and political cleansing', *New Left Review*, N. 235, 1999, p. 31. For a reliable account of this genocide, see also Paul B. Paboudjian and Raymond H. Kévorkian, *Les Arméniens dans l'Empire Ottoman à la veille du Génocide*, Paris, Arhis, 1992, particularly pp. 47–77, passim. Turkey has been very inflexible in dealing with this issue. It could very well have admitted its mistake, while making clear that this genocidal policy had taken place in the context of the imperialistic politics of the West European Powers during the First World War, whose chief aim was to partition Anatolia using as a pretext the presence of large Christian minorities there.

59. It is worth noting that powerful factions within the Turkish military oppose the country's entry into the EU on the basis of the implementation of the *acquis* principle. They consider that any reform of the Turkish state along this principle will force Turkey to accept a certain administrative, civil and cultural autonomy for the Kurds in South-eastern Turkey. In addition, the accession of Cyprus to the EU will put pressure on Turkey to allow some 180,000 Greek-Cypriot refugees to return to their homes in the Northern occupied areas even under Turkish administration. We shall deal extensively with these issues in the next chapters.

60. See 'Turkey: On the crest of the wave', *The Economist*, October 30, 1999, pp. 50–3.

61. 'Russia's ultimatum', *Guardian*, December 7, 1999, p. 21.

62. James Riordan, *A Biography of Oliver Stone*, London, Aurum Press, 1996, p. 133.

63. Steel, 'Instead of NATO', p. 22.

64. See, among others, Matthew Campbell and Stephen Grey, 'US fears force will break up NATO', *Sunday Times*, December 12, 1999, p. 2; François Heisbourg, 'Europe's strategic ambitions: The limits of ambiguity', *Survival*, V. 42, N. 2, Summer 2000, pp. 5–15.

65. See Lena Jonson, 'Russia, NATO and the handling of conflicts at Russia's Southern periphery: At a crossroads?', *European Security*, V. 9, N. 4, Winter 2000, pp. 45–72; 'Vladimir Putin's long, hard haul', *The Economist*, May 18, 2002, pp. 25–7.

66. George Papandreou, 'Greece wants Turkey to make the grade', *International Herald Tribune*, December 10, 1999, p. 8. For an informed outline

of the economic policy to be pursued by the West for the reconstruction of the Balkans see, among others, Task Force Report, *Promoting Sustainable Economies in the Balkans*, New York, Council on Foreign Relations, 2000; Benn Steil and Susan L. Woodward, 'A European "New Deal" for the Balkans', *Foreign Affairs*, N. 6, 1999, pp. 95–105; Constantine P. Danopoulos and Emilia Ianeva, 'Poverty in the Balkans and the issue of reconstruction: Bulgaria and Yugoslavia compared', *Journal of Southern Europe and the Balkans*, V. 1, N. 2, November 1999, pp. 185–98.

67. See in particular Ben Soetendorp, *Foreign Policy in the European Union*, London, Longman, 1999, pp. 95–113.

68. See, *inter alia*, Guicherd, 'International Law and the War in Kosovo', who argues in favour of institutionalising the principle of humanitarian intervention; Adam Roberts, 'NATO's "Humanitarian War" over Kosovo', *Survival*, V. 41, N. 3, Autumn 1999, pp. 102–23, who offers a more balanced account, although he refrains from presenting a straightforward critique of NATO's intervention over Kosovo. The overall strategic rationale of NATO expansion is given in Zbigniew Brzezinski's statement *The Grand Chessboard*.

69. Mandelbaum, 'A Perfect Failure', p. 8.

Chapter 4

1. Bruce R. Kuniholm, *The Origins of the Cold War in the Near East: Great Power Conflict and Diplomacy in Iran, Turkey and Greece*, Princeton, Princeton University Press, 1980, p. xv.

2. Rouhollah Ramazani, *The Northern Tier: Afghanistan, Iran and Turkey*, Princeton, Princeton University Press, 1966, pp. 8–10.

3. Kuniholm, *The Origins of the Cold War in the Near East*, p. 380.

4. In this context, it is worth remembering that during the last phase of the Civil War in 1948–9, the leader of the Greek Communist Party (KKE), Nikos Zachariades, managed to pass a resolution according to which the KKE should fight for an autonomous and independent Macedonia and Thrace. This could accommodate Tito's and Dimitrov's views for an independent Macedonian state, later to be divided between Yugoslavia and Bulgaria, a fact that would have split Greece's territorial integrity and thus its common frontier with pro-Western Turkey. In addition, such a development would have facilitated the USSR's penetration into the Eastern Mediterranean.

5. American strategists had put forward policy plans under the code names 'Griddle', 'Broiler' and 'Halfmoon', in which Turkey and its role with regard to securing oil featured prominently in case of war with the USSR; see Melvyn P. Leffler, 'Strategy, diplomacy and the Cold War: the United States, Turkey and NATO, 1945–1952', *Journal of American History*, V. 71, N. 4, 1985, pp. 813–18.

6. Bruce R. Kuniholm, *The Near East Connection: Greece and Turkey in the Reconstruction and Security of Europe, 1946–1952*, Massachusetts, Hellenic College Press, 1984, p. 16.

7. The best work we possess in this vein is that by Ekavi Athanassopoulou, *Turkey: Anglo-American Security Interests (1945–1952) and the First Enlargement of NATO*, London, Frank Cass, 1999.

8. Theodore Couloumbis, *The United States, Greece and Turkey: the Troubled Triangle*, New York, Praeger, 1983, p. 178. The most perceptive and detailed study of the EOKA struggle is by Robert Holland, *Britain and the Revolt in Cyprus*, Oxford, Clarendon, 1998; on the international and regional security dimensions of the Cyprus issue during the same period, see Evanthis Hatzivassiliou, *Britain and the International Status of Cyprus*, Minneapolis, University of Minnesota Press, 1997.

9. Ronald R. Krebs, 'Perverse Institutionalism: NATO and the Greco-Turkish Conflict', *International Organisation*, V. 53, N. 2, Spring 1999, p. 364. 'From 1946 to 1985', with the exception of the countries who fought wars (Israel, South Vietnam and South Korea), 'Turkey was the world's first largest recipient of US military assistance, garnering a total of $7,857.8 million'; see Marios Evriviades, 'Turkey's role in United States strategy during and after the Cold War', *Mediterranean Quarterly*, V. 9, N. 2, Spring 1998, p. 35. Drawing from Amikam Nachmani's *Israel, Turkey and Greece: Uneasy Relations in the East Mediterranean* (London, Frank Cass, 1987), Evriviades also points out that in 1958, with US blessing, Turkey and Israel formed a secret pact calling 'for joint military action in the event that Aden, which lay on the route of the oil tankers, fell into Nassir hands', p. 40.

10. Efforts to balance this unequal distribution of military assistance were made by institutionalising a 7:10 ratio between Greece and Turkey. However, even this principle was challenged in the 1980s and 1990s; see Tamar Gabelnick, William D. Hartung and Jennifer Washburn, *Arming Repression: US Arms Sales to Turkey During the Clinton Administration*, A Joint Report of the World Policy Institute and the Federation of American Scientists, <http://www.fas.org/asmp/library/reports/turkeyrep.htm>, October 1999.

11. Theodor Herzl, a Jewish journalist and playwright from Vienna, had published his *Der Judenstaat* (The Jewish State) in 1896. He advocated the foundation of a Jewish state in Palestine, and the immigration of Jewish populations and the acquisition of land there; see Shlomo Avineri, *The Making of Modern Zionism: the Intellectual Origins of the Jewish State*, New York, Basic Books, 1981.

12. Kenneth W. Stein, *The Land Question in Palestine, 1917–1939*, Chapel Hill, University of North Carolina Press, 1984, pp. 6–8.

13. British Colonial Secretary Malcolm MacDonald reformed the previous legislation of James Arthur Balfour (1917), producing a White Paper (1939) that limited Jewish immigration to 15,000 per year. Understandably enough, this outraged the European Jews, who were at the time under the pogrom of the Nazis.

14. Schulze, *The Arab–Israeli Conflict*, p. 9. The original members of the League were Egypt, Iraq, Lebanon, Saudi Arabia, Transjordan, Yemen and the Palestinians. Libya joined in 1953, Sudan in 1956, Tunisia and Morocco in 1958, Kuwait in 1961, Algeria in 1962, South Yemen in 1968, Bahrain, Qatar, the Trucial States and Oman in 1971, Mauritania in 1973, Somalia in 1974 and the PLO in 1976. In 1978 Egypt's membership was suspended, following the Camp David Accord between

Israel and Egypt, a peace agreement providing for the restoration of the Sinai peninsula to Egypt. Egypt re-entered the League in 1987.

15. In this first war between Israel and the Arabs, some Arab states were indeed more interested in acquiring Palestinian territory themselves, and/or in affirming leadership in the Arab world, than in undoing the foundation of Israel; see Mark Tessler, *History of the Israeli–Palestinian Conflict*, Bloomington, Indiana University Press, 1994.

16. See Benny Morris, *The Birth of the Palestinian Refugee Problem, 1947–1951*, Cambridge, Cambridge University Press, 1987.

17. Quoted in Stephen Ambrose and Douglas Brinkley, *Rise to Globalism: American Foreign Policy since 1938*, London, Penguin, 1997, p. 254.

18. 'In such a case', Van Coufoudakis wrote, 'the Eastern Mediterranean and the Persian Gulf constituted a unified strategic basin for the United States'. See his perceptive essay 'The solution of the Cyprus problem and its security implications for the United States and Europe', in Andreas Theophanous and Nicos Peristianis (eds), *The Cyprus Problem: Its Solution and the Day After*, Nicosia, Intercollege Press, 1998, p. 14.

19. In 1954 Iraq signed a military assistance agreement with the US, and the following year it concluded the Baghdad Pact with Turkey. Britain joined the Baghdad Pact in April 1955, Pakistan in September 1955 and Iran in October. The US, although never a signatory, was basically 'the principle paymaster and promoter of the project'; see, *inter alia*, Hale, *Turkish Foreign Policy*, p. 126.

20. The plan, agreed in the form of a secret protocol signed in Sèrves on October 24, 1956, determined that Israel would seize the Canal, then Britain and France would ask both Egypt and Israel to cease hostilities and withdraw. If Egypt refused to do so, which was almost certain, Britain and France would intervene to protect the Suez; see in particular Anthony Gorst and Lewis Johnman, *The Suez Crisis*, London, Routledge, 1997, pp. 93–102.

21. See Ambrose and Brinkley, *Rise to Globalism*, p. 157.

22. US plans came somewhat into fruition in August 1959, when 'the remains of the Baghdad Pact were reconstructed as a purely northern tier alliance of Britain, Turkey, Iran and Pakistan, with the US continuing its observer status, known as the Central Treaty Organisation (CENTO)', Hale, *Turkish Foreign Policy*, p. 127.

23. Ambrose and Brinkley, *Rise to Globalism*, p. 151, passim.

24. In 1943–4, the 'Big Three' (Churchill, Roosevelt, Stalin) were instrumental in dividing the Balkan states into spheres of influences. Yugoslavia, unlike Greece (10 per cent pro-Soviet, 90 per cent pro-Western), Romania and Bulgaria (both: 10 per cent pro-Western, 90 per cent pro-Soviet), was broken down equally between the West and the East; see Gavin Scrase, 'The Balkans and international politics in the 1940s: on the Eden–Gusev pre-percentages agreement', *Journal of Southern Europe and the Balkans*, V. 2, N. 2, November 2000, pp. 163–76.

25. Woodward, *The Balkan Tragedy*, p. 25.

26. See James A. McHenry, *The Uneasy Partnership on Cyprus, 1919–1939*, New York, Garland Publishing, 1987, pp. 48–9.

27. Ibid., p. 49.

28. For an interpretation of the events and a discussion on the background to the 1974 crisis see my 'Reflections on the Cyprus issue and the Turkish invasions of 1974', *Mediterranean Quarterly*, V. 12, N. 3, Summer 2001, pp. 98–127.

29. House of Commons, Parliamentary Debates 1953–54, 531, col. 508, July 28, 1954, quoted in Claude Nicolet, *United States Policy Towards Cyprus, 1954–1974: Removing the Greek–Turkish Bone of Contention*, Mannheim, Bibliopolis, 2001, p. 42.

30. See in particular ibid. Although at times he assesses Makarios's strategy improperly, Nicolet's meticulously researched book is the most perceptive historical account of the US policy in Cyprus to date.

31. We have ample evidence about this type of British colonial policy of 'divide and rule' in Cyprus; see, *inter alia*, Tozun Bahcheli, *Greek–Turkish Relations since 1955*, Boulder CO, Westview Press, 1990, p. 37, passim; Fouskas, 'Reflections'.

32. Quoted in Makarios Drousiotis, *The Dark Side of EOKA* (in Greek), Athens, Stachi, 1998, pp. 187–90.

33. See the perceptive article by S. Victor Papacosma, 'More than rocks: the Aegean's discordant legacy', *Mediterranean Quarterly*, V. 4, N. 4, Fall 1996, p. 81 ff.

34. See William Mallinson, 'Reality versus morality', *Defensor Pacis*, N. 7, January 2001, p. 44.

35. Coufoudakis, 'The solution', p. 15.

36. See Suha Bolukbasi, 'The Johnson letter revisited', *Middle Eastern Studies*, V. 29, N. 3, July 1993, pp. 505–25.

37. The Cuban crisis and the way in which the US dealt with it by disregarding Turkey's security interests had left Turkey totally unsatisfied. See, among others, Evriviades, 'Turkey's role', p. 41, Gareth M. Winrow, 'NATO and the out-of-area issue: the positions of Turkey and Italy', *Il Politico* (University of Pavia, Italy), anno LVIII, n. 4, 1993, pp. 631–52.

38. Suha Bolukbasi, 'Behind the Turkish–Israeli alliance: a Turkish view', *Journal of Palestine Studies*, V. XXIX, N. 1, Autumn 1999, p. 26.

39. Winrow, 'NATO and the out-of-area issue', p. 636; see also the penetrating study by Michael B. Oren, *Six Days of War: June 1967 and the Making of the Modern Middle East*, Oxford, Oxford University Press, 2002.

40. Among others, Brendan O'Malley and Ian Craig, *The Cyprus Conspiracy*, London, I.B. Tauris, 1999, p. 144.

41. Acheson was Secretary of State from January 1949 until January 1953. He assumed the role of US–Cyprus special mediator during Summer 1964 and was in close collaboration with Ball, deputy Secretary of State from 1961 until 1967.

42. It should be noted here that George Papandreou was very moderate and ready to accept versions of Ball–Acheson schemes, but under the influence of Andreas the American efforts proved indeed fruitless; see in particular, Andreas Papandreou, *Democracy at Gunpoint: the Greek Front*, London, Andre Deutsch, 1970.

43. Coufoudakis, 'The solution', p. 14.

44. See, *inter alia*, Van Coufoudakis, 'US foreign policy and the Cyprus question: an interpretation', *Millennium*, V. 5, N. 3, 1976–77, pp. 245–68; Vassilis Fouskas, 'Reflections'.

45. Kissinger is sincere at least on this point; see Henry Kissinger, *Years of Renewal*, New York, Simon & Schuster, 1999, pp. 195 ff. Claude Nicolet (*United States Policy Towards Cyprus*, pp. 402–47) is too apologetic with regard to Kissinger's attitude. Although Nicolet admits that we still have no hard evidence proving Kissinger's complicity in the Turkish invasions, he seems to be anxious to find evidence that supports Kissinger's innocence. This self-imposition of the 'neutralist' position, even if 'some sort of evidence is not neutral', is one of the most serious drawbacks of Nicolet's text.

46. The 1959–60 settlements prohibited both *enosis* (the Greek Cypriot demand) and *taksim* (partition, the Turkish Cypriot claim). More to the point, Article 4 of the Treaty of Guarantee stated that 'in the event of a breach of the provisions of the present Treaty, Greece, Turkey and the UK undertake to consult together with respect to the representations or measures necessary to ensure observance of those provisions. In so far as common or concerned action may not prove possible, each of the three guaranteeing powers reserves the right to take action with the sole aim of re-establishing the state of affairs created by the present Treaty.' It is interesting to note that the second sentence, never honoured by Turkey, was nevertheless added at the insistence of the Turkish delegation during the negotiations. It is this sentence that deprived Turkey of any legal ground to justify the two invasions and the situation created in the occupied zone since; see Fouskas, 'Reflections', p. 116.

47. I owe this insight to a Labour Party MP, who prefers his name not to be disclosed.

48. See, *inter alia*, Richard Clogg, 'Greek–Turkish relations in the post-1974 period', in Dimitri Constas (ed.), *The Greek–Turkish Conflict in the 1990s*, London, Macmillan, 1991, pp. 12–23; Aldo Chircop et al. (eds), *The Aegean Sea after the Cold War*, London, Macmillan, 2000.

49. Papacosma, 'More than rocks', p. 88. The 1958 Geneva Convention states that islands, like the mainland, do have continental shelves, that is 'submerged off-coast lands extending between the outer limits of a nation's territorial waters and a water depth of two hundred meters or beyond that to a depth at which the water above the submerged lands permits exploitation of those lands', ibid., p. 82. Turkey denies continental shelf to the Eastern Aegean islands and the Dodecanese, because it argues that they rest on the shelf of Asia Minor. Turkey's argument lacks legal grounds and is rather political, based on Turkey's regional military superiority in the wake of its success in Cyprus.

50. As a Turkish economist put it: 'The extension of the EEC membership to Greece ... put Turkey at a disadvantage and required readjustments on the part of both sides', Z.Y. Hershlag, *The Contemporary Turkish Economy*, London, Routledge, 1988, p. 86. It is worth mentioning that Turkey's opposition to Greece's re-entry in NATO was eased after the Generals' coup of September 12, 1980.

51. See Canan Balkir, 'The customs union and beyond', in Libby Rittenberg (ed.), *The Political Economy of Turkey in the Post-Soviet Era*, Connecticut, Praeger, 1998, pp. 66–7.

Chapter 5

1. Fraser Cameron, *The Foreign and Security Policy of the European Union*, Sheffield, Sheffield Academic Press, 1999, p. 84.

2. Javier Solana, 'The globe's most important relationship', *Wall Street Journal Europe*, May 2, 2002, p. A10. Solana, the EU high representative for common foreign and security policy, wrote this article in the run up to the EU–US summit in Washington in May 2002. He tried, rather unsuccessfully, to play down the differences between the US and the EU, by emphasising the vague policy issues that they share and pursue in common.

3. Former EU trade commissioner Leon Britain went as far as to say that George W. Bush's decision to impose tariffs on steel will undermine wider transatlantic co-operation, see his 'No way to treat an ally', *Financial Times*, March 19, 2002, p. 25; on the issue of EU–US policy divergence in the post-Cold War Middle East, see Hadar, 'Meddling in the Middle East?'.

4. 'The future of NATO: A moment of truth', *The Economist*, May 4, 2002, p. 27.

5. See, among others, Spyros A. Sofos, 'Reluctant Europeans? European integration and the transformation of Turkish politics', *South European Society and Politics* (special issue on 'Europeanisation and the Southern Periphery'), V. 5, N. 2, Autumn 2000, pp. 243–60.

6. Among others, Fuad Aleskerov, Hasan Ersel and Yavuz Sabuncu, 'Power and coalition stability in the Turkish parliament, 1991–99', *Turkish Studies*, V. 1, N. 2, Autumn 2000, pp. 21–38.

7. See, for example, the misleading thesis by Christopher Brewin, who argues that the Turkish secular elite, including the army, supports unconditionally the country's entry into the EU; Christopher Brewin, *The European Union and Cyprus*, Cambridge, The Eothen Press, 2000, p. 120, passim, and my review of Brewin's book in *The International History Review*, V. XXIII, N. 3, September 2001, pp. 740–42.

8. Ian O. Lesser, 'Changes on the Turkish Domestic scene and their foreign policy implications', in Zalmay Khalilzad et al. (eds), *The Future of Turkish–Western Relations: Towards a Strategic Plan*, Arlington VA, RAND, 2000, p. 16.

9. See 'A general speaks his mind', *The Economist*, March 16, 2002, pp. 46–8.

10. On this issue, the fervently pro-Turkish statement by Norman Stone is particularly instructive, see his 'Talking Turkey', *The National Interest*, N. 61, Fall 2000, pp. 66–73.

11. See Judith S. Yaphe, 'Turkey's domestic affairs: shaping the US–Turkey strategic partnership', Strategic Forum, Institute for National Strategic Studies, National Defence University, Policy Paper 121, July 1997, <http://www.ndu.edu/inss/strforum/forum121.html>.

12. Among others, Hale, *Turkish Foreign Policy*, p. 148 ff.

13. See Bulent Aras, 'Turkey's policy in the former Soviet South: Assets and options', *Turkish Studies*, V. 1, N. 1, Spring 2000, p. 38.

14. Among others, Eric Rouleau, 'Turkey's dream of democracy', *Foreign Affairs*, V. 79, N. 6, November–December 2000, pp. 100–14.

15. F. Stephen Larrabee, 'Turkish foreign and security policy: new dimensions and new challenges', in Khalilzad et al., *The Future of Turkish–Western Relations*, p. 26; see also Christos Iacovou, 'Ethnicity and politics: Turkey and the Turkic peoples after the collapse of the Soviet Union', in Christodoulos K. Yiallourides and Panagiotis Tsakonas (eds), *Greece and Turkey after the End of the Cold War*, Athens, Aristide D. Caratzas, 2001, pp. 2–19.

16. Aras, 'Turkey's policy in the former Soviet South', p. 39. Aras's source is Mehmet Sukuroglu, Head of Energy Studies at the Centre for Eurasian Studies in Ankara.

17. Ibid.; see also Idil Tuncer, 'The security policies of the Russian federation: the "Near Abroad" and Turkey', *Turkish Studies*, V. 1, N. 2, Autumn 2000, pp. 95–112.

18. It should be noted that 'Turkey has pinned its hopes for playing a major political role in the Caucasus and Central Asia on the construction of the [Baku–Ceyhan] pipeline, which it sees as the linchpin of its Central Asian and Caspian strategy. However, [the project] has been plagued by delays and financing problems and it is unclear whether it will ever be built', ibid., p. 30.

19. Altunisik, 'Turkey and the changing oil market in Eurasia', p. 164.

20. Turkey is dependent on Iran's natural gas, without which it will become almost wholly dependent on Russia for gas. In addition, Russia is Turkey's second largest trade partner after Germany.

21. The phrase belongs to Graham E. Fuller, 'The Institutional framework of US–Turkish relations' (Conference Report), paper presented to the Conference 'The Parameters of Partnership: Germany, the US and Turkey', American Institute for Contemporary German Studies, The Johns Hopkins University, Washington DC, October 24, 1997, p. 5.

22. Let us offer one example showing the possibility of change in the Middle Eastern balance of force, in the event that Iran becomes pro-American. A thaw in US–Iranian relations would not only liberate Iran's energy market, but it could also 'open up prospects for shipping Caspian oil through Iran, a route that is favoured by many Western companies because it would be cheaper. This would significantly reduce the interest of Western investors in the Baku–Ceyhan route, thus diminishing the geo-political importance of Turkey'; see Larrabee, 'Turkish foreign and security policy', p. 31.

23. *Inter alia*, Brzezinski, *The Grand Chessboard*, pp. 135–50, passim.

24. It is not true that Turkish Kurdistan is underdeveloped because of the Turco-Kurdish war in the 1980s and 1990s. Turkish Kurdistan is under-developed and backward because of the lack of economic (e.g. fixed capital investment) and social (e.g. development of welfare and cultural programmes) backing by the Turkish governments since 1923. Needless to say, the Kurdish problem has not gone away with the capture of Abdullah Ocalan in February 1999. The affair has simply widened existing European concerns regarding the Turco-Kurdish conflict, which is taking place in the very sensitive security perimeter of Europe; see in particular Dietrich Jung and Wolfango Piccoli, *Turkey at the Crossroads: Ottoman Legacies and a Greater Middle East*, London, Zed Books, 2001.

25. See Heinz Kramer, 'The institutional framework of German–Turkish relations', paper presented to the Conference 'The Parameters of Partnership', pp. 10–31.
26. See in particular Sukru Elekdag, 'Two and one-half war strategy', *Perceptions*, V. 1, N. 1, 1996, pp. 33–57. Syria and Greece figure prominently as the 'two fronts' that want to envelop Turkey, excluding her from the Eastern Mediterranean, whereas the 'half-one' was the war of Turkey against the separatism of the Kurdish Workers' Party (PKK). The missing link in this argument is the Russian and Iranian contingencies, which Elekdag does not take into account. The author is former Under-secretary of the Turkish Ministry of Foreign Affairs and served as Ambassador of Turkey to the United States and Japan.
27. On the Imia crisis, cf., Vassilis Fouskas, 'The Left and the crisis of the Third Hellenic Republic, 1989–97', in Donald Sassoon (ed.), *Looking Left: European Socialism after the Cold War*, London, I.B. Tauris, 1997, pp. 64–87; Ekavi Athanassopoulou, 'Blessing in disguise? The Imia crisis and Turkish–Greek relations', *Mediterranean Politics*, V. 2, N. 3, Winter 1997, pp. 76–101.
28. Brzezinski, *The Grand Chessboard*, pp. 41, 47.
29. Sabri Sayari, 'Turkish perspectives toward German and US foreign policy', paper presented to the Conference 'The Papameters of Partnership', p. 34.
30. Fuller, 'The institutional framework of US–Turkish relations', p. 7.
31. There have been several indications and trends confirming the power of the euro in relation to some policy facts taking place in the US and the globe. For instance, the power of the dollar was declining after September 11 and, following several corporate scandals in the US, trader and investor confidence began running low. David Roche, president of Independent Stategy, a consulting firm in London, argued that 'US financial assets are no longer as attractive as those of Europe or Japan and will seem even less so if the US goes it alone in attacking Iraq', see Michael R. Sesit, 'Investors lose their faith in a strong US Dollar', *Wall Street Journal Europe*, May 14, 2002, p. A1.
32. Gowan, *The Global Gamble*, p. 159.
33. Ian O. Lesser, 'Bridge or Barrier? Turkey and the West After the Cold War', in Graham E. Fuller and Ian O. Lesser (eds), *Turkey's New Geopolitics: From the Balkans to Western China*, Oxford, Westview Press/A RAND Study, 1993, p. 125.
34. It is worth noting that since 1984 Turkey has been in a defence pact with Jordan, similar to that with Israel since 1995–6.
35. Larrabee, 'Turkish foreign and security policy', p. 25.
36. Ibid., p. 46.
37. Greece has objected to this decision, as it was taken outside the institutional framework of the EU. Although an official EU opinion is still pending, the fact remains that Turkey has managed to pull off a favourable agreement that will carry substantial weight in any future development of the ESDI.
38. See BBC Monitoring, 'Cakmakoglu comments on Turkey's efforts for ESDP compromise', Anatolia–Brussels, May 14, 2002.

39. Beyond the Commission's regular opinion reports on Turkey regarding progress in meeting the Copenhagen political criteria, see the four interesting Memos submitted to the Foreign Affairs Committee of the House of Commons, UK, by William Hale (TKY 1, no date), Philip Robins (TKY 16, January 21, 2002), William Park (TKY 5, January 2002) and Amnesty International (TKY 6, January 2002). Of all four Memos, the one by Amnesty appears to be the least conducive to Turkey's European membership; London, House of Commons Foreign Affairs Select Committee on Turkey, file no: TKY, February 2002.
40. Further support for our thesis is given by Alan Makovsky, 'Turkey's faded European dream', paper presented to the Conference 'The Parameters of Partnership', p. 58. Makovsky is a Senior Fellow at the Washington Institute for Near Eastern Policy.
41. This phrase was used by a former Turkish Ambassador while commenting on the statement of General Kilinc, who suggested the shifting of the Turkish alliance system toward Russia and Iran, see 'A general speaks his mind', *The Economist*, p. 48.

Chapter 6

1. Apart from the works by Claude Nicolet, Eventhi Hatzivassiliou, James A. McHenry, Robert Holland, Brendan O'Malley and Ian Craig that have already been cited, I would also like to mention the following monographs: Diana Weston Markides, *Cyprus 1957–1963: From Colonial Conflict to Constitutional Crisis*, Minneapolis, University of Minnesota Press, 2001; Michael Attalides, *Cyprus: Nationalism and International Politics*, Edinburgh, Q Press, 1979; Farid Mirbagheri, *Cyprus and International Peace-Making*, London, Hurst, 1998; Suha Bolukbasi, *The Superpowers and the Third World: Turkish–American Relations and Cyprus*, New York, University of Virginia Press, 1988; Ioannis Stefanidis, *Isle of Discord: Nationalism, Imperialism and the Making of the Cyprus Problem*, London, Hurst, 1999; Christopher Hitchens, *Hostage to History – Cyprus: From the Ottomans to Kissinger*, London, Verso, 1997.
2. In fact, Britain had at least twice offered Cyprus to Greece in return for Greece's participation in the war on the side of the allies and by way of assisting Serbia against Germany's and Bulgaria's combined attack. But Greece, facing serious domestic problems, declined the offer; see Sir David Hunt, 'Cyprus: A study in International Relations', The 1980 Montague Burton Lecture on International Relations, University of Edinburgh, Edinburgh, October 28, 1980; Michael Llewellyn Smith, *Ionian Vision: Greece in Asia Minor, 1919–1922*, London, Hurst, 1998, p. 15.
3. I would like to stress that what we know on the Cyprus issue is largely from the archival work done in Britain, in the US, in Cyprus, in the Greek Ministry of Foreign Affairs and in the archives of the American Embassy in Athens (see the extraordinary work by Alexis Papachelas, *The Rape of the Greek Democracy: the American Factor, 1947–1967* (in Greek), Athens, Estia, 1997). We know practically nothing as regards, for example, the USSR's policy in Cyprus from the beginnings of the Cold War, and

through the Turkish invasions of summer 1974 to the present day. Also, there is a lot of work to be done from the files of the National Security Council of Turkey (Milli Gubenlik Kurulu – MGK) and in the Greek Ministry of Defence but, admittedly, access to them is rather difficult.

4. For instance, Kevin Featherstone's sober and instructive account accepts that a solution to the Cyprus issue cannot be disentangled from a 'multidimensional chess game', but his chosen focus is rather the institutional dimension of EU–Cyprus relations and the way in which the EU is strategically used by the Cypriot political class on security grounds; Kevin Featherstone, 'Cyprus and the onset of Europeanisation: Strategic Usage, Structural transformation and institutional adaptation', *South European Society and Politics*, Special Issue on 'Europeanisation and the Southern Periphery', V. 5, N. 2, Autumn 2000, pp. 141–62. Another case is the account by Nathalie Tocci and Michael Emerson, both at the Centre for European Policy Studies, Brussels, who presented a pedagogical recipe on Cyprus on its joining of the Union, *Cyprus as Lighthouse of the East Mediterranean: Shaping EU Accession and Re-unification Together*, Brussels, CEPS, 2002.

5. This is, for example, the main theme of Neill Nugent's, otherwise very interesting, 'EU enlargement and the "Cyprus problem"', *Journal of Common Market Studies*, V. 38, N. 1, March 2000, pp. 130–50, of Oliver Richmond's 'A perilous catalyst? EU accession and the Cyprus problem', *The Cyprus Review*, V. 13, N. 2, Fall 2001, pp. 125–31, and of Heinz Kramer's, 'The Cyprus problem and European security', *Survival*, V. 39, N. 3, Autumn 1997, pp. 16–32. Although I have personally benefited from reading these texts, they nevertheless tend to be highly speculative, if not at times alarmist. See also Clement H. Dodd, *Storm Clouds over Cyprus*, Cambridge, The Eothen Press, 2001 and Christopher Brewin, 'European Union perspectives on Cyprus Accession', *Middle Eastern Studies*, V. 36, N. 1, January 2000, pp. 21–34. For two altogether bad cases of presenting alarmist scenarios and partiality of views, see Nanette Neuwahl, 'Cyprus and the EU', Cambridge MA, Jean Monnet Working Paper 4, Harvard Law School, 2000, and Michael Stephen, *The Cyprus Question*, London, Northgate Publications, 2001.

6. I repeat, this should be read only as a tentative concluding remark, simply because we do not possess hard evidence on the part of the Greek side that this was and is the case. Nevertheless, to the extent that the witness of an insider can be used as a reliable source of evidence by the researcher while approaching 'historical truth', I should mention the public discussion I held with Christos Stylianides in London (March 17, 2002), former Government Spokesman of the Republic of Cyprus, who admitted that in 1993–6 these strategic debates about the role of Germany and France that could potentially underpin Cyprus' EU bid, were held in the Greek Ministry of Foreign Affairs, at the time under the influence of Theodore Pangalos and Yiannos Kranidiotis; see also Michalis Ellinas, 'A Lobby for Cyprus seminar on Cyprus and the EU', *Eleftheria* (London edition, in Greek), March 21, 2002, p. 6. I will be more specific on these issues below.

7. Brzezinski, *The Grand Chessboard*, p. 74.

8. Hadar, 'Meddling in the Middle East?', p. 48.
9. See European Commission, *Strengthening the Mediterranean Policy of the European Union: Establishing a Euro-Mediterranean Partnership*, Luxembourg, Bulletin of the European Union, Supplement 2, 1995; also, Fulvio Attina and Stelios Stavridis (eds), *The Barcelona Process and Euro-Mediterranean Issues from Stuttgart to Marseille*, Milano, Dott. A. Giuffre Editore, 2001. See also the work edited by Richard Gillespie based around the UK-based journal *Mediterranean Politics*, as well as his *The Euro-Mediterranean Partnership: Political and Economic Perspectives*, London, Frank Cass, 1997; a more recent work is that edited by Marc Maresceau and Erwan Lannon, *The EU's Enlargement and Mediterranean Strategies*, London, Palgrave, 2001.
10. Hadar, 'Meddling in the Middle East?', p. 49.
11. Ibid., p. 52.
12. Brzezinski, *The Grand Chessboard*, p. 66 (footnote).
13. 'Cyprus shipping improves its image', *Cyprus News*, N. 152, London, Cyprus High Commission, April 2002, p. 3.
14. See 'Gas pipeline decisions looming', *Cyprus News*, N. 150, London, Cyprus High Commission, February 2002, p. 3.
15. For further comments on this, see Tozun Bahcheli, 'Turkish Cypriots, the EU option and resolving ethnic conflict in Cyprus', in Andreas Theophanous et al. (eds), *Cyprus and the European Union*, Nicosia, Intercollege Press, 1996, pp. 108, 119.
16. Many authors fail to see this aspect of the Luxembourg summit, instead attributing Turkey's exclusion to Greece's opposition alone; see, among others, William Park, 'Turkey's European Union candidacy: from Luxembourg to Helsinki – to Ankara?', *Mediterranean Politics*, V. 5, N. 3, Autumn 2000, p. 35; Jean-François Drevet, *Chypre en Europe*, Paris, L'Harmattan, 2000, pp. 261–70; Aylin Guney, 'Turkey: Beyond the customs union?', in Attina and Stavridis, *The Barcelona Process*, pp. 201–25.
17. See Alan Makovsky, 'Turkey's faded European dream', paper presented to the Conference 'The Parameters of Partnership', p. 52.
18. Ibid., p. 59. Sabri Sayari also notes ('Turkish perspectives toward German and US foreign policy', p. 40) that 'the US was a key player in pushing for the conclusion for the customs union agreement between Brussels and Ankara' but at Luxembourg it was 'unable to change the opposition, led by Germany and Greece, to Turkey's full membership of the EU'.
19. Makovsky, 'Turkey's faded European dream', p. 55.
20. William Wallace, 'Rare optimism on Cyprus', *Wall Street Journal Europe*, February 21, 2002, p. A9.
21. Tozun Bahcheli fails to see the dual geo-political and institutional/global dimension of the Greek–Turkish dispute, thus confining himself to the obvious assertion that EU states 'would prefer to stay clear of Greek–Turkish disputes, but Greece's membership has made this impossible'. In essence, Bahcheli discards the independent role of Germany at the Luxembourg summit altogether, see 'Turkish Cypriots', p. 119.

22. Henri J. Barkey and Philip H. Gordon, 'Cyprus: the predictable crisis', *The National Interest*, N. 66, Winter 2001/02, <http://nationalinterest.org/issues/66/BarkeyGordon.html>, p. 10.

23. Many analysts have made that mistake, including Barkey and Gordon (ibid., p. 4). The Greek–Turkish *rapprochement* has been a long and protracted process of half-hearted initiatives on behalf of both countries, and began with the lifting of the Greek veto over Turkey's customs union agreement with the EU. As far as the Greek side is concerned, the strategic mind behind both the *rapprochement* and Cyprus' European bid was Nikos Kranidiotis, the Cypriot-born Greek deputy Minister of Foreign Affairs, who was killed in a plane accident in Romania in 1999; see also the views expressed by Christos Stylianides, in Ellinas, 'A Lobby for Cyprus'.

24. Derogations from the fundamental principles of the *acquis* are possible and are rather easily obtainable when they are temporary (e.g. the case of purchase of second holiday homes in Austria). Some permanent derogations are also possible and regard items without a serious political impact, such as the issue of tobacco snuff in Sweden. The most extreme form of derogation to date has been that awarded to Finland regarding the Aland islands. These Baltic Sea islands (some 6,500) belong to Finland, but the majority of their population is Swedish, and various agreements since 1922 stipulate that a regional citizenship applies to them and that Finnish people need five years permanent residence to be able to buy real estate and start doing business there. The whole issue 'posed major difficulties for the EU during negotiations, but the Accession Treaty for Finland maintained the restrictions on real estate ownership, establishment, exercise of profession and services for those not having regional citizenship, but held that these would be non-discriminatory and would apply to all the citizens of the Union'; see Costas Apostolides, ' The European *acquis communautaire* and a federal Cyprus', in R.C. Sharma and Stavros A. Epaminondas (eds), *Cyprus: In Search of Peace and Justice*, New Delhi, Somali Publications, 1997, pp. 258–9.

25. Editorial, 'Cyprus surprise', *Financial Times*, January 18, 2002, p. 14.

26. Coufoudakis, 'The solution', pp. 17–18.

27. See European Union, *2001 Regular Report on Cyprus's Progress Towards Accession*, Brussels, Office for Official Publications of the European Communities, COM, 2001, pp. 3–34; see also the legal opinion on the issue of settlers delivered by an international team of ten professors of International Law, Christopher Greenwood, Alain Pellet, Gerhard Hafner et al., *Legal Issues Arising from Certain Population Transfers and Displacements on the Territory of the Republic of Cyprus in the Period Since 20 July 1974*, London, Press and Information Office, Cyprus High Commission, June 30, 1999.

28. European Union, *2001 Regular Report*, pp. 5, 21, passim.

29. See *Cyprus*, Appendix B, 'Draft Treaty of Guarantee', Nicosia, Cmnd 1093, Republic of Cyprus, July 1960, p. 86.

30. See James Crawford, Alain Pellet and Gerhard Hafner, 'Republic of Cyprus: Eligibility for membership', United Nations, A/52/481,

S/1997/805, October 17, 1997. Turkey has twice, unsuccessfully tried to reply with an opinion written by Professor Maurice Mandelson, supporting the view that Cyprus' application is illegal (see, for example, Turkey–Maurice Mandelson, UN A/56/451, S/2001/953, October 5, 2001). Crawford, Pellet and Hafner replied again reinforcing their arguments further; see their 'The eligibility of the Republic of Cyprus for EU membership', London, Press and Information Office, Cyprus High Commission, January 2002.

31. Jack Straw and Matthew Hamlyn, 'On Cyprus', FCO/FAC/002–02, London, House of Commons, March 12, 2002, pp. 1–2.

32. Barkey and Gordon, 'Cyprus', p. 5.

33. Cf., Bolukbasi, 'Behind the Turkish–Israeli alliance', pp. 26 ff., and Marios Evriviades, 'The Turkish–Israeli axis: Alliances and alignments in the Middle East', *Orient*, V. 39, N. 4, 1998, pp. 565–82. Evriviades's analysis is deeper and more sophisticated than that by Bolukbasi, although both writers seem to agree that the Turkish–Israeli military axis comes a long way (this is more pronounced in the analyses of Evriviades). It should also be noted that, whereas in the 1950s the Turkish–Israeli axis was initiated by Israel, in the 1990s it was the Turks that had begun courting the Israelis.

34. *Inter alia*, Khalilzad et al., *The Future of Turkish–Western Relations*, passim.

35. Carl Schmitt, in his classic *Der Begriff des Politischen* ([The Concept of the Political], Berlin, Dunker & Humbolt, 1932) develops a comprehensive theory of the political instance, in which the defining terrain of politics is not simply the element of hostility, but the distinction between Friend and Enemy. This distinction, applicable to both domestic and foreign affairs, constitutes an accumulation of power relations that determines the terms of the real sovereignty. But legal documents, susceptible to moral and legal issues, do not always reflect the realities of power. *Real power belongs to those who are capable of imposing onto the political terrain a state of emergency.* On this issue, I am mostly indebted to the analyses developed by Peter Gowan in his, 'The twisted road to Kosovo', pp. 74–5; see also Gopal Balakrishnan, *The Enemy: An Intellectual Portrait of Carl Schmitt*, London, Verso, 2000. Schmitt, who died in 1982, was the leading Nazi jurist during the interwar period. His philosophy should thus be seen as an attempt to lay the foundations of the Nazi dominance of Europe by force. Despite this political shortcoming, Schmitt's work is widely recognised as one of the most important and penetrating analyses in the field of modern political theory.

36. Ismail Cem, 'A common vision for Cypriots', *International Herald Tribune*, March 14, 2002, p. 6. A better elaborated view of this notion is developed by Ergun Olgun, undersecretary to Rauf Denktash, in his 'Time running out for the détente in Cyprus', *The European Voice*, May 8–15, 2002. The Greek Foreign Minister, George Papandreou, responded with an article that was characteristically entitled 'A unified Cyprus is essential for European unity', *International Herald Tribune*, May 2, 2002.

37. For a good background of the events and analysis, see Makarios Drousiotis, 'S-300 and other myths' (in Greek), *Archeio*, N. 1, December 1999.

38. There is a wide consensus that the military deployment of missiles would have had a minor impact on the overall relationship of military force

on Cyprus. Nevertheless, Turkey opposed their installation for preventive reasons; see, for instance, Dan Lindley, 'The military factor in the Eastern Mediterranean', in Clement H. Dodd (ed.), *Cyprus: the Need for New Perspectives*, Cambridge, The Eothen Press, 1999, pp. 195–230; on the issue of military balance in Cyprus before the case of SS-300 broke out, see Aristos Aristotelous, *Greece, Turkey and Cyprus: the Military Balance, 1995–96*, Nicosia, Cyprus Centre for Strategic Studies, 1995.

39. In essence, the political solution Turkey wants in Cyprus is a Turkish state in the North and a Greco-Turkish state in the South; see, *inter alia*, Andreas Theophanous, *Cyprus in the European Union and the New International Environment* (in Greek), Athens, I. Sideris, 2000, pp. 103–04, passim.

40. This joint defence doctrine between Greece and Cyprus, among others, stipulates that any further advance of the Turkish forces in Cyprus would be a *casus belli* for Greece. France has a listening post in Cape Gkreko, South-eastern Cyprus, and it also transmits from there radio programmes in both French and Arab in the Middle East. France has held this site since 1970. I am obliged to former Cypriot diplomat Nikos Makris for this invaluable information.

41. See in particular European Union, *2001 Regular Report*, p. 21. After strong diplomatic pressure on Turkey, the Greek Cypriot was finally released in April 2001.

42. Erbakan, who was known for his anti-Semitic views, signed the pact under strong pressure from the military, only to be overthrown by it with the mini-coup of June 1997. From whichever angle ones examines the issue of Islam in Turkey, the fact remains that it is bad news politically for the US and, therefore, for the secular military.

43. See Muhamoud A-Shaikh, 'US–Israel–Turkey exercises could be a blessing in disguise', <http://www.muslimedia.com/archives/oaw98/blessing.htm>.

44. Evriviades argues that the formation of that security forum institutionalised the relationship between Turkey and Israel, and is thus the most important long-term aspect of their alliance, 'The Turkish–Israeli axis', p. 569.

45. Among others, Soetendorp, *Foreign Policy in the European Union*, pp. 95–113; Schulze, *The Arab–Israeli Conflict*; European Commission, Directorate General External Relations, 'The EU and the Middle East peace process', <http://europe.eu.int/comm/external_relations/mepp/index.htm>, 2002.

46. This is also the main theme of Samuel Limone, a retired Israeli General, in his 'Security issues in the Eastern Mediterranean and Europe: A view from Israel', in Theophanous et al., *Cyprus and the European Union*, pp. 189–96.

Chapter 7

1. Terry Eagleton, *The Ideology of the Aesthetic*, Oxford, Basil Blackwell, 1990, p. 24.

2. Nearly 70 per cent of the required $3.3 billion for the construction of the pipeline may be sought from taxpayers, primarily in Europe, Japan

and the US through public lending institutions, such as various export agencies and the World Bank.

3. See 'Germany sees greater role for Europe in Asia', NATO Enlargement Daily Brief, <http://groups.yahoo.com/group/nedb/messages>, June 26, 2002.

4. 'China feels encircled', *The Economist*, June 8, 2002, p. 65.

5. John Vogler, 'The European Union and September 11', in Bulent Gokay and R.B.J. Walker (eds), *11 September 2001: War, Terror and Judgement*, Keele, Keele European Research Centre, Keele University, 2002, pp. 88–9.

6. By 'interests' I mean the three instances of 'class', 'state-bureaucratic' and 'national interest'. All three of them enjoy both an overlapping artic-ulation and a relative autonomy. In this respect, what exemplifies the functioning of 'class' might be the competing interests not only between a US and an Italian firm, but also between two US firms. The 'state-bureaucratic' instance represents the material interests of the state's own administrative elites, whereas the 'national interest' is mainly a balancing act between 'class' and 'bureaucracy', between class interests and the state's bureaucratic apparatuses. In this context, there are several forms of conflict between the EU bureaucracy and the national bureau-cracies of EU states, and this should be seen as an additional obstacle to the political and fiscal integration of the EU.

7. The permanent members of the Security Council are: France, the UK, Russia, the US and China. China is the only country not affiliated with NATO. Each Security Council member has the power to veto resolutions, a privilege denied to the ten rotating members, whose presence on the Council lasts for two years only.

8. Brzezinski, *The Grand Chessboard*, p. 23.

9. 'The acceptability of American power' (Present at the Creation: A Survey of America's World Role), *The Economist*, June 29, 2002, p. 8.

10. Christopher Lasch, *The Culture of Narcissism*, New York, Norton, 1978; see also his *Haven in a Heartless World: the Family Besieged*, New York, Norton, 1977.

11. Youth crime and general social unrest are not always reducible to conditions of poverty and deprivation. Ronald Huff, who chaired an advisory committee that made recommendations to the administration of Bush junior in 2002, admitted that there is not always a connection between crime and poverty in Los Angeles: 'What law enforcement agencies and the courts fail to understand is that these are kids. Yes, some of them have done horrible things. But they are suffering an identity crisis. How else do you explain the fact that even in Beverly Hills – a place full of millionaires – you find white gangs?'; see Burhan Wazir, 'Lost Angeles', *Observer*, July 7, 2002, p. 30 ('The Observer Magazine').

12. The best work on the pre-1917 Russian populist tradition is by Franco Venturi, *Il populismo Russo*, V. I–III, Torino, Einaudi, 1972. I have discussed these issues, as well as the impact of radical populism on bolshevism and the Russian Revolution in my *Populism and Modernisa-tion: the Exhaustion of the Third Hellenic Republic, 1974–1994* (in Greek), Athens, Ideokinissi, 1995.

13. Ludwig Wittgenstein, *Tractatus Logico-Philosophicus*, London, Routledge, 1990, p. 32.

Bibliography

I include here only the sources that are cited in the text as it is impossible to list all the material that I have consulted while writing the book.

Aleskerov, Fuad, Hasan Ersel and Yavuz Sabuncu, 'Power and coalition stability in the Turkish parliament, 1991–99', *Turkish Studies*, V. 1, N. 2, Autumn 2000.

Ali, Tariq (ed.), *Masters of the Universe? NATO's Balkan Crusade*, Verso, London, 2000.

Ambrose, Stephen and Douglas Brinkley, *Rise to Globalism: American Foreign Policy since 1938*, Penguin, London, 1997.

Anderson, Perry and Peter Gowan (eds), *The Question of Europe*, Verso, London, 1997.

Aras, Bulent, 'Turkey's policy in the former Soviet South: Assets and options', *Turkish Studies*, V. 1, N. 1, Spring 2000.

Aristotelous, Aristos, *Greece, Turkey and Cyprus: the Military balance, 1995–96*, Cyprus Centre for Strategic Studies, Nicosia, 1995.

A-Shaikh, Muhamoud, 'US–Israel–Turkey exercises could be a blessing in disguise', <http://www.muslimedia.com/archives/oaw98/blessing.htm>.

Asmus, Ronald D. and Robert C. Nurick, 'NATO enlargement and the Baltic states', *Survival*, V. 38, N. 2, Summer 1996.

Athanassopoulou, Ekavi, 'Blessing in disguise? The Imia crisis and Turkish–Greek relations', *Mediterranean Politics*, V. 2, N. 3, Winter 1997.

——, *Turkey: Anglo-American Security Interests (1945–1952) and the First Enlargement of NATO*, Frank Cass, London, 1999.

Attalides, Michael, *Cyprus: Nationalism and International Politics*, Q Press, Edinburgh, 1979.

Attina, Fulvio and Stelios Stavridis (eds), *The Barcelona Process and Euro-Mediterranean Issues from Stuttgart to Marseille*, Dott. A. Giuffre Editore, Milan, 2001.

Avineri, Shlomo, *The Making of Modern Zionism: the Intellectual Origins of the Jewish State*, Basic Books, New York, 1981.

Bahcheli, Tozun, *Greek–Turkish Relations since 1955*, Westview Press, Boulder CO, 1990.

Bahree, Bhushan and Marc Lifsher, 'Venezuela's capacity crunch threatens key crude partners', *Wall Street Journal Europe*, April 18, 2002.

Balakrishnan, Gopal, *The Enemy: An Intellectual Portrait of Carl Schmitt*, Verso, London, 2000.

Barkey, Henri J. and Philip H. Gordon, 'Cyprus: the predictable crisis', *The National Interest*, N. 66, Winter 2001/02, <http://nationalinterest.org/issues/66/BarkeyGordon.html>.

Baun, Michael J., *An Imperfect Union*, Westview Press, Oxford, 1996.

BBC Monitoring, 'Cakmakoglu comments Turkey's efforts for ESDP compromise', Anatolia–Brussels, May 14, 2002.

Bebler, Anton A. (ed.), *The Challenge of NATO Enlargement*, Praeger, New York, 1999.

Benjamin, Daniel, 'US troops must stay in the Balkans', *International Herald Tribune*, December 28, 2000.

Betts, Richard K. and Thomas J. Christensen, 'China: getting the questions right', *The National Interest*, N. 62, Winter 2000–01.

Blackburn, Robin, 'Kosovo: the war of NATO expansion', *New Left Review*, N. 235, 1999.

Blinken, Antony J., 'New mood threatens NATO enlargement', *International Herald Tribune*, April 3, 2001.

Bolukbasi, Suha, *The Superpowers and the Third World: Turkish–American Relations and Cyprus*, University of Virginia Press, New York, 1988.

——, 'The Johnson letter revisited', *Middle Eastern Studies*, V. 29, N. 3, July 1993.

——, 'Behind the Turkish–Israeli alliance: a Turkish view', *Journal of Palestine Studies*, V. XXIX, N. 1, Autumn 1999.

Boulton, Leyla, 'Turkey aims to aid Moslem brethren', *Financial Times*, April 8, 1999.

Brewin, Christopher, 'European Union perspectives on Cyprus Accession', *Middle Eastern Studies*, V. 36, N. 1, January 2000.

——, *The European Union and Cyprus*, The Eothen Press, Cambridge, 2000.

Britain, Leon, 'No way to treat an ally', *Financial Times*, March 19, 2002.

Brown, Michael, 'Minimalist NATO: a wise alliance knows when to retrench', *Foreign Affairs*, N. 3, 1999.

Brzezinski, Zbigniew, *The Grand Chessboard: American Primacy and its Geo-strategic Imperatives*, Basic Books, New York, 1997.

Buchan, David and Andrew Jack, 'A return to Russia', *Financial Times*, April 25, 2002.

Buszynski, Leszek, 'Russia and the West: Towards renewed geo-political rivalry?', *Survival*, V. 37, N. 3, Autumn 1995.

Cameron, Fraser, *The Foreign and Security Policy of the European Union*, Sheffield Academic Press, Sheffield, 1999.

Campbell, Matthew and Stephen Grey, 'US fears force will break up NATO', *Sunday Times*, December 12, 1999.

Carpenter, Ted G., *NATO Enters the 21st Century*, Frank Cass, London, 2001.

Castellina, Luciana (ed.), *La Nato nei Balcani*, Riuniti, Rome, 1999.

Cem, Ismail, 'A common vision for Cypriots', *International Herald Tribune*, March 14, 2002.

Chircop, Aldo et al. (eds), *The Aegean Sea after the Cold War*, Macmillan, London, 2000.

Clément, Sophia, *Conflict Prevention in the Balkans: Case Studies of Kosovo and the FYR of Macedonia*, Chaillot Paper 30, Institute for Security Studies, Western European Union, Paris, December 1997.

Commission of the European Communities, 'Towards a European strategy for the security of energy supply', Green Paper, COM (2002), 769 final, November 29, 2000.

Conference Papers Collection, 'The Parameters of Partnership: Germany, the US and Turkey', American Institute for Contemporary German Studies, The Johns Hopkins University, Washington DC, October 24, 1997.

Constas, Dimitri (ed.), *The Greek–Turkish Conflict in the 1990s*, Macmillan, London, 1991.

Constitutional Arrangements, *Cyprus*, Appendix B, 'Draft Treaty of Guarantee' Cmnd 1093, Republic of Cyprus, Nicosia, July 1960.

Cook, Steven A., 'US–Turkey relations and the war on terrorism', Analysis Paper 9, November, 2001, <http://www.brook.edu>.

Cottrell, Robert, et al., 'Russian unease as US war on terror shifts to Caucasus', *Financial Times*, February 28, 2002.

Coufoudakis, Van, 'US foreign policy and the Cyprus question: an interpretation', *Millennium*, V. 5, N. 3, 1976–77.

Couloumbis, Theodore, *The United States, Greece and Turkey: the Troubled Triangle*, Praeger, New York, 1983.

Cox, Michael, 'American power before and after 11 September', *International Affairs*, V. 78, N. 2, April 2002.

Crawford, James, et al., 'Republic of Cyprus: Eligibility for membership', United Nations, A/52/481, S/1997/805, October 17, 1997.

——, 'The eligibility of Cyprus for EU membership', Press and Information Office, Cyprus High Commission, London, January 2002.

Daalder, Ivo H. and James M. Lindsay, 'Nasty, brutish and long: America's war on terrorism', *Current History*, December 2001, <http://www.brook.edu>.

Danopoulos, Constantine P. and Emilia Ianeva, 'Poverty in the Balkans and the issue of reconstruction: Bulgaria and Yugoslavia compared', *Journal of Southern Europe and the Balkans*, V. 1, N. 2, November 1999.

Dempsey, Judy and Richard Wolffe, 'In from the Cold', *Financial Times*, May 15, 2002.

Dobbs, Michael, 'US indicates preference for just 3 new NATO states', *Washington Post*, May 30, 1997.

Dodd, Clement H. (ed.), *Cyprus: the Need for New Perspectives*, The Eothen Press, Cambridge, 1999.

——, *Storm Clouds over Cyprus*, The Eothen Press, Cambridge, 2001.

Donnelly, Jack, *Realism and International Relations*, Cambridge University Press, Cambridge, 2000.

Drevet, Francois-Jean, *Chypre en Europe*, L'Harmattan, Paris, 2000.

Drousiotis, Makarios, *The Dark Side of EOKA* (in Greek), Stachi, Athens, 1998.
, 'S-300 and other myths' (in Greek), Archeio, N. 1, December 1999.

Eagleton, Terry, *The Ideology of the Aesthetic*, Basil Blackwell, Oxford, 1990.

Economist Intelligence Unit, Country Forecast, *Russia*, London, 3rd Quarter, 1998.

Elekdag, Sukru, 'Two and one-half war strategy', *Perceptions*, V. 1, N. 1, 1996.

Ellinas, Michalis, 'A Lobby for Cyprus seminar on Cyprus and the EU', *Eleftheria* (London edition, in Greek), March 21, 2002.

European Commission, *Strengthening the Mediterranean Policy of the European Union: Establishing a Euro-Mediterranean Partnership*, Bulletin of the European Union, Supplement 2, Luxembourg, 1995.

European Commission, Directorate General Extended Relations, 'The EU and the Middle East peace process', <http://europa.eu.int/comm/ external_ relations/mepp/index.htm>, 2002.

European Union, *2001 Regular Report on Cyprus's Progress Towards Accession*, Office for Official Publications of the European Communities, COM, Brussels, 2001.

Evriviades, Marios, 'The Turkish–Israeli axis: Alliances and allies in the Middle East', *Orient*, V. 39, N. 4, 1998.

——, 'Turkey's role in United States strategy during and after the Cold War', *Mediterranean Quarterly*, V. 9, N. 2, Spring 1998.

Featherstone, Kevin, 'Cyprus and the onset of Europeanisation: Strategic usage, structural transformation and institutional adaptation', *South European Society and Politics*, Special Issue on 'Europeanisation and the Southern Periphery', V. 5, N. 2, Autumn 2000.

Feffer, John, 'Globalisation and militarisation', *Foreign Policy in Focus*, V. 7, N. 1, February 2002.

Fisher, Keith, 'A meeting of blood and oil: the Balkan factor in Western energy security, *Journal of Southern Europe and the Balkans*, V. 4, N. 1, May 2002.

Fouskas, Vassilis, *Populism and Modernisation: the Exhaustion of the Third Hellenic Republic, 1974–1994* (in Greek), Ideokinissi, Athens, 1995.

——, *The Internationalisation of Economic Relations and the State*, Working Paper Series 5, Business School, University of Hertfordshire, Herts, 1998.

——, *Italy, Europe, the Left: the Transformation of Italian Communism and the European Imperative*, Ashgate, Aldershot, 1998.

——, 'Reflections on the Cyprus issue and the Turkish invasions of 1974', *Mediterranean Quarterly*, V. 12, N. 3, Summer 2001.

——, 'Review of *The European Union and Cyprus* by Christopher Brewin', *The International History Review*, V. XXIII, N. 3, September 2001.

Fraser, Maurice (ed.), *Britain in Europe*, Strategems Publishing Ltd., London, 1998.

Fuller, Graham E. and Ian O. Lesser (eds), *Turkey's New Geopolitics: From the Balkans to Western China*, Westview Press/A RAND Study, Oxford, 1993.

Gabelnick, Tamar, William D. Hartung and Jennifer Washburn, *Arming Repression: US Arms Sales to Turkey During the Clinton Administration*, A Joint Report of the World Policy Institute and the Federation of American Scientists, October, 1999, <http://www.fas.org/asmp/library/reports/ turkeyrep.htm>.

Gaddis, John Lewis, 'History, grand strategy and NATO enlargement', *Survival*, V. 40, N. 1, Spring 1998.

——, *The United States and the Origins of the Cold War*, Columbia University Press, New York, 2000.

Gedmin, Jeffrey, 'The alliance is doomed', *Washington Post*, May 20, 2002.

George, Alan and William Simons (eds), *The Limits of Coercive Diplomacy*, Westview Press, New York, 1994.

Giddens, Anthony, *The Third Way*, Polity Press, London, 1999.

Gillespie, Richard (ed.), *The Euro-Mediterranean Partnership: Political and Economic Perspectives*, Frank Cass, London, 1997.

Glennon, Michael J., 'The new interventionism: the search for a just international law', *Foreign Affairs*, N. 3, 1999.

Global Environment, *1998 Strategic Assessment*, <http://www.ndu.edu/inss/sa98/sa98ch1.html>.

Gokay, Bulent, 'Introduction: oil, war and geo-politics from Kosovo to Afghanistan', *Journal of Southern Europe and the Balkans*, V. 4, N. 1, May, 2000.

——, 'Oil, War and Global Hegemony', unpublished paper, Keele University, Keele, February 28, 2002.

Gokay, Bulent and R.J.B. Walker (eds), *11 September, 2001: War, Terror and Judgement*, Keele European Research Centre, Keele University, Keele, 2002.

Gorodetsky, Gabriel, *The Grand Delusion: Stalin and the German Invasion of Russia*, Yale University Press, New Haven, 1999.

Gorst, Anthony and Lewis Johnman, *The Suez Crisis*, Routledge, London, 1997.

Gould-Davies, Nigel and Ngaire Woods, 'Russia and the IMF', *International Affairs*, V. 75, N. 1, 1999.

Gowan, Peter, 'The NATO powers and the Balkan tragedy', *New Left Review*, N. 234, March–April 1999.

——, 'The twisted road to Kosovo', *Labour Focus on Eastern Europe* (single issue), N. 62, 1999.

——, *The Global Gamble: Washington's Faustian Bid for World Dominance*, Verso, London, 1999.

Greenwood, Christopher, et al., *Legal Issues Arising from Certain Population Transfers and Displacements on the Territory of the Republic of Cyprus in the Period Since 20 July 1974*, Press and Information Office, Cyprus High Commission, London, June 30, 1999.

Griffin, Michael, *Reaping the Whirlwind: the Taliban Movement in Afghanistan*, Pluto Press, London, 2001.

Guicherd, Catherine, 'International law and the war in Kosovo', *Survival*, V. 41, N. 2, Summer 1999.

Hadar, Leon T., 'Meddling in the Middle East? Europe challenges US hegemony in the region', *Mediterranean Quarterly*, V. 7, N. 4, Fall 1996.

Hale, William, *Turkish Foreign Policy 1774–2000*, Frank Cass, London, 2000.

Hasegawa, Tsuyoshi and Alex Pravda (eds), *Perestroika: Soviet Domestic and Foreign Policies*, Sage–Royal Institute of International Affairs, London, 1990.

Hashi, Iraj, 'The disintegration of Yugoslavia: Regional disparities and the nationalities question', *Capital and Class*, V. 48, Autumn 1992.

Hassan, Shawaluddin W., 'The response of Muslim countries to the Bosnian crisis', paper presented to the 40th annual convention of the International Studies Association, Washington DC, February 16–20, 1999.

Hatzivassiliou, Evanthis, *Britain and the International Status of Cyprus*, University of Minnesota Press, Minneapolis, 1997.

Hedges, Chris, 'Kosovo's next masters?', *Foreign Affairs*, N. 3, 1999.

Heisbourg, François, 'Europe's strategic ambitions: The limits of ambiguity', *Survival*, V. 42, N. 2, Summer 2000.

Herd, Graeme P. and Fotios Moustakis, 'Black Sea geo-politics: a litmus test for the European security order?', *Mediterranean Politics*, V. 5, N. 3, Autumn 2000.

Hershlag, Z.Y., *The Contemporary Turkish Economy*, Routledge, London, 1988.

Hill, Fiona, 'Pipeline politics, Russo-Turkish competition and geo-politics in the Eastern Mediterranean', *The Cyprus Review*, V. 8, N. 1, Spring 1996.

Hirst, Paul and Grahame Thompson, *Globalization in Question*, Polity Press, Cambridge, 1996.

Hitchens, Christopher, *Hostage to History – Cyprus: From the Ottomans to Kissinger*, Verso, London, 1997.

Hofheinz, Paul, 'EU urged to revamp voting at IMF to counterbalance US', *Wall Street Journal Europe*, April 19–21, 2002.

Holland, Robert, *Britain and the Revolt in Cyprus*, Clarendon, Oxford, 1998.

House of Commons, Foreign Affairs Select Committee on Turkey, file No: TKY, London, 2002.

Howard, Michael, 'An unhappy successful marriage: Security means knowing what to expect', *Foreign Affairs*, N. 3, 1999.

Hunt, Sir David, 'Cyprus: A study in international relations', The 1980 Montague Burton Lecture on International Relations, University of Edinburgh, Edinburgh, October 28, 1980.

Hyland, William G., *Clinton's World: Remaking American Foreign Policy*, Praeger, New York, 1999.

International Affairs and Defence Section, *11 September 2001: The Response*, Research Paper 01/72, House of Commons, London, October 3, 2001.

International Institute for Strategic Studies, 'Germany's "new" foreign policy', *IISS Strategic Comments*, V. 7, N. 9, November 2001.

Johnstone, Diana, 'Notes on the Kosovo problem and the international community', *Labour Focus on Eastern Europe*, N. 63, 1999.

Jonson, Lena, 'Russia, NATO and the handling of conflicts at Russia's Southern periphery: At a crossroads?', *European Security*, V. 9, N. 4, Winter 2000.

Jung, Dietrich and Wolfango Piccoli, *Turkey at the Crossroads: Ottoman Legacies and a Greater Middle East*, Zed Books, London, 2001.

Kennedy, Paul, 'The eagle has landed' (FT Weekend), *Financial Times*, February 2–3, 2002.

Keohane, Robert O. and Helen V. Milner (eds), *Internationalisation and Domestic Politics*, Cambridge University Press, Cambridge, 1996.

Keynes, John M., *The General Theory of Employment, Interest and Money*, Macmillan, London, 1973.

Khalilzad, Zalmay et al. (eds), *The Future of Turkish–Western Relations: Towards a Strategic Plan*, RAND, Arlington VA, 2000.

Khodarenok, Mikhail, 'Russia surrounded with US military bases and Moscow still do not know if this is good or bad', *NATO Enlargement Daily Brief*, CDI Russian Weekly, April 8, 2002.

King Jr, Neil et al., 'Iraq war would alter the economics of oil and politics of OPEC', *Wall Street Journal Europe*, September 19, 2002.

Kissinger, Henry, *Years of Renewal*, Simon & Schuster, New York, 1999.

Kramer, Heinz, 'The Cyprus problem and European security', *Survival*, V. 39, N. 3, Autumn 1997.

Krebs, Ronald R., 'Perverse institutionalism: NATO and the Greco-Turkish conflict', *International Organisation*, V. 53, N. 2, Spring 1999.

Kuniholm, Bruce R., *The Origins of the Cold War in the Near East: Great Power Conflict and Diplomacy in Iran, Turkey and Greece*, Princeton University Press, Princeton, 1980.

——, *The Near East Connection: Greece and Turkey in the Reconstruction and Security of Europe, 1946–1952*, Hellenic College Press, Massachusetts, 1984.

Kux, Dennis, 'The Pakistani pivot', *The National Interest*, N. 65, Fall 2001.

Lasch, Christopher, *Haven in a Heartless World: the Family Besieged*, Norton, New York, 1977.

——, *The Culture of Narcissim*, Norton, New York, 1997.

Leffler, Melvyn P., 'Strategy, diplomacy and the Cold War: the United States, Turkey and NATO, 1945–1952', *Journal of American History*, V. 71, N. 4, 1985.

Lesser, Ian O., *NATO Looks South: New Challenges and New Strategies in the Mediterranean*, Project Air Force–RAND, Washington DC, 2000.

Luttwak, Edward, 'NATO flatters', *Sunday Telegraph*, April 11, 1999.

Macintyre, Ben, 'Clinton rejected warnings of fiasco', *The Times*, April 2, 1999.

Mallinson, William, 'Reality versus morality', *Defensor Pacis*, N. 7, January 2001.

Mandelbaum, Michael, 'A perfect failure: NATO's war against Yugoslavia', *Foreign Affairs*, N. 5, 1999.

Mandelson, Maurice, 'On Cyprus's eligibility', UN A/56/451, S/2001/953, October 5, 2001.

Mann, Michael, 'The dark side of democracy: The modern tradition of ethnic and political cleansing', *New Left Review*, N. 235, 1999.

Maresceau, Marc and Erwan Lannon (eds), *The EU's Enlargement and Mediterranean Strategies*, Palgrave, London, 2001.

Maull, Hanns W., 'Germany in the Yugoslav crisis', *Survival*, V. 37, N. 4, Winter 1995–6.

Mazower, Mark, 'The G-word: Review of *The Treatment of Armenians in the Ottoman Empire, 1915–16*, (Document Series edited by Ara Sarafian, Gomidas Institute, December 11, 2000)', *London Review of Books*, February 8, 2001.

McHenry, James A., *The Uneasy Partnership on Cyprus, 1919–1939*, Garland Publishing, New York, 1987.

McKenzie, Mary M., 'Constructing European security: Security conceptions, institution building, and transatlantic relations', paper presented for the 38th Annual Convention of the International Studies Association, Toronto, Canada, March 18–22, 1997.

Mikhailov, Nick, 'Russian oil pipelines set for expansion', *Oil and Gas Journal*, March 25, 2002.

Mirbagheri, Farid, *Cyprus and International Peace-Making*, Hurst, London, 1998.

Morgenthau, Hans, *Politics Among Nations: The Struggle for Power and Peace*, Alfred A. Knopf, New York, 1948.

Morris, Benny, *The Birth of the Palestinian Refugee Problem, 1947–1951*, Cambridge University Press, Cambridge, 1987.

Morse, Edward L. and James Richard, 'The battle for energy dominance', *Foreign Affairs*, March–April 2002.

Nachmani, Amikam, *Israel, Turkey and Greece: Uneasy Relations in the East Mediterranean*, Frank Cass, London, 1987.

Neuwahl, Nanette, 'Cyprus and the EU', Jean Monnet Working Paper 4, Harvard Law School, Cambridge MA, 2000.

Nicolet, Claude, *United States Policy Towards Cyprus, 1954–1974: Removing the Greek–Turkish Bone of Contention*, Bibliopolis, Mannheim, 2001.

Nugent, Neill, 'Redefining Europe', *Journal of Common Market Studies*, Annual Review Issue, V. 33, 1995.

——, 'EU enlargement and the "Cyprus problem"', *Journal of Common Market Studies*, V. 38, N. 1, March 2000.

Nye, Joseph, 'The new Rome meets the new barbarians', *The Economist*, March 23, 2002.

——, *The Paradox of American Power: Why the World's Only Superpower Can't Go it Alone*, Oxford University Press, Oxford, 2002.

O'Malley, Brendan and Ian Craig, *The Cyprus Conspiracy*, I.B. Tauris, London, 1999.

Office of International Security Affairs, *United States Strategy for the Middle East*, Department of Defence, Washington DC, May 1995.

Olgun, Ergun, 'Time running out for the détente in Cyprus', *The European Voice*, May 8–15, 2002.

Oren, Michael B., *Six Days of War: June 1967 and the Making of the Modern Middle East*, Oxford University Press, Oxford, 2002.

Ozturk, Ahmet, 'From oil pipelines to oil Straits: the Caspian pipeline politics and environmental protection of the Istanbul and the Canakkale Straits', *Journal of Southern Europe and the Balkans*, V. 4, N. 1, May 2002.

Paboudjian, Paul B. and Raymond H. Kévorkian, *Les Arméniens dans l'Empire Ottoman à la veille du Génocide*, Arhis, Paris, 1992.

Palloix, Christian, *Les Firmes Multinationales et le Procès d'Internationalisation*, François Maspero, Paris, 1973.

Papachelas, Alexis, *The Rape of the Greek Democracy: the American Factor, 1947–1967* (in Greek), Estia, Athens, 1997.

Papacosma, S. Victor, 'More than rocks: the Aegean's discordant legacy', *Mediterranean Quarterly*, V. 4, N. 4, Fall 1996.

Papandreou, Andreas, *Democracy at Gunpoint: the Greek Front*, Andre Deutsch, London, 1970.

Papandreou, George, 'Greece wants Turkey to make the grade', *International Herald Tribune*, December 10, 1999.

——, 'A unified Cyprus is essential for European unity', *International Herald Tribune*, May 2, 2002.

Park, William, 'Turkey's European Union candidacy: from Luxembourg to Helsinki – to Ankara?', *Mediterranean Politics*, V. 5, N. 3, Autumn 2000.

Parthasarathy, Gopalaswami, 'War against terrorism and the oil and gas dimensions', <http://www.rediff.com/news/gp.htm>.

Peel, Quentin, 'Putin plays a weak hand well', *Financial Times*, March 18, 2002.

Petras, James and Morris Morley, 'Contesting hegemons: US–French relations in the "New World Order"', *Review of International Studies*, N. 1, 2000.

Pettifer, James, *The New Macedonian Question*, Macmillan, London, 1999.

Pfaff, William, 'For Europe, a tough call on defence co-operation', *International Herald Tribune*, May 18, 2002.

Poulantzas, Nicos, *L'État, le Pouvoir, le Socialisme*, Presses Universitaires de France, Paris, 1978.

Poulton, Hugh, *The Balkans: Minorities and States in Conflict*, Minority Rights Group, London, 1991.

——, 'The struggle for hegemony in Turkey: Turkish nationalism as a contemporary force', *Journal of Southern Europe and the Balkans*, V. 1, N. 1, 1999.

Ramazani, Rouhollah, *The Northern Tier: Afghanistan, Iran and Turkey*, Princeton University Press, Princeton, 1966.

Richmond, Oliver, 'A perilous catalyst? EU accession and the Cyprus problem', *The Cyprus Review*, V. 13, N. 2, Fall 2001.

Riordan, James, *A Biography of Oliver Stone*, Aurum Press, London, 1996.

Rittenberg, Libby (ed.), *The Political Economy of Turkey in the Post-Soviet Era*, Praeger, Connecticut, 1998.

Roberts, Adam, 'NATO's "Humanitarian War" over Kosovo', *Survival*, V. 41, N. 3, Autumn 1999.

Rouleau, Eric, 'Turkey's dream of democracy', *Foreign Affairs*, V. 79, N. 6, November–December, 2000.

Sassoon, Donald, *One Hundred Years of Socialism: the West European Left in the 20th Century*, I.B. Tauris, London, 1996.

——, *Social Democracy at the Heart of Europe*, IPPR, London, 1996.

—— (ed.), *Looking Left: European Socialism after the Cold War*, I.B. Tauris, London, 1997.

Schulze, E. Kirsten, *The Arab–Israeli Conflict*, Longman, London, 2000.

Schwarz, Benjamin and Christopher Layne, 'For the record', *The National Interest*, N. 57, 1999.

Scrase, Gavin, 'The Balkans and international politics in the 1940s: on the Eden–Gusev pre-percentages agreement', *Journal of Southern Europe and the Balkans*, V. 2, N. 2, November 2000.

Sesit, Michael R., 'Investors lose their faith in a strong US Dollar', *Wall Street Journal Europe*, May 14, 2002.

Setinc, Marjan, 'Slovenia and Europe: Whatever happened to the enlargement of the European Union?' [memo], ERC, Kingston University, London, November 21, 2000.

Sharma, R.C. and Stavros A. Epaminondas (eds), *Cyprus: In Search of Peace and Justice*, Somali Publications, New Delhi, 1997.

Smith, Julianne and Martin Butcher, *A Risk Reduction Strategy for NATO: Preparing for the Next 50 Years*, British American Security Information Council – Basic Research Report, 1, London, 1999.

Smith, Martin A. and Graham Timmins, *Building a Bigger Europe: EU and NATO Enlargement in Comparative Perspective*, Ashgate, Aldershot, 2000.

Smith, Michael Llewellyn, *Ionian Vision: Greece in Asia Minor, 1919–1922*, Hurst, London, 1998.

Soetendorp, Ben, *Foreign Policy in the European Union*, Longman, London, 1999.

Sofos, Spyros A., 'Reluctant Europeans? European integration and the transformation of Turkish politics', *South European Society and Politics* (special issue on 'Europeanisation and the Southern Periphery'), V. 5, N. 2, Autumn 2000.

Solana, Javier, 'The globe's most important relationship', *Wall Street Journal Europe*, May 2, 2002.

Steel, Ronald, 'Instead of NATO', *The New York Review of Books*, January 15, 1998.

Stefanidis, Ioannis, *Isle of Discord: Nationalism, Imperialism and the Making of the Cyprus Problem*, Hurst, London, 1999.

Steil, Benn and Susan L. Woodward, 'A European "New Deal" for the Balkans', *Foreign Affairs*, N. 6, 1999.

Stein, Kenneth W., *The Land Question in Palestine, 1917–1939*, University of North Carolina Press, Chapel Hill, 1984.

Stephen, Michael, *The Cyprus Question*, Northgate Publications, London, 2001.

Stone, Norman, 'Talking Turkey', *The National Interest*, N. 61, Fall 2000.

Straw, Jack and Matthew Hamlyn, 'On Cyprus', FCO/FAC/002–02, House of Commons, London, March 12, 2002.

Task Force Report, *Promoting Sustainable Economies in the Balkans*, Council on Foreign Relations, New York, 2000.

Tessler, Mark, *History of the Israeli–Palestinian Conflict*, Indiana University Press, Bloomington, 1994.

Theophanous, Andreas, *Cyprus in the European Union and the New International Environment* (in Greek), I. Sideris, Athens, 2000.

Theophanous, Andreas et al. (eds), *Cyprus and the European Union*, Intercollege Press, Nicosia, 1996.

Theophanous, Andreas and Nikos Peristianis (eds), *The Cyprus Problem: Its Solution and the Day After*, Intercollege Press, Nicosia, 1998.

Tocci, Nathalie and Emerson Michael, *Cyprus as Lighthouse of the East Mediterranean: Shaping EU Accession and Re-unification Together*, CEPS, Brussels, 2002.

Tsoukalis, Loukas, *The New European Economy Revisited*, Oxford University Press, Oxford, 1997.

Tuncer, Idil, 'The security policies of the Russian Federation: the "Near Abroad" and Turkey', *Turkish Studies*, V. 1, N. 2, Autumn 2000.

Tyler, Patrick E., 'Abkhazia hastens break with Georgia', *International Herald Tribune*, March 1, 2002.

Unsigned Editorial, 'Cyprus surprise', *Financial Times*, January 18, 2002.

Unsigned Editorial, 'George Bush and the axis of evil', *The Economist*, February 2, 2002.

Unsigned Editorial, 'Messy war, messy peace', *The Economist*, June 12, 1999.

Unsigned Editorial, 'Russia's ultimatum', *Guardian*, December 7, 1999.

Unsigned, 'A general speaks his mind', *The Economist*, March 16, 2002.

Unsigned, 'A Survey of NATO' (special insert), *The Economist*, April 30, 1999.

Unsigned, 'China feels encircled', *The Economist*, June 8, 2002.

Unsigned, 'Cyprus shipping improves its image', *Cyprus News*, N. 152, Cyprus High Commission, London, April 2002.

Unsigned, 'Don't mention the O-word', *The Economist*, September 14, 2002.

Unsigned, 'Flaring up?', *The Economist*, April 13, 2002.

Unsigned, 'Gas pipeline decisions looming', *Cyprus News*, N. 150, Cyprus High Commission, London, February 2002.

Unsigned, 'Germany sees greater role for Europe in Asia', NATO Enlargement Daily Brief, <http://groups.yahoo.com/group/nedb/messages>, June 26, 2002.

Unsigned, 'Kosovo: State in embryo', *The Economist*, December 3, 1999.

Unsigned, 'Old friends and new', *The Economist*, June 1, 2002.

Unsigned, 'Present at the Creation: A Survey of America's World Role', *The Economist*, June 29, 2002.

Unsigned, 'Presidential pique', *The Economist*, May 4, 2002.

Unsigned, 'The future of NATO: A moment of truth', *The Economist*, May 4, 2002.

Unsigned, 'Turkey: On the crest of the wave', *The Economist*, October 30, 1999.

Unsigned, 'Turkey and Greece', *The Economist*, April 13, 2002.

Unsigned, 'Vladimir Putin's long, hard haul', *The Economist*, May 18, 2002.

Unsigned, *Bosnia Report*, series 8, The Bosnian Institute, London, January–March, 1999.

Van der Wee, Herman, *Prosperity and Upheaval: the World Economy, 1945–1980*, Viking, London, 1986.

Vassiliev, Alexei, *Central Asia: Political and Economic Challenges in the Post-Soviet Era*, Saqi Books, London, 2001.

Venturi, Franco, *Il populismo Russo*, V. I–III, Einaudi, Torino, 1972.

Wagstyl, Stefan, 'Profile: LUKoil; process of growth is the main target', *Financial Times* ('Russia', special insert), April 15, 2002, p. VII.

Wallace, William, 'Rare optimism on Cyprus', *Wall Street Journal Europe*, February 21, 2002.

Waltz, Kenneth N., *Theory of International Politics*, Random House, New York, 1979.

——, 'Globalisation and American power', *The National Interest*, N. 59, Spring 2000.

Wazir, Burhan, 'Lost Angeles', *Observer*, July 7, 2002 ('The Observer Magazine').

Weber, Max, 'Legitimate authority and bureaucracy', in Pugh D.S. (ed.), *Organisation Theory*, Penguin, Harmondsworth, 1971.

Weston, Diana Markides, *Cyprus, 1957–1963: From Colonial Conflict to Constitutional Crisis*, University of Minnesota Press, Minneapolis, 2001.

Williams, Michael C. and Iver B. Neumann, 'From alliance to security community: NATO, Russia and the power of identity', *Millennium*, V. 29, N. 2, 2000.

Winrow, Gareth M., 'NATO and the out-of-area issue: the positions of Turkey and Italy', *Il Politico* (University of Pavia, Italy), anno LVIII, N. 4, 1993.

Wittgenstein, Ludwig, *Tractatus Logico-Philosophicus*, Routledge, London, 1990.

Woodward, Susan, *The Balkan Tragedy*, The Brookings Institution, Washington DC, 1995.

Woollacott, Martin, 'How the man we could-do-business-with is becoming the man we must destroy', *Guardian*, April 3, 1999.

Yaphe, Judith S., 'Turkey's domestic affairs: Shaping the US–Turkey strategic partnership', Strategic Forum, Institute for National Strategic Studies, National Defence University, Policy Paper 121, July, 1997, <http://www.ndu.edu/inss/strforum/forum121.html>.

Yiallourides, Christodoulos K. and Panagiotis Tsakonas (eds), *Greece and Turkey after the End of the Cold War*, Aristide D. Caratzas, Athens, 2001.

Yost, David S., *NATO Transformed*, United States Institute of Peace Press, Washington DC, 1998.

Index

Compiled by Sue Carlton